Modernisation of India and China Defence

With Special Reference to Enhancing Infrastructure on South Asia Border

MODERNISATION OF INDIA AND CHINA DEFENCE

With Special Reference to Enhancing Infrastructure on South Asia Border

Col. S.C. Narang (Retd.)

PRASHANT PUBLISHING HOUSE
DELHI-110094

Published by :
Prashant Publishing House
C-34, 28 Foota Road, Gali-3,
West Karwal Nagar, Delhi-110094
Phone : 011-22963970, Mob. : 9810396373
e-mail.: prashantpublishinghouse@gmail.com

Modernisation of India and China Defence
With Special Reference to Enhancing Infrastructure on South Asia Border

First Published 2015

ISBN 978-93-80565-59-0

PRINTED IN INDIA
Published by Mr. R.K. Jha M/s Prashant Publishing House and Published at H.S. Offset House Press, Delhi.

Contents

Preface

The road will connect sparsely populated and poorly-connected hill communities living in four large frontier districts of Arunachal Pradesh. It will also help farmers in the mountainous region to transport their organic crops and medicinal herbs to low-lying and busy markets in neighbouring Assam state. "This road will not boost our defences but help connect far flung communities for economic development denied to them for so long," says India's junior home minister Khiren Rijiju, himself a resident of Arunachal Pradesh.

But Indian military officials say the road will help consolidate Indian defences. This represents a change in Indian military thinking that has so far opposed developing roads near the border, in case it is used by the Chinese during a conflict for speedy movement inside Indian territory. The road, however, could could ignite fresh tensions between India and China. The world's two most populous countries disagree over the demarcation of several Himalayan border areas and fought a brief war in 1962.

The rise of China, whether in terms of economic growth or military build-up, is bound to have a regional implication. Different countries, however, have their own interpretation and response. As neighbouring states, each is affected, some positively and some negatively, by China's military power, posture, strategic thinking, and evolving role. China thus shapes in a major way the regional balance of power and security environment. Although India and South Asia are not central to China's foreign relations and policy priorities at present, this is a growing area of Beijing's interest. For New Delhi, however, whether positive or negative, "China's military doctrines, forced deployment postures and economic interests are a matter of interest to India."

In India there is a general understanding that the main focus of China's grand strategy and military capability development is the competition with the United States, India's concerns regarding force modernisation of China, arise primarily from what Robert Kaplan calls the "collapse of distance brought about by advances in military technology," allowing countries to encroach on each other's sphere of influence.

Although China tends to underplay the threat from India, both in terms of India's military modernisation and existing capabilities, Beijing has recently exhibited a tendency to look at these capabilities from the larger perspective of strategic collusion between India and the United States. This tendency reflects a mindset that increasingly perceives India as a "near peer competitor", one acting in concert with the United States, that could in the future challenge China's regional and global aspirations for preeminence. This is despite repeated assertions by the Indian leadership that India does not have major security issues with China other than the boundary dispute.

Future conventional conflict on the Indian sub-continent will in all probability result from the ongoing low-intensity limited war on the Line of Control (LoC) with Pakistan or the unresolved territorial and boundary dispute with China and will be predominantly a land conflict. The Indian Army seriously lacks a potent firepower punch, especially in the mountain sector. Precision-guided munitions (PGMs) have still to enter service in numbers large enough to make a real difference. The reconnaissance, surveillance and target acquisition (RSTA) assets necessary for the optimum exploitation of even the existing firepower assets are grossly inadequate. Automated command and control and decision support systems have been on the drawing boards for several decades but are yet to mature.

As the book addresses this crucial issue quite deftly, it is hoped that it would prove to be a source of great information for the reader.

—*Editor*

1

Political Economy of Infrastructure Development in the Sino-Indian Border Areas

China occupies a growing space in the daily imagination of ordinary Indians. While they might be not be conscious of the presence of Chinese components in their mobile phones, Indians are increasingly aware of the wide gulf that exists with China in the provision of such essentials as good physical infrastructure. And nowhere, perhaps, is this consciousness stronger than along India's underdeveloped borders areas with China. From Ladakh in the west to Arunachal Pradesh in the east, border communities are aware of the stark differences in road, telecom and other forms of physical and social infrastructure between what is available on the Indian side and in Tibet.

In the run-up to the 1962 border conflict with China, the Indian government did take note of the shortcomings of physical infrastructure in the border regions but was unable to get various agencies of the central and state governments to function in a coordinated and timely manner to plug the gaps. Following the conflict, however, the combination of an Indian official psyche scarred by defeat and general ignorance of Chinese intentions and capabilities created a policy of infrastructure development in the border areas that was remarkable for its shortsightedness. The policy involved keeping India's border areas deliberately underdeveloped and lacking in roads and telecommunications in order to prevent another instance of easy access to the plains for the Chinese army.

Indian policy has since been reversed due to many factors. These include greater confidence in the country's military abilities, increased understanding of China's own intentions and weaknesses, the availability of economic resources for infrastructure development in the border areas, and, the need to address the development deficit in these far-flung border areas. The question is, of course, what is the level of priority accorded to each of these reasons?

There is still in the Indian military establishment, a dominant sense of suspicion involving China – a legacy of 1962. Combined with economic liberalization and India's improved relations with the West, particularly the United States, India has greater access to Western military technology and equipment. A major justification for such acquisitions is the 'China threat' theory buttressed by the experience of 1962. But such justifications would not matter if there was not also a concomitant effort to be seen as being ready to employ such newly-acquired capabilities in case of another Chinese attack. Hence, infrastructure development in the border regions – from roads to telecom is as much a military imperative as it is an issue of facilitating local development.

There are still other considerations that the huge investments in infrastructure development come alloyed with. Primarily, these are political objectives and possibilities for economic rent-seeking as is the case in other parts of India.

A local political leader is expected to share the goods of political office with other members of his community or tribe. These goods include those derived from corruption in the form of siphoning off of funds from various development projects, including infrastructure projects. Further, in Arunachal Pradesh, which has several tribes but often each very small in number, such corruption is often seen as 'democratic' since the benefits percolate down to practically every member.

However, low education levels, lack of awareness and, to an extent inter-tribal competition among other factors, also combine to create obstacles for infrastructure development. In this context, it is worth remembering that all land in a state like Arunachal Pradesh is private land, belonging either to the individual or the community. Thus, individuals or groups in the quest for greater compensation can hold up land acquisition for infrastructure development.

These factors are especially germane when one moves to discussion about infrastructure development that is being carried out with private sector participation, especially dams in Arunachal. These dams are part of the Indian state's desire to establish first-user rights on the waters of the Siang (as the Yarlung Tsangpo is called on entering Arunachal) and the other tributaries of the Brahmaputra, in competition with the projects of dam-building and water-diversion projects that the Chinese are believed to be engaged in upstream. The central and state governments have a preference for mega hydroelectric dams that would produce far in excess of what either Arunachal or the rest of the Northeast India could conceivably use given the region's poor industrial capacity. Further, some of the Indian private companies involved possess little experience of such infrastructure development but have been attracted by the huge monies involved.

However, if they imagined that land acquisition and construction would be easier in an economically underdeveloped and socially backward region, they have been disabused of the notion by a host of local environmental and cultural preservation movements as well as opposition from the central government's own Environment Ministry. It is somewhat noteworthy, then, that the central government recently replaced its Environment Minister with the Minister for Petroleum and Natural Gas.

Across India's border regions, development initiatives and fears about their consequences have led to splits – inter-generational and political – within various communities. In Ladakh, for example, there are concerns among certain interest groups that better infrastructure actually creates opportunities for an influx of domestic Indian tourists who are not as high value customers as Western tourists, and who could create greater environmental impact than the considerably limited numbers that currently visit the region. Meanwhile, Arunachal's planned infrastructure development requires the entry of labourers from elsewhere in India and this, it is feared, will overwhelm smaller local populations. These developments are particularly fraught for what is the largest state in Northeast India, a region that is already the site of various forms of political instability, including ethnic insurgencies.

In the end, it remains to be seen whether the Indian state is able to find a balance in its infrastructure development projects between the imperatives of national security, political accommodation, cultural sensitivity and environmental sustainability.

THE THREAT FROM CHINA'S BORDER INFRASTRUCTURE

Eyes on strategic as well as economic gains, China is making all endeavours to build networks of rail and road links along Sino-India frontier and beyond. Besides the economic benefi ts, this colossal border infrastructure build-up makes it possible for Beijing to gather a huge number of troops at the border in double-quick time, whenever it needs. In contrast, Indian troops have to struggle with sloppy infrastructure to reach at the border.

Over the years, China has built an envious network of road and rail links along the border while napping India failed to comprehend the significance of border connectivity. Now with the change in policy in recent years, New Delhi is floundering to execute its own relatively modest plans to match the Chinese moves. India's recent declaration to upgrade the road infrastructure in Arunachal Pradesh and develop the rail connectivity between Ladakh and Himachal Pradesh has been conceived as an effort to go with the Chinese.

China is way ahead to India on infrastructure development along the border. As China is reaching its railway almost near Arunachal Pradesh and Sikkim border, India is struggling to locate Gangtok and Itanagar in Indian Railways map. Chinese frontier city Nyingchi (near Arunachal border) is expected to link with main land through Chinese railway network while all Indian frontier cities along the Sino-India border are still bereft of rail links. In Middle Himalaya, after linking Lhas a with Kathmandu by road, Chinese rail is knocking at Sino-Nepal border. Contrary to it, most of the India-Nepal Railway projects are not even pushed beyond the feasibility studies. On western front, China has already built strategic Karakoram road and now planning to construct rail network across the inaccessible Karakoram whereas India is still waiting to connect Srinagar to rest of the nation by rail.

KARAKORAM HIGHWAY: STRATEGIC AND ECONOMIC GAINS FOR CHINA

India's loss of strategic segments of high Himalayas and part of Karakoram to Pakistan and China in 1947-48 put China and Pakistan into advantageous position in the region. And later on, both augmented the strategic gains by opening of Karakoram Highway (KKH).

The KKH, not far from the Line of Control (LoC), is strategically key asset for the China and Pakistan. This highway along with the Chinese road running in Aksai Chin provides major avenues of collaboration against Indian by troops of all weather friends 'China' and 'Pakistan'.

The KKH, the highest paved international road in the world, was completed in 1986 after 20 years of rigorous efforts. The highway, connecting the Northern Areas of Pakistan to the ancient Silk Road, runs approximately 1,300 km from Kashgar-a city in the Uygur Autonomous Region of Xinjiang-to Havelian, located in the Abbottabad District of Pakistan. An extension of the highway meets the old Grand Trunk Road at Hasan Abdal, about 40 km northwest of Islamabad. Now, the Chinese are heavily engaged in the upgrading of K arakoram Highway, from the existing 10 meters width to 30 meters to allow heavier vehicles to pass throughout the year.

The Highway passes through the confluence zone of Asian and Indian subcontinents where the Pamir, Kunlun, Hindukush, Karakoram and Great Himalaya ranges are knotted together and China, Tajikistan, Afghanistan, Pakistan and India all come within 250km of each other can also serve as a link between China and the Central Asian states.

China and Pakistan are also planning to connect strategic Gwadar port with the broadened Karokaram Highways. The link is intended to enhance Chinese economic influence in Central Asia and West Asian region as well as strategic access to the People's Liberation Army in politically sensitive areas. In near future, the link would act as land-locked and resource-rich Central Asia's gateway to the outside world as the newly constructed dry port at Sost on Karakoram Highway has the potential to act as a channel of trade for Central Asian countries. China-built Gwadar port close to the strategic 'Straits of Hormuz' will be the entry point for energy supplies to China, bypassing the Malacca Straits. Linking Western China with the Arabian Sea means China's strategic reach to the Indian Ocean as well as greater economic benefits to Xinjiang province.

Moreover, the highway has also been emerged as 'highway of nuclear and missile proliferation'. Some years back, American satellites detected the movement of 12 consignments of Chinese missiles to Pakistan via Karakoram highway. The silkworm missiles that China got in trouble for selling to Pakistan came only through Karakoram route, whose bridges are reconstructed to handle heavy freights. Also, North Korea received Uranium enrichment equipment from the A Q Khan network through this route only.

India seems to be apprehensive as Chinese intend to establish strategic link-up with Pakistan in parts of Jammu and Kashmir under occupation by both the countries, saying this could have direct military implications. The Defence Ministry's Annual Report for 2008-09 tabled in Rajya Sabha last year noted with concern the possibility of China's growing connectivity with Pakistan through the territory in Jammu and Kashmir, illegally occupied by both these nations.

While China begun the infrastructural development programme across the Trans Himalaya and Karakoram range programme many years ago, India took some initiatives to connect Himalayan border to the mainland in recent years only. New Delhi's recent decisions to develop border infrastructure like; building a more reliable second approach to Ladakh with the upgrading the Manali-Leh road and construction of Rohtang tunnel, and development of railway networks in border areas of Jammu & Kashmir and linking it with other part of the nation, indicates that it intends to improve transport network along its borders with China in the region.

Aiming the round-the-year lines of communication to eastern Ladakh, the Cabinet Committee (CCS) recently approved the pending proposal of building an 8.8-km-long Rohtang tunnel. The proposal was waiting for approval from CCS since 2002. At present, due to heavy snowfall at the Rohtang Pass (13,050 feet), the road connectivity for Leh from Himachal Pradesh remains disrupted during winter season. Since another link road to Leh-Srinagar-Leh road-is vulnerable to Pakistani shelling, as was witnessed during the Kargil conflict, an alternative route to Leh and eastern Ladakh for military as well as civilian purpose is obligatory.

Moreover, New Del hi is also looking ahead to set off a new railway project to link Ladakh region with rest of the India. The strategic rail link is proposed between Leh and Bilaspur in Himachal Pradesh. Six passenger trains and nine goods trains are planned on the 498 km-long section. According to some recent reports, the Indian Railways has already completed a reconnaissance survey of this ambitious rail link. The project has been conceived as an effort to counterbalance China's strategic advantage along the Sino-Indian border.

In addition, India also got the success to make its military presence along the Chinese border in Ladakh. Following the strategy to build communication infrastructure on the Chinese border, the Indian Air Force has successfully converted one of its old landing grounds in Ladakh, in the vicinity of the Sino-Indian border, into an operational airstrip where military transport planes can land.

India is also on mission to complete one of its most challenging railway projects by construct a rail tracks to connect valley of Kashmir with the Himalayan foothills. The idea of bringing organised transport to the Kashmir Valley is nothing new but the ambitious Kashmir railway project initiated after declaring it as National Priority Project in 2001. Though the rail link was planned to be fully opened in 2009, all that has been opened so far is the section in the flat terrain of the Kashmir. Quite the opposite, China finished a similar high-altitude railway line (Golmund-Lhasa) in adjacent Tibet in the remarkably short period of five years. It commenced work on the 1142 km Golmud-Lhasa rail route in 2001, just as India ordered faster work on the Kashmir railway, and inaugurated the track on July 01, 2006.

TRANS KARAKORAM RAILWAY: CONNECTING GWADAR AND CHAHBHAR

While Indian Railway is facing hitches in building the rail link between the Srinagar valley and the rest of the nation, China is about to commenced own rail line to the parts of Jammu and Kashmir under Pakistan's control. Islamabad has already awarded a contract of US $ 1.2 million to an international consortium to carry out a feasibility study for this ambitious rail project. The Pakistan-China rail link is intended to connect Havelian, the northern limit of Pakistan's railways, to the Kasghar of China's Xin Xiang region via Northern Areas of Jammu and Kashmir. The proposed rail link is expected to roughly follow the Karakorum Highway route.

It is noteworthy that by extending its East-West Railway from the Chinese border town of Kashi to Peshawar in Pakistan's northwest region, Beijing can receive cargo to and from Gwadar along the shortest route, from Karachi to Peshawar. This rail link could be used not only for trade purposes but also to transport energy from the Persian Gulf to Xinjiang, in case a pipeline is not a viable option. Pakistan's exiting rail link is also enabling China to get rail access to Iran. The only problem is difference in rail gauge. There is possibility of Chinese involvement in construction of a rail link from the north-western city of Mashhad along Iran's eastern border to the port of Chabahar. According to a recent report, Tehran is in negotiations with two Chinese companies to build a 1,100 kilometers long railway in eastern Iran to connect Mashhad with Chabahar.

Besides roads and rail links, Beijing and Islamabad are ready to construct oil and gas pipeline across Karakoram to connect Gwadar to land-locked Xinjiang. A Memorandum of Understanding

(MoU) has already been signed with Pakistan for the feasibility study to build the energy corridor to China. According to a news paper report, a Chinese state firm is examining building a pipeline to carry Gulf oil from Gwadar to western China. This route will not only cut freight costs and supply time but also help China to by pass Malacca Straits. Chinese government is also planning to construct oil-refining and storage facilities at the Gwadar.

Train to Nepal

China has already instigated the construction of a rail network connecting Tibetan capital of Lhasa with the market town of Khasa on the Sino-Nepal border. The 770 km proposed Lhasa –Khasa rail link is an extension of the world's highest railway, which runs between Golmund, a city in China's Quinghai province and Lhasa. The project, planned to be completed by 20 13, is expected to follow Lhasa-Kathmandu Friendship Highway route. The proposed rail link, a Chinese scheme to improve its transport infrastructure in isolated Himalayan region, is likely to strengthen Nepal's strategic and economic engagement with China and reduce its dependence on old traditional friend 'India'.

Chinese plans are not limited to railways but include the plans for six additional highways to link up with Nepal, the development of cross-border energy pipelines and optical fibre.

Anxious to Chinese involvement in infrastructure projects in Nepal, India has recently launched a Rs-1,700 crore road-and-rail infrastructure initiative in the terai region of the Himalayan country. India is thinking over expanding its rail links with Nepal through at least five technically and financially feasible routes: Nautanwa-Bhairahawa, Nepalgunj Road-Nepalgunj, Jogbani-Biratnagar, New Jalpaiguri-Kakarbhitta and Jayanagar-Bardibas. Currently, there is one rail link between the two countries that connects Raxaul (India) with container inland port at Birganj (Nepal). India does plan to expand the existing rail link up to Kathmandu. A train from Birganj to Kathmandu that cuts through the mountains will be a mere 80 km, cutting travel time and costs. At present Birganj is connected to Kathmandu by road only and distance between the cities is about 261 Km.

India worries that building an extensive transport network along Nepal's northern borders and other ambitious plans to develop road and rail network in Bangladesh, Pakistan and Myanmar will help China making inroads into South Asia, posing a threat to India's security and economy. And, that is expected to happen if Delhi fails to develop its own transport network in the border area to compete the Chinese 12. New Delhi also needs to initiate the pending proposal for construction of a trans national network to put Nepal, Pakistan, and Bangladesh in its railway network. According to a news paper report "India is courting its three immediate neighbours with a proposal f or construction of a trans-national network to bring together all of South Asia. Details of the plan are soon to be finalised by a multinational expert group".

CHINESE EYES ON INDIA'S EASTERN BORDER

Beijing is planning to extend the newly launched Golmund-Lhasa rail link up to Xigaze, south of Lhasa and from there to Yatung, a traditional trading centre situated at the mouth of the chumbi valley just a few kilometres away from strategic Nathu La pass. Anticipating the China's strategic gain across the Sikkim, India approved a long pending proposal of rail link for this landlocked Himalayan State. The project, expected to be completed by 2015-16, will provide much-needed rail connectivity to Sikkim with the rest of the nation. The rail links at Gangtok and the respective Chinese link across the border will not only boost bilateral trade, but also counter each other on military movement.

There is another Chinese proposal too to extend the Golmund-Lhasa line to Nyingchi, an important trading town north of the Indian state of Arunachal Pradesh, at the tri-junction with Myanmar 15. From Nyingchi this rail link is further scheduled to link up to Dali in Yunnan province, extension of this rail link up to Dali will complete the circuit of the Chinese national rail n etwork. And connecting it up with the existing western railway network will grant strategic as well as economic benefits to China.

From Chinese Military point of view, this Lhasa-Nyingchi-Dali route is significant as it runs in an east-west direction almost parallel and quite close to the Arunachal border, means quick and easier deployment of military along the Sino-Indian border. "It will enable the 14 Group of the Chinese Army located at Kunming, with its divisions at Dali, Kaiyuanand and Kunming to rapidly move westwards from Yunnan to Tibet Autonomous Region (TAR) by railway. Similarly, the 13 Group Army (Unit 56005) from its locations in the Sichuan province shall be able to utilise this linked railway network to move to TAR".

While China is reaching its railway almost near Arunachal Pradesh, Indian response is only limited to planning and feasibility studies. The Indian Railways' network is yet to make a way into Arunachal Pradesh. In January 2008, Prime Minister Manmohan Singh took an initiative and announced the package to construct rail link between Harmuti 18 and Itanagar. The project, vital for national security, will also boost the local economy.

India has lately woken up to China's aggressive infrastructure building along the eastern border. After years of hiccups, in 2006, India reversed its earlier policy to keep the weak roadways infrastructure in Arunachal, and planned out a building of seven new strategic roads in the region. The rationale behind earlier policy was that the feeble infrastructure in border area would deter the Chinese to obtaining an easy territorial access into the region. Later, aiming to improve the road connectivity in Arunachal Pradesh, a new plan called trans-Arunachal Highway project was announced by Prime Minister Manmohan Singh in 2008. The 1840 km long Trans Arunachal Highway is planned to interconnect its 11 district headquarters, while an additional 847 km 2-lane road would connect the remaining 5 districts. The project signifies the beginning of a new strategic vision of well-connected borders. Improved road and rail links would not only better connect the people of peripheral areas but also ensure greater security and economic progress.

Road to progress

New Delhi needs to formulate an enormous plan to build up its own connectivity along and across the long frontier with Tibet. Although in recent years it has made some progress on this front but still requires more roads and rail links to secure the border and revivify the economic and cultural linkages across the borders. The atrocious state of road and railways network along the border is also an outcome of a deliberate policy in New Delhi over the last many decades, not to develop connectivity in states bordering China.

India feared that roads and railways in these Himalayan states would help the Chinese penetrate deep into India.

Along with good planning, India needs unrelenting efforts to improve the connectivity in border states.

Almost all border road and rail projects are running behind the schedule. Besides the inhospitable terrains, other impediments like, lack of compulsory environmental clearances, bureaucratic hurdles and delays in allocation of funds are, however, proving to be major obstruction in completion of these ambitious projects.

Contrary to India, China has already demonstrated that it will not let any difficulties in the way of its attempt to transform its frontier regions and extend its economic influence across borders. India should learn to adapt the Chinese initiatives instead of opposing it, and ability to convert strategic assets into economic opportunities.

China's trans-border infrastructures build-up are no longer mere for military leverages but also an instruments for the expansion of Chinese economic influence into the Subcontinent.

Well-developed infrastructures of roads and railways in frontier region would supplement India's vision of greater economic engagement with border states.

Connectivity is much needed to enhance its economic sway in Tibet, Central Asia and South East Asia as well as accelerate the development of peripheral states. In and across the Trans Himalayan region, India needs to reinstate its connectivity to Kashgar. It is reasonable to connect Ladakh to Xinjiang region and further north with the development of access road to Karakoram pass to boost the economy of Ladakh and other parts of the Jammu & Kashmir. A well-developed transport infrastructure in India's North-East states can also provide vital transportation link to Southeast Asia on account of its geographic immediacy to the region.

INDIA'S WORRYING BORDER INFRASTRUCTURE DEFICIT

Even as China's road and rail network in Tibet inches towards thedisputed Sino-Indian border, India's plans to repair dilapidated border roads and construct new roads and railway lines are running wekk behind schedule, with some infrastructure projects not only missing completion deadlines but also failing to move beyond the drawing board.

As Parliament's Standing Committee on Defence, 2013-2014, noted in a recent report, India's air, road and rail network near its border with China is in a "very dismal" state. Of the 73 all-weather roads that were identified for construction in 2006, just 18 have been completed so far. Of the 27 roads that were to be constructed by the Indo-Tibetan Border Police, just one is complete, the report pointed out, adding that "as many as eleven roads are behind schedule" with even their detailed project reports not yet finalized. As for construction of 14 strategic railway lines that were to be laid near the border, these have registered "nil achievement," the report said.

The roughly 3488 km Line of Actual Control (LAC), which snakes through the Himalayas, serves as the de facto border between India and China. Besides differences over where the LAC runs, India and China have territorial claims over chunks of territory. In the western sector, India accuses China of occupying 38,000 sq km of its territory in Aksai Chin and of holding 5,180 sq km of land in Kashmir that Pakistan gifted Beijing in 1963. China lays claim to around 90,000 sq km of land in India's northeast, roughly approximating the Indian state of Arunachal Pradesh, which Beijing refers to as "Southern Tibet."

The two countries fought a border war in 1962, which China won. Besides violent skirmishes at Nathu La, a mountain pass that connects Tibet with the Indian state of Sikkim, in 1967, and at Sumdurong Chu Valley in Arunachal in 1987, as well as periodic "incursions" at various points of the LAC over the years, the Sino-Indian frontier has been largely quiet as bilateral relations have improved significantly in recent decades.

Still the possibility of a future military confrontation cannot be ruled out and it is in this context that India's poor connectivity to the LAC is reason for concern.

The difference in infrastructure on the Indian and Chinese sides is "stark," Rajeswari Rajagopalan, Senior Fellow at the Observer Research Foundation in New Delhi told *The Diplomat*, pointing to the "tremendous improvements" China has made over the past decade in linking the LAC to the rest of the country. Tibet has a 40,000 km road network and roads run up to the LAC, unlike roads on the Indian side, which stop 60 to 80 km short of the border, she pointed out.

China's railway infrastructure is expanding rapidly, too. The Golmud-Lhasa railway line, inaugurated in 2006, is being extended to Xigaze, and also to Yatung, a TRADING center that is just a few kilometers from Nathu La. There are also plans to extend this railway line up to Nyingchi, a trading town north of Arunachal Pradesh.

Sikkim and Arunachal figure prominently on the radar of Sino-Indian territorial disputes. Yet India's overland connectivity to the LAC here is abysmal.

Recalling her trip to the McMahon Line (as the Arunachal part of the LAC according to India is called) in the summer of 2013, Monika Chansoria, Senior Fellow and Head of the China-study program at the Centre for Land Warfare Studies in New Delhi, spoke of the "pathetic" condition of the road running to Tawang, an important bone of contention between India and China. This is an area that experiences heavy rains and landslides throughout the year. Yet the road lacks a system for drainage, rendering it a slushy stretch, she told *The Diplomat*. As for the road from Tawang to Bumla (the last border post on the Indian side), it takes a "grueling" three hours to cover this 40 km stretch, she says, "making it perhaps the worst and most unpleasant of all journeys by road."

In contrast is the "smooth, maintained, metal track road on the Chinese side" that one can see from Bumla. This road comes to within 4 km of the LAC, she says "further magnifying the dismal state of roads in India's eastern sector." According to locals it takes the Chinese a mere 45 minutes to reach the Bumla Post from the town of Sonajung, which lies 37 km from the McMahon Line on the Chinese side.

The infrastructure in Sikkim is as decrepit. On a trip to Sikkim in 2009, this correspondent found that the state capital Gangtok was linked to Nathu La by one single-lane, pot-holed, avalanche-prone road, while one landslide-prone, narrow road links Sikkim to the rest of India. Connectivity has improved only marginally since.

The yawning gap in the quantity and quality of India and China's infrastructure near the LAC has multiple implications. Militarily, those implications for India are far reaching.

According to Rajagopalan, with the improved infrastructure, China is in a position to deploy and sustain 30 to 32 divisions, including five or six rapid reaction divisions,COMPARED with the 20 to 22 divisions it could have sent earlier. What is more, all-weather roads have changed the scenario completely, as such mobilization will be possible year round. Moreover, while mobilization would have taken more than six months in the past, it can now be done in six weeks with the improved infrastructure. Apart from extensive road and rail networks, China has also built oil depots. Together, these suggest that China will not only be able to amass troops and supplies to the LAC rapidly in the event of war but will also be able to sustain operations over a longer period of time. "Multiple air bases and forward airstrips near the border areas are additional advantages to China," she said.

In contrast, India's lack of road and rails on its side will undermine Delhi's capacity to rush reinforcements to the LAC. This could prove costly especially in the initial stages of a possible war.

There are economic consequences too for India. Border trade at Nathu La was resumed in 2006. As a Sikkim government official told this correspondent in 2008, "When trade takes off in a big way in a few years, goods by the train-load will arrive at Nathu La from China. India will be in a position then to send back mere truck-loads."

Indian officials are quick to point an accusing finger at each other to explain the delays in the execution of road and rail projects near the LAC. A senior official in the Border Roads Organization (BRO), a quasi military organization responsible for building and maintaining border roads, told *The Diplomat* that besides the "very difficult terrain and hostile weather conditions in which roads in the Himalayas have to be built are the unrealistic deadlines" set by the government.

An official in Uttarakhand – the LAC in Uttarakhand falls under the middle sector – blamed challenges like land acquisition and environmental clearances for delays in projects not taking off. In Uttarakhand and Arunachal Pradesh, for instance, "much of the required land is held jointly by tribal communities, complicating its acquisition for border road construction," he said.

Similar buck-passing has stalled India's grand plans for building strategic railway lines. While the Indian Railways has refused to fork out the massive amount needed for the border projects on the plea that these lines are "not commercially viable," the Ministry of Finance has blamed the economic slowdown for its tightfistedness.

An important reason why India is lagging far behind China with regard to roads and rail near the LAC is their very different perceptions of border infrastructure.

Road and rail building has been a key component of China's grand strategy for the Himalayan region for decades. Building drivable roads into Tibet topped Beijing's agenda as early as 1950 and in the run up to the annexation of Tibet, Mao Zedong called on the People's Liberation Army to "advance while building roads."

Multiple roads were constructed thereafter into Tibet against all odds and at enormous human cost. But it enabled Beijing to pour troops into Tibet to quell unrest and to eventually firm its grip. Railway lines soon followed.

Roads and railway lines in Tibet had an economic component, too, as they helped Beijing usher in economic development.

If in previous decades Beijing's road and rail building activity was focused on integrating Tibet with China, the southward expansion of this infrastructure towards borders with India, Nepal and Bhutan are with an eye on South Asian markets. China has been working assiduously to flatten the Himalayan barrier to its overland trade with South Asia. Contrast this with India's perception of border roads and rails. Since its humiliating defeat in the 1962 war with China, India perceived the building of roads near the LAC as facilitating the advance of China's troops into India in the event of another invasion.

It was only in 2006 that the country's Cabinet Committee on Security, its topmost policy making body on national security, ordered among other things the construction of 73 strategic roads and airstrips near the LAC.

The inordinate delay in improving connectivity to the LAC signals that even if India has shed its old defensive mindset, it still lacks the political will and the energy to match China.

INDIA, CHINA HOPE TO STRENGTHEN BORDER MECHANISM

India and China on Friday began their annual defence dialogue, which is expected to earmark four additional points of emergency interaction between border personnel in the Ladakh sector, and establish new nodes for confidence building, including joint forays to tackle humanitarian disasters at sea.

Highly placed sources told *The Hindu* that discussions could be wrapped up on designating Track Junction, Pangang Tso Lake, Demchock and Chumar — all in Ladakh — as points for emergency meetings between the border personnel, during talks. The Indian delegation to the dialogue is led by Defence Secretary, R.K. Mathur.

The day-long interaction hopes to strengthen institutional mechanisms to prevent a flare up of border tensions from impeding growing economic and regional partnership between New Delhi and Beijing. "The talks are focused on improving border management through a web a Confidence Building Measures (CBMs)," the sources said. The stability of the border has been undermined in the past because of the varying perceptions of the Line of Actual Control (LAC) by either side.

Both sides have already demonstrated their intent to stabilise the border first, rather than seek a quick resolution of the boundary issue. In an interview published on the eve of the talks, Prime

Minister Narendra Modi said that, "Insofar as the border is concerned, the most important point right now is that peace and tranquility must not be disturbed." Chinese foreign ministry spokesperson Hua Chunying also observed on Thursday that New Delhi and Beijing "should make joint efforts to maintain peace tranquility of the border area and create favourable conditions for the negotiation of the boundary question".

With focus on CBMs, the two delegations are expected to discuss Kibithoo in eastern Arunachal Pradesh and Mana Pass in Uttarakhand as additional points for the annual meeting of border personnel. Senior officers from the two countries already meet at least four times a year, to celebrate their national holidays at Bumla in Arunachal Pradesh, Nathula in Sikkim and Chushul in Ladakh.

The dialogue in Beijing is also considering specialised military training exchanges in the defence academies in the two countries. The Chinese side has been keen on training exchanges, in order to build a culture of confidence and openness at all levels. Last month Air Marshal PP Reddy, Chief of Integrated Defence Staff to the Chairman Chiefs of Staff Committee (CISC), visited Beijing, and narrowed down the nuts and bolts of military exchanges with his Chinese counterparts.

China considers counter-terrorism as its top priority, in view of escalating terror attacks in its Xinjiang province, which is the vital gateway for implementing Beijing's ambitious Silk Road projects.

Both sides also want to ensure that Afghanistan does no reignite as fulcrum of regional extremism. Thus, the annual China-India hand-in-hand exercise, which is primarily focused on counterterrorism, is expected to acquire greater sophistication in the future. Ahead of the talks, the Chinese side is signaling the possibility of collaborating with India in tackling humanitarian emergencies abroad. The Chinese defence ministry has posted a Xinhua report on its website, which dilates on the possibility of the two countries working together, following their success in evacuation of their citizens, as well as from other nationalities, during the crisis in Yemen.

Observers say that the backdrop to the defence dialogue is rapidly changing, with China poised to become a major investor in India, and the two countries emerging as founding members of the Asian Infrastructure Investment Bank (AIIB), which is slated to finance infrastructural projects along the Asian segment of China's, Eurasia-centered, "belt and road" initiative. India is likely to become a full-member, later this year of the Shanghai Cooperation Organisation (SCO), which has a security core, centered on counterterrorism, and is pillared by China and Russia. Consequently, going beyond an essentially bilateral focus, the defence dialogue appears to be broadening in view of the security impact of developments in Eurasia.

2

India's Military Modernization: Plans and Strategic Underpinnings

As a key player in Asia and a large democracy with which the United States shares common interests, India is emerging as an important U.S. strategic partner. There is a broad national consensus in India on the contours of this emerging relationship with Washington, particularly with respect to enhanced defense and civil nuclear energy cooperation. During his visit to New Delhi in June 2012, U.S. defense secretary Leon Panetta identified India as a "linchpin" in Washington's emerging "rebalancing" strategy in the Asia-Pacific region. While there was no reaction from the Indian government, it is clear that these two large democracies need to work together militarily in order to maintain freedom of the seas in the Indian Ocean region and to ensure peace and stability in the Asia-Pacific more generally. Should China experience political instability or behave irresponsibly in asserting its territorial rights—as it has shown a tendency to do in the South China Sea—both India and the United States will need strong strategic partners to face worst-case scenarios effectively.

In order to meet future threats and challenges and achieve interoperability with U.S. and other friendly armed forces for joint operations in India's area of strategic interest, the Indian military needs to modernize and create force structures that are capable of undertaking network-centric warfare on land, at sea, and in the air. Gradually, but perceptibly, the Indian armed forces are upgrading their capabilities, enhancing their kinetic effectiveness and command and control, and improving interoperability. This brief analyzes the threats and challenges that India must address, the measures being adopted to modernize the country's armed forces, and the strategic underpinnings behind this slow but steady modernization effort.

PREPARING FOR A TWO-FRONT WAR

South Asia is among the world's most unstable regions due to the ongoing war against al Qaeda and the Taliban in Afghanistan and on the Afghanistan-Pakistan border. In addition, growing fundamentalist terrorism; creeping "Talibanization" in Pakistan; political instability in Bangladesh, Myanmar, Nepal, and Sri Lanka; unrest in Tibet and Xinjiang; narcotics trafficking; and the proliferation of small arms and light weapons are also destabilizing factors. Unresolved territorial and boundary disputes with China and Pakistan, over which India has fought four wars; internal security challenges in Jammu and Kashmir (J&K) and the northeastern states; and the rising tide of the Maoist insurgency in the heartland further vitiate India's strategic environment. Further, many Indian security analysts worry that China is engaged in the strategic encirclement of India through its nuclear and missile nexus with Pakistan; the sale of military hardware to Bangladesh, Nepal, Myanmar, and Sri Lanka; and a "string of pearls" strategy to surround India with naval bases in the northern Indian Ocean region.

India-China relations are stable at the strategic level. Resolution of the territorial dispute is being discussed by India's national security adviser and China's vice foreign minister, military confidence-building measures are holding up, bilateral TRADE has increased to $60 billion, and both countries are cooperating in international forums like the World Trade Organization and the UN Climate Change Conference. However, the relationship is more contentious at the tactical level. For example, China refuses to issue proper visas to Indian citizens of Arunachal Pradesh, Beijing denied the commander-in-chief of India's Northern

Command a visa for an official visit because it believes that J&K is a disputed territory, and the People's Liberation Army (PLA) has been making frequent forays across the Line of Actual Control into Indian territory simply to push Chinese territorial claims. China has also rapidly developed military infrastructure in Tibet to allow for quicker induction of troops and their sustenance over a longer period of time. Another destabilizing factor is the large Chinese presence in the Gilgit-Baltistan area of Pakistan-occupied Kashmir. These developments do not augur well for long-term peace and stability.

The prevailing strategic environment has forced India's armed forces to prepare for the possibility of a "two front" war, while the army and other security forces are engaged in fighting an ongoing "half front" internal security war. Even though the probability of conventional conflict remains low due to steadily improving relations and military confidence-building measures with China and Pakistan, this possibility cannot be completely ruled out. Nuclear deterrence also plays a positive role in conflict avoidance, but the prevailing wisdom in India is that there is space for conventional conflict below the nuclear threshold. There is now increasing realization that unless India takes immediate measures to accelerate the pace of its military modernization, the gap with China, which is only a quantitative gap at present, will soon become a qualitative gap, given the rapid rate of PLA modernization. Likewise, the slender edge that the Indian armed forces now enjoy over the Pakistani armed forces in conventional conflict is being eroded as Pakistan is spending considerable sums of MONEY on its military modernization under the garb of fighting radical extremism.

Although the Indian armed forces have drawn up elaborate plans for modernizing and qualitatively upgrading their capabilities for future combat, including the ability to secure the sea lanes of communication and project power in India's area of strategic interest, the pace of modernization has been slow due to the lack of adequate FUNDING, delayed decision-making, and a low-tech defense industrial base. India's defense budget is pegged at less than 2% of its GDP at present, and the bulk of the expenditure is on the revenue account—that is, pay and allowances, rations, fuel, oil and lubricants, ammunition, and vehicles. Very little remains in the capital account to be spent on modernization. In the case of the army, spending on modernization is as little as 20% to 25% of total capital expenditure in 2012–13. According to Indian defense minister A.K. Antony, "New procurements have commenced...but we are still lagging by 15 years." Nonetheless, an inadequate defense industrial base—imports constitute 70% of defense acquisitions—and bureaucratic inefficiency, rather than lack of FUNDS, are the main causes of the slow pace of modernization. India is expected to procure defense equipment worth $100 billion, most of it imported, over the next two five-year plans. Simultaneously, however, efforts are being stepped up to enhance indigenous capabilities and thereby reduce India's dependence on imports by an order of magnitude.

MILITARY MANPOWER AND STRATEGIC ENVIRONMENT

India's regional security environment is marked by Afghanistan's endless civil war despite US-led North Atlantic Treaty Organization (NATO) intervention and the overthrow of the despotic Taliban regime and its tense relations with Iran and the Central Asian Republics (CARs). Pakistan's half-hearted struggle against the remnants of the al Qaeda and the Taliban, the fissiparous tendencies in Balochistan and the Pushtun heartland, the continuing rise of the cancer of radical extremism and creeping Talibanisation, the unstable civilian government, the floundering economy and, consequently, the nation's gradual slide towards becoming a 'failed state', pose a major security threat to India.

The collusive nuclear weapon-cummissile development programme of China, North Korea and Pakistan and Iran's quest for nuclear weapons are issues of concern. Sri Lanka's inability to find a lasting solution to its ethnic problems despite the comprehensive defeat of the LTTE (Liberation Tigers of Tamil Eelam) has serious repercussions for India. Bangladesh's emergence as the new hub of Islamist fundamentalist terrorism even as it struggles for economic upliftment to subsistence levels, could trigger a new wave of terrorism in India.

The Maoist ascendancy in Nepal and its adverse impact on Nepal's fledgling democracy, as also Nepal's newfound inclination to seek neutrality between India and China, are a blow to what has historically been a stable relationship. Simmering discontentment in Tibet and Xingjian against China's repressive regime is gathering momentum and could result in an open revolt. The peoples' nascent movement for democracy in Myanmar and several long festering insurgencies may destabilise the military Junta. The spill over of religious extremism and terrorism from Afghanistan and political instability in the CARs (Central Asian Republics) are undermining development and governance. Other vitiating factors impacting regional stability in India's neighbourhood is unchecked proliferation of small arms which has been nurtured and encouraged by large-scale narcotics trafficking.

India's unresolved territorial and boundary dispute with China and an un-demarcated Line of Actual Control (LAC) on the India-Tibet border do not augur well for long-term peace and stability between these two Asian giants. Though the border is relatively stable, a future border war with China, though improbable, cannot be ruled out.

China's carefully orchestrated plan aimed at the strategic encirclement of India is evident from its unjustifiable opposition to India's nuclear weapons programme; its strong military support to the ruling regime in Myanmar; its diabolical assistance to the LTTE in Sri Lanka; its increasing proclivity to build and acquire ports in the Bay of Bengal and the Arabian Sea – the so-called "string of pearls" strategy; its attempts to isolate India in the ASEAN Regional Forum (ARF) and to prevent India's entry to the Shanghai Cooperation Organisation (SCO); and, its relentless efforts to increase its influence in Nepal, Bhutan and Bangladesh.

Clearly, China's growing power and influence in Asia poses a long-term strategic challenge to India as a competing regional power. The 60-year old dispute over Jammu and Kashmir (J&K) continues to bedevil India-Pakistan relations. The Line of Control (LoC) in J&K and the Actual Ground Position Line (AGPL) at Siachen Glacier were perpetual flashpoints and witnessed active military hostilities for most of these 60 years. Violations of the LoC, such as the intrusions engineered by Pakistan in the Kargil district of J&K in the summer months of 1999, are fraught with danger and have the potential to lead to full-scale conventional conflict. Also, India accuses Pakistan of sponsoring a "proxy war" through terrorist outfits nurtured by the Inter-Services Intelligence (ISI) Directorate in J&K.

With the military continuing to drive from the backseat in Pakistan, the recurrence of such misadventures remains likely, particularly if the domestic political and security situations continue to deteriorate. Pakistan's 450,000 combatant personnel remain India's foremost military threat. Progress on the India-Pakistan Composite Dialogue process has been stalled due to Pakistan's disinclination to bring to justice the perpetrators of the Mumbai terror attacks. The only positive factor is that a mutually respected cease-fire has been in place on the LoC since November 25, 2003.

Though it is an ancient civilisation, India is a young nation state that is still engaged in the process of nation building. This process has been marked by ethnic tensions, fissiparous tendencies and socio-economic challenges. India has been saddled with a long-drawn low level insurgency in J&K due to its inability to fully integrate all parts of the state with the national mainstream.

Failure to find an amicable solution and end the alienation of the people of the Kashmir Valley, in particular, could have widespread repercussions in other parts of the country and in the region. Similarly, several of India's north-eastern states have been in turmoil for many decades due to political and economic neglect, poor governance and, consequently, inadequate socio-economic development. Left Wing Extremism or Maoist terrorism is the latest manifestation of India's internal instability. These internal security challenges are likely to continue to prevail over the next two decades.

The end of the Cold War led to what could be characterised as an era of strategic uncertainty. Defence planning has become more difficult in several ways. The sources and types of conflicts for which planning must be carried out have become more diverse and less predictable even as the number of potential adversaries continues to grow. The range of missions that armed forces need to undertake is expanding to include those likely to be assigned in sub-conventional conflict, including low-intensity border wars and insurgency fuelled by foreign powers. And, the global security agenda has expanded in functional terms.

Yesterday's peripheral challenges such as the security of energy sources and the threat from mass migrations now compete with conventional threats for a share in the defence pie.

Systemic changes in the structure of the global economy, communications and military technologies are likely to alter the strategic stakes. These changes in the security paradigm are changing the strategic terms in which policymakers, military leaders and defence analysts must address long-term defence planning so as to evolve defence capabilities that will be relevant to the emerging threats.

The asymmetric character of contemporary conflict challenges conventional thinking and demands fresh responses. General Rupert Smith has identified six key trends that define modern warfare:1 the growing role of non-state actors as well as multinational forces as combatants; looking for creative new uses for old weapons; emphasis on force protection rather than using force at any cost; the prolonged nature of modern wars; a new focus on winning the hearts and minds of people; and, a shift from absolute objectives to more flexible ones.

He writes that in the Clausewitzian trinity (army, state and people), the balance between the three has changed.

"There was a time when armies dominated — as they still do in the country of warlords; later, states were able to command the complete obedience of their people.

Now it is the people who are in charge and the strategic objective is their hearts and minds." The aim of this book is to examine the salient issues affecting the recruitment, training and retention of suitable personnel in the Indian armed forces, understanding the linkage between manpower and technology and recommending measures to reduce the cost of manpower in the light of India's strategic environment. The chapter also takes stock of similar re-structuring issues across major Western armies.

INDIA'S POLY/MULTI-ALIGNED DIPLOMACY

The India that China defeated in 1962 was guided by a foreign policy doctrine called *non-alignment* vis-à-vis the superpower rivalry, and it remained the cornerstone of India's international diplomacy for more than four decades. However, this foreign policy paradigm underwent a U-turn when it metamorphosed into *poly/multi-alignment* under the new leadership in New Delhi in 1998. The new foreign policy outlook broadly had two components, namely, *improving relations with the US* and its *Look East Policy-II.*

The turnaround in India-US relations from being "estranged democracies" during the Cold War to "engaged democracies" in the 2000s has played a central role in bringing out a shift in China's India posture over the last decade. The anti-China element in the dramatically improving Indo-US relations was not very difficult to discern. Chinese scholar Jing-Dong Yuan notes that the warming of US-Indian relations took place at a time when China-US relations were undergoing serious setbacks in the late 1990s. In 1999, NATO bombed the Chinese embassy in the former Yugoslavia (the only embassy that it targeted); in May of that year, the Cox Report charged Chinese nationals with nuclear espionage and accused China of proliferation activities. hostile attitude toward the PRC further exacerbated tensions in early 2001. Also, the revised Nuclear Posture Review (NPR) included China as a nuclear target.

Meanwhile, in a diametrically opposite turn of events, India-US relations suddenly displayed signs of dramatic improvement. US President Bill Clinton visited India in March 2000 (the first presidential visit since Carter's visit in 1978). The US' National Security Strategy Report of 2002 released by the White House redefined India-US relations, stating that because of "India's potential to become one of the great democratic powers of the twenty-first century," the United States would "invest time and resources [for] building strong bilateral relations with India," and "work hard to transform our relationship accordingly." Consequently, the years 2002-03 witnessed a series of high-level meetings and substantial cooperation between the two democracies. Yet another contrast was the U.S.'s approval of Israel's sale of the

Phalcon airborne warning and control systems to India in 2003 after the blockage of a similar sale to China in 2000.

Another Chinese security analyst Du Youkang argues that the US strategy of maintaining the balance of power in South Asia during the Cold War has gone beyond the balance of power and has tilted toward India. He cites the Clinton administration's pro-India attitude during the Kargil conflict, and his subsequent official tour to South Asia, where he spent six days in India compared to five hours in Pakistan. The growing strategic ties between the two countries provides a dangerous historical precedent for Beijing. During the Cold War, China perceived India-USSR relations in terms of an anti-China alliance in South Asia. So the strategic partnership between India and the US in the 2000s is, from China's perspective, the revival of the same anti-China alliance – the only difference being that the US has replaced the Soviet Union. Zhang Guihong compared the US-India Western Pacific.

The other pedestal of India's multi-aligned diplomacy included its *Look East Policy-II*. India's Look East Policy-I was officially initiated in 1992. Like most of the previous Indian policies it was reactionary and an outcome of ad hoc-ism. The main driver behind this policy was the economic doldrums of early 1990s, and India saw Southeast Asia as a springboard to join unfolding globalization. However, India displayed an uncharacteristic proactiveness in projecting the Look East policy in its second incarnation in the first-ever India ASEAN summit in Phnom Penh, Cambodia in 2002. India added a politico-security dimension to this policy. It developed security ties with the ASEAN group. From ASEAN's perspective, developing such ties with India (apart from the US presence in the region) provided them a sense of strategic reassurance given their territorial disputes in the South China Sea with a rapidly growing, authoritarian China.

An important highlight of India's Look East Policy-II, from China's viewpoint, has been a transformational improvement in India-Japan relations. Although the ice between their relations was broken with the visit of Prime Minister Mori Yoshiro to India in August 2000, their relations broadened and deepened in the second phase. The April 2005 joint statement issued during Koizumi Junichiro's visit to India introduced a "strategic" dimension to the partnership. The establishment of the Strategic and Global Partnership between India and Japan in December 2006 elevated relations to a new level. In 2006 Japan became only the second country with which India had a bilateral annual summit apart from Russia. When then Prime Minister Shinzo Abe visited India in August 2007, the joint statement sought to provide a roadmap for new dimensions to the strategic and global partnership. The October 2008 joint statement during Prime Minister Manmohan Singh's visit to Japan mentioned the advancement of the strategic and global partnership, making Japan the only country Partnership Agreement (CEPA) which came into force in August of the same year. In late December 2011 India's External Affairs minister visited Japan in October 2011 for the Fifth round of the India-Japan Strategic Dialogue. Japanese PM Yoshihiko Noda visited India for the sixth annual meeting of the leaders of India and Japan. It was the success of India's Look East Policy-II (and not Look East Policy I) that made China remark that India's Look East Policy is "look to encircle China."

India Emerging as an Economic Giant

India and China had similar per capita income by 1974. However, China surged well ahead of India thanks to its deep economic engagement with the US after the Policy of Reform and Open Up (*gaige kaifang*) by Deng Xiaoping in 1978. While China's Open Door policy was a well-thought-out initiative, India, following its legacy of taking radical initiatives only while in crisis, embarked upon its own version of Open Door policy in 1991. The much-needed reforms removed obstacles to economic freedom, and India began to play catch-up, steadily re-integrating into the global economy. A Goldman Sachs report from 2007 found another watermark in India's economic history since 1991 when it pointed out that since 2003 India has been one of the fastest growing major economies, leading to rapid increases in per capita income, demand, and integration with the global economy.

The story of India's economic success has captivated Chinese attention over the last decade. Among Chinese scholars a new discourse has begun over India's economic success story, especially in the IT and consensus that China is a great success in exports, inside China, focusing on China's lag in information technology, Chinese researchers ask why India has become so competitive in the international software market when India has many unattractive features."

Chinese scholars now debate an "Indian Model" as an alternative to the "Chinese model" for developing countries. The Indian model, as understood by Chinese scholars, is characterized by avoiding its weaknesses and exploiting its strengths. For example, India leapfrogged from the primary sector (agriculture) to the tertiary sector (services) by exploiting its inherent advantages in the IT sector which includes a vast, young English-speaking population, the entrepreneurial genius of its private sector, computer literacy, a sound banking sector, and a culture that respects the rule of law. Chinese analysts have especially taken notice of what they call "India New Economy" which is acting like an engine to the Indian Model. Ma Jiali argues that although India is a baby elephant in the manufacturing industry, it is a "doughty tiger" in the information sector. Another set of scholars attributed India's success in this sector to its diaspora. It opined, "India's IT success is also attributed to the large cohort of educated overseas Indians who have good connections and invested heavily in their home country in recent years as a result of favourable government policies. The dynamism brought by the overseas Indians was comparable to the boost brought by the overseas Chinese since the 1978 economic reform in China."

India's Growing Soft Power

The drivers triggering a shift in China's India posture can be placed under the rubric of India's *hard power*. However, India's (re)rising *soft power* has also contributed to this shift in China's outlook a country's ability to alter the behavior of others through attraction rather than sticks or carrots. India has been a democracy right since its birth as a modern nation-state in 1947. However, its sluggish economic growth and weak military profile that led to its defeat in 1962 seriously tarnished this aspect of India's soft power. With the rising India story, its democracy as an important component of its soft power has again come into the global limelight. India has more than 1 billion people. It is linguistically, culturally, racially, and religiously diverse, and it is growing economically at an enviable pace under democratic governmental institutions (except for the emergency period of 1975-77 when civil liberties were undermined). Its culture values peaceful coexistence, nonviolence, and religious tolerance. All of these factors, combined with the largest pool of English speakers outside the US, has increased India's power of attraction without need for coercion or persuasion, a fact not lost on an envious, hard power-minded China. The country to which India has projected most of its soft power is the US, through the export of highly skilled manpower, consisting mainly of software developers, engineers, and doctors. China has been keeping a close watch on the rising influence of the Indian community in the United States, especially over the last decade. In order to improve its own soft power in the United States, China has sent far more students to the United States than India. As per the Institute of International Education's annual report in the academic year 2009-10, out of 690,932 international students in the United States nearly 128,000 of them, or more than 18 percent, were from China while India sent only 107,897 students in the same academic year. However, with Oct 2011, educational exchanges between India and the US would rise much faster in the future.

MODERNISATION PREPAREDNESS OF THE INDIAN MILITARY

Despite the army leadership's best efforts, the ongoing Revolution in Military Affairs (RMA) had, till recently, almost completely bypassed the Indian Army. For well over a decade the army's efforts to modernise had been thwarted due to political neglect and lack of adequate budgetary support. The funds made available for modernisation are extremely limited and a large portion of these funds is surrendered year after year. For Financial Year 2006-07, a sum of Rs 3,000 crore was surrendered as unspent. The fact that 155 mm ammunition for the Bofors howitzer had to be imported from South Africa during the Kargil conflict in 1999 tells its own tale of persistent shortages. Had the conflict not been confined to the 150 km frontage of the Kargil sector, T-72 and 130 mm medium gun ammunition too would have run short and it would have been politically embarrassing for the government as well as the army. In the plains the army would have had to fight with obsolete Vijayant tanks and several other vintage equipment that were unsuitable for combat. However, sustained efforts by Army HQ have now borne fruit and the army's modernisation drive is once again well underway.

In the prevailing era of strategic uncertainty, while terrorism has become the primary threat, the external and internal threats and challenges faced by India are such that a large army is still required to be maintained. Also, a high degree of preparation and operational readiness is still necessary as conventional war, though improbable, cannot be categorically ruled out. At the same time, heavy capital investments in modern defence equipment are undoubtedly a drain on a developing economy that is ill-equipped to handle the burgeoning defence expenditure. Several eminent analysts have recommended that qualitative upgradation should be accompanied by quantitative downsizing of personnel strength of the army. However, given its responsibilities for border management and the manpower-intensive low intensity conflict that the army is involved in, this is easier said than done.

Future conventional conflict on the Indian sub-continent will in all probability result from the ongoing low-intensity limited war on the Line of Control (LoC) with Pakistan or the unresolved territorial and boundary dispute with China and will be predominantly a land conflict. The Indian Army seriously lacks a potent firepower punch, especially in the mountain sector. Precision-guided munitions (PGMs) have still to enter service in numbers large enough to make a real difference. The reconnaissance, surveillance and target acquisition (RSTA) assets necessary for the optimum exploitation of even the existing firepower assets are grossly inadequate. Automated command and control and decision support systems have been on the drawing boards for several decades but are yet to mature.

In a future conventional war that will be fought under the nuclear shadow, manoeuvre will be extremely limited. This restriction will lead to much greater emphasis being placed on firepower to achieve the laid down military aim. Hence, it is imperative that artillery modernisation is undertaken with alacrity so as to generate firepower asymmetries on the future battlefield. After a long spell of keeping the powder dry, action on modernisation of the Indian artillery is livening up once again. Since January 2008, the Ministry of Defence (MoD) has issued three global tenders for 155mm guns and howitzers for the mountains, the plains and self-propelled guns for the deserts. Summer and winter trials are expected to be held over the next one year and, red tape permitting, contracts may be awarded as early as in the first half of 2010.

Artillery firepower had paved the way for victory during the Kargil conflict. Despite the lessons learnt in Kargil, modernisation of the artillery had continued to lag behind. The last major acquisition of towed gun-howitzers was that of about 400 pieces of 39-calibre 155mm FH-77B howitzers form Bofors of Sweden in the mid-1980s. This gun had proved its mettle in the Kargil conflict. Just when a contract for 120 tracked and 180 wheeled self-propelled (SP) 155mm guns was about to be concluded after years of protracted trials, South African arms manufacturer Denel, a leading contender for the contract, was alleged to have been involved in a corruption scam in an earlier deal for anti-material rifles (AMRs). The other two howitzers in contention, from Soltam of Israel and BAE (Bofors) of Sweden did not meet the laid down criteria according to the COAS and Army HQ recommended fresh trials, setting the programme back at least three to four years. Another key issue was that the howitzers that had been offered were technology demonstration models and not guns that were in actual service with the home country armies.

The probability of the next conventional war breaking out in the mountains is far higher than that of a war in the plains. With this in view, the artillery recently conceptualised a requirement for a light-weight towed howitzer of 155mm calibre for employment in the mountains. Neither the present Bofors howitzer nor its replacement will be capable of operations in the mountains. A light-weight 45-calibre 155mm howitzer weighing less than 5,000 kg, with a light but adequately powered prime mover, is ideal for the mountains. The gun-train should be capable of negotiating sharp road bends without the need to unhook the gun from the prime mover. The two British 45-calibre 155mm howitzers that competed for the US contract for a similar howitzer some years ago – the UFH (Ultra-lightweight Field Howitzer) and the LTH (Light-weight Towed Howitzer) – could be considered for licensed production with transfer of technology.

In January 2008, the MoD floated a Request for Proposal (RfP) for 140 pieces of ultra-light 39 calibre 155mm towed howitzers for use by the Indian Army's mountain formations and, presumably, by its rapid reaction divisions – as and when these are raised as it will be easy to transport by air. 140 howitzers will be adequate to equip seven medium artillery regiments and will cost approximately Rs 3,000 crore.

The RfP has been reportedly issued to UK's BAE Systems (which now owns Bofors), for the M777 howitzer claimed to be the lightest in the world at under 4,220 kg, and to Singapore Technologies for the Pegasus SLWH.

India has floated a global tender for the purchase of 400 155mm towed artillery guns for the Army, to be followed by indigenous manufacture of another 1,100 howitzers, in a project worth a whopping Rs 8,000 crore. The RFP was issued to eight prospective bidders including BAE, General Dynamics, Nexter (France), Rhinemetall (Germany) and Samsung (South Korea). An RfP has also been issued for 180 wheeled self-propelled guns for around Rs 4,700 crore for employment by mechanised forces in the plains and semi-desert sectors.

Since the Bofors 155mm Howitzer was introduced into service, the indigenously designed and manufactured 105 mm Indian Field Gun (IFG) and its (not so) light version, the Light Field Gun (LFG), have joined the 75/24 Indian Mountain Gun, the 100mm Russian field gun and the 122mm Russian howitzer on the obsolescence list. Approximately 180 pieces of 130mm M46 Russian medium guns have been successfully "up-gunned" to 155mm calibre with ordnance supplied by Soltam of Israel. The new barrel length of 45 calibres has enhanced the range of the gun to about 40 km with extended range ammunition.

A contract for the acquisition of two regiments of the 12-tube, 300mm Smerch multi-barrel rocket launcher (MBRL) system with 90 km range was reported to have been signed with Russia's Rosoboronexport in early-2006. This will be a major boost for the long-range firepower capabilities of the army. If this weapon system had been available during the Kargil conflict, Pakistan's brigade HQ and forward airfield at Skardu and other targets deep inside POK could have been hit with impunity. Extended range (ER) rockets are being introduced for the 122 mm Grad MBRL that has been in service for over three decades. The ER rockets will enhance the weapon system's range from 22 to about 40 km. A Rs 5,000 crore contract has also been signed for the serial production of the Pinaka MBRL weapon system, another DRDO project plagued by time delays and completed with help from Larsen and Toubro and the Tatas.

The modernisation plan of tube artillery alone is likely to cost Rs 13,000 crore. The major acquisitions will be of initial lots of 400 towed howitzers of 155mm calibre, with a barrel length of 52 calibres, costing about Rs 4,000 crore, 140 ultra-light weight 155mm towed howitzers, with a barrel length of 45 calibres, costing Rs 3,000 crore and 180 SP 155mm howitzers costing Rs 5,000 crore. The "Shakti" project for a command and control systems for the artillery, called Artillery Combat Command and Control System (ACCCS), has reached the stage of maturity and is now being fielded up to the regimental level.

The BrahMos supersonic cruise missile (Mach 2.8 to 3.0), with a precision strike capability, very high kill energy and range of 290 km, was inducted into the army in July 2007. It is a versatile missile that can be launched from TATRA mobile launchers and silos on land, aircraft and ships and, perhaps in future, also from submarines. Fifty BrahMos missiles are expected to be produced every year. Efforts are underway to further increase its strike range. BrahMos Aerospace has orders worth Rs 3,500 crore from the army and the navy, which has opted for the anti-ship as well as the land attack cruise missile (LACM) versions. These terrain hugging missiles are virtually immune to counter measures due to their high speed and very low radar cross section and are far superior to sub-sonic cruise missiles like Pakistan's Babur. Chile,

Kuwait, Malaysia and South Africa have shown interest in acquiring this missile.

The Indian army is extensively engaged in ongoing internal security (IS) and counter-insurgency operations (CI) and simultaneously needs to prepare itself for a future border conflict that may spill over to a larger conventional war in the plains. In keeping with these twin requirements, Army HQ have apparently decided to upgrade the IS and CI capabilities of infantry battalions as well as enhance their Infantry firepower-mobility-EW (electronic warfare) punch for a possible war in the plains against Pakistan or in the mountains against China. The Army Chief's modernisation vision is to "adapt to high-end technology, improve night-fighting capability... (and) information technology, information warfare and network centric warfare."

Despite its large-scale employment on border management and extensive commitments in Internal Security and Counter Insurgency operations, infantry modernisation had been languishing for several decades when the Ministry of Defence (MoD) finally cleared a visionary plan to modernise the army's infantry battalions by according "in principle" approval in the form of Modification 4B to the war establishment (WE) of a standard infantry battalion in 1998. However, no funds were specially sanctioned for this purpose till the BJP-led NDA government approved the expenditure of Rs 3,500 crore in September 2003. Thereafter, approval had to be sought on file for each new weapon system or piece of equipment on a "case-by-case" basis as has become the norm. It is by now well-known how each such case chronicles the saga of an uphill struggle to get approval first from the MoD, then MoD (Finance) and, finally, the Ministry of Finance (MoF). All this is only possible after the DRDO has first certified that the weapon system or equipment in question cannot be developed and manufactured indigenously and such a certificate is hard to come by.

While 250 Kornet-E anti-tank guided missiles (ATGMs) with thermal imaging sights have substantially increased the anti-tank capability of infantry battalions, most efforts to modernise the equipment held by infantry and Rashtriya Rifles (RR) units are aimed at enhancing their capability for surveillance and target acquisition at night and boosting their firepower for precise retaliation against infiltrating columns and terrorists holed up in built-up areas. About 200 hand-held BFSRs with practical ranges up to seven to eight km where clear line of sight is available, 2,000 hand-held thermal imaging devices (HHTIs) with ranges up to 2,000 metres for observation at night and stand-alone infra-red, seismic and acoustic sensors with varying capabilities have enabled infantrymen to dominate the Line of Control so completely that infiltration has come down to almost a trickle.

The newly acquired weapons, which complement these surveillance and observation devices, include: 1,500x84 mm rocket launchers, including some disposable ones; 1,000 AMRs (anti-material rifles); 8,000 UBGLs (under-barrel grenade launchers); 4,000 new generation carbines; 300 bullet proof vehicles; and, several hundred accurate sniper rifles. However, the numbers acquired and the ammunition stocks are still inadequate and need to be made up more rapidly. While the INSAS 5.56 mm assault rifles have now been in service for almost 10 years and proved to be effective, the light machine gun (LNG) version is still facing teething problems and the carbine version for close quarter battle has not found favour with the army. New 5.56 mm assault rifles of bull-pup design with an integrated laser range finder and grenade launcher are under development. Efforts are also being made to provide infantry platoons and sections with integrated GPS-based navigation system, secure light-weight walkie-talkie radio sets and better protective gear with a helmet that incorporates a built-in head-up display.

The mechanised infantry is now equipped with the BMP-2 ICV Sarath of which over 1,000 have been built since 1987. A new variant is the 81 mm Carrier Mortar Tracked Vehicle (CMTV) that is based on the chassis of the Sarath ICV and has been indigenously developed to enhance the integral firepower available to mechanised infantry battalions. Other variants include a command post, an ambulance, armoured dozer and engineer and reconnaissance vehicles. Mechanised reconnaissance and support battalions need better surveillance radars, fire-and-forget ATGMs and effective night fighting capability. However, their capabilities can be upgraded on a lower priority compared with infantry battalions that are engaged in border management and IS/CI operations.

The army's infantry battalions also need their own mini or micro UAVs like Elbit's Skylark or Rafael's Skylite, among others, to partly reduce the extent of patrolling necessary in internal security environment and to improve their surveillance capability in conventional conflict. These UAVs should have a range of about 10 to 15 km, should be light-weight (less than 10 kg), hand-launched, carry a single payload, e.g. a daylight video camera or infra-red camera for night operations, and should be inexpensive enough to be dispensable. A mini ground control station should be authorized at battalion HQ for planning and control. Ideally, these should be indigenously designed and developed and locally manufactured.

A new DRDO project, that is reported to be ongoing, aims to equip future soldiers with lightweight force multipliers. Soldiers of the future will have miniaturised communication and GPS systems, small power packs, weapon platforms and smart vests with fibre-optic sensors. The soldiers will also have better and lighter combat fatigues, boots, belts, ammunition pouches, rucksacks and rations in the form of meals-ready-to-eat. Though somewhat akin to the US Army's Land Warrior programme, the Indian Army programme for modernisation of infantry battalions will result in only incremental changes. However, these would be significant enough to make a difference on the battlefields of the Indian sub-continent. The infantryman's average combat load is approximately 27 kg, including the 3.06 kg 5.56 mm INSAS assault rifle and its "on weapon" ammunition. If this can be reduced by even a few kg, it will enable the soldier to improve his agility in battle and counter-insurgency operations. Ultimately an infantryman has to be prepared to engage in hand-to-hand combat and agility can make a difference between life and death.

For over 350 infantry battalions, plus about 150 Rashtriya Rifles, Assam Rifles and Territorial Army battalions, these major changes will be extremely costly to implement and will spill over at least 10 to 12 years – that is, if the funds can be found. What is certain is that there is no alternative to making the financial commitment that is necessary to enhance the operational capabilities of the army's infantry battalions. Without modernising this cutting edge of its sword, the army will soon begin to resemble the armies of India's lesser neighbours.

The indigenously designed Arjun main battle tank (MBT) has been in the pipeline for over two decades. Though the tank has many good features, it has consistently failed to meet the army's GSQR for an MBT and orders have been placed for only 124 tanks to be manufactured. The lack of progress on the Arjun MBT had slowed down the pace of armour modernisation. India then signed a deal with Russia to acquire 310 T-90S tanks in the year 2000. Subsequently, India began to assemble these tanks at Avadi. It has recently been reported that in addition to these, India has decided to acquire another 347 T-90S tanks and assemble them within the country.

The first Indian assembled T-90S (Bhishma) rolled off the production line on January 8, 2004. While T-90S Russian tanks have provided new teeth to India's strike formations in the plains and corrected the imbalance that had resulted from Pakistan's acquisition of T-80 UD from Ukraine and the Al Khalid tanks jointly designed with China, a large number of T-72 (Ajeya) tanks are still awaiting modernisation. The lack of a suitable fire control system and night fighting capability are major handicaps. As soon as the obsolescent Vijayanta tanks are phased out of service, it will be time to also discard the old T-55s as well as they can no longer be either upgraded or modernised. Armour modernisation is now proceeding apace and can be classified as a success story.

The air defence (AD) of mechanised forces is another area that is crying for attention. The Kvadrat missile system that has been the backbone of AD for strike formations since the early 1970s are now ageing and need urgent replacement. With the DRDO's indigenous Akash medium-range and Trishul short-range missile projects not making major headway, it is time to start looking at import substitutes. In fact, the assets of Army Air Defence corps of the army are grossly inadequate to provide effective protection against enemy aircraft during war. This young corps requires substantial capital infusion to really come into its own.

Another DRDO project that is way behind schedule is the Nag anti-tank missile system. The antiquated Jonga-mounted SS-11 B1 anti-tank guided missile (ATGM) system has been replaced in missile battalions by MILAN shoulder-fired ATGMs. However, a vehicle-mounted missile system like the Nag is definitely necessary for reconnaissance and attrition tasks. The experimental Plan AREN tactical communications system for strike formations needs early replacement.

The ability to carry broadband data needs to be enhanced in particular. Even the more recent static communications network called ASCON lacks ISDN capability for the real-time transmission of maps and streaming video.

While some Stentor long-range BFSRs have been in service for over a decade, medium-range radars are still to be acquired. At least about 30 to 40 weapon locating radars (WLRs) are required for effective counter-bombardment, especially in the plains, and only a few have been procured so far. Israeli Searcher-I unmanned aerial vehicles (UAVs) have been introduced into service but these are few in number and it will be a long time before these will really make a difference by providing a real-time surveillance capability so that ground forces can initiate action even as a fresh input is received. Only a small number of Searcher – II UAVs, with an upper ceiling that makes them suitable for the mountains, have been acquired.

An automated command and control and decision support system for use by the General Staff is still a far cry and so are supporting systems like the battlefield surveillance system and air space management system. The urgent requirement of real-time satellite reconnaissance systems has still not been accepted despite the nuclear overhang under which the armed forces now operate. Even though the cameras on India's remote sensing and cartographic satellites now have sharply enhanced resolutions, less than one metre, military-grade photographs of still better resolution are needed to be purchased from the open market. These sources may dry up quickly during war.

A "system of systems" approach must be followed so that scarce RSTA and communications resources can be synergistically configured and optimally exploited. The war in Iraq fought in March-April 2003 was based on the concept of "network-centric warfare" in which surveillance sensors, targeting systems and "shooters" are fused together in a seamless "system of systems" that reduced response time between the acquisition of a target and its destruction to 15 to 20 minutes. While such a system may take over a decade to establish, a beginning must be made right away.

PGMs are increasingly gaining currency as weapons of choice in conflict on land, both to accurately destroy critical hard targets quickly as well as to avoid or at least minimise collateral damage. During the Gulf War I in 1991, despite all the CNN-generated hype of smart bombs flying unerringly through ventilators, PGMs formed less than 10 percent of the total high explosive dropped over Iraq and were rather inaccurate. The "collateral" destruction of an air raid shelter harbouring women and children has been too well documented to bear recounting. The coalition forces did not destroy a single Iraqi Scud missile launcher. In Kosovo, PGMs accounted for about 30 per cent of the ordnance dropped and accuracies had improved considerably by 1999. In the post-September 11, 2001 retribution inflicted on the Taliban militia and its al Qaeda supporters in Afghanistan, the share of PGMs had risen to nearly 60 percent. In Gulf War II in Iraq, the ratio of PGMs went up to nearly 70 per cent. The Indian artillery does not have any PGMs worth the name. Only limited quantities of the Russian Krasnopol PGM have been imported for the Bofors 155 mm howitzer. Among others, the Bofors Bonus PGM is a suitable candidate, subject to successful trials in the deserts and the mountains.

Finally, the approach to army modernisation must be more focused; the priorities must be clearly established and then adhered to. The government must give a firm commitment in terms of funds and the Ministry of Defence must streamline its procedures and processes for speedy procurement of high priority weapons and equipment. It is time to institute a rolling, non-lapsable defence modernisation fund of Rs. 25,000 crores as a viable method of ensuring that defence procurement is not subjected to the vagaries of annual budgets. The present situation is disturbing and, if allowed to go on indefinitely, will seriously compromise the army's preparedness to fight the next border war that inimical neighbours like Pakistan can be expected to thrust on India.

MODERNISING THE INDIAN INFANTRY

Why has it taken the Army so long to conceive an upgrade package for the oldest, most potent and intensely employed fighting arm, the Infantry, even after the so-called revolution in military affairs? The foot soldier, the original and most versatile weapon system that is always taken for granted, has emerged from the dubious shock and awe strategy of recent campaigns as its ultimate arbiter. India has paid dearly for the neglect of its infantry in terms of cost, casualties and over-stretch of battle. But the Infantry has never let us down. Kargil was its finest hour. Gen VP Malik, the Army Chief of the time, wryly noted: "We will fight with what we have."

So when for the first time an international conference of Army and defence industry was launched last week to put the forgotten soldier centre-stage, some misgivings were natural. While Army Chief Gen JJ Singh outlined his vision for the soldier system of the future, the conspicuous and total absence of Government-MoD-robbed the conference of any sanctity. In sharp contrast, for a MoD-sponsored defence finance seminar earlier in the month, Government officials and ministers were stepping over each other at Vigyan Bhavan.

Free India's Army came into being in 1947 and within weeks, the Infantry soldiers landed in Srinagar to save J&K from being gobbled up by Pakistani tribal raiders. Since then, the Infantry has not ceased fighting proxy wars there and later, elsewhere too. A former Army Chief, Gen SR Choudhury, who was not from the Infantry, described the Infantry as the Army and vice versa. Field Marshal Montgomery said: An army is considered only as good as its Infantry.

The experience of four wars, several border skirmishes, two out-of-area missions, the ceaseless campaign to counter cross-border terrorism in Kashmir, numerous other insurgencies in the North-East, internal stability operations elsewhere in the country and UN peace keeping operations make the Indian Infantry the most battle-hardened and combat rich force in the world. The simple and uncomplaining infantryman has given so much to so many for so little. The modernisation of the infantry was first attempted-halfheartedly-in the mid-1980s by the Perspective Planning branch of the Army Headquarters. The bias for mechanised warfare, zealously pursued by Gen Sundarji, was so pronounced that the Infantry modernisation plan was skipped altogether. Guns, tanks, APCs were the weapons in demand. The Infantry was ignored. Had a modest upgrade package been undertaken at that time, infantry would have been more combat contemporary and effective.

Instead, till recently, some soldiers were still using World War II equipment and clothing. Shameful as it was, soldiers had to buy rucksacks and other accoutrements from the market. DRDO is still to come out with a light bulletproof vest. The Army failed to accurately visualize the nature of combat it would fight in the future. Pakistan-sponsored insurgency in Punjab did not alert the nation and the Army to the proxy war brewing in J&K. We defaulted on both counts-anticipating low intensity conflict and cross border terrorism and preparing the Infantry for it.

Despite the sustained counter-insurgency and counter-terrorism campaign in J&K and the North-East since the 1990s, the Army was sluggish in investing in the infantry. The first Gulf War reintroduced the fiction that wars could be won from the air. The air campaigns in Bosnia and Kosovo temporarily turned fiction into reality. But 9/11 broke the myth of supremacy of air power. Operation Enduring Freedom in Afghanistan lasted 76 days; 65 of these were air operations.

The 11-day land offensive secured a temporary and incomplete victory against the Taliban. Operation Iraqi Freedom on the other hand, fought for 20 days was bereft of any preparatory air campaign though a secret air war preceded it. Unhappily for the US/NATO-led coalition forces, despite their pyrrhic military victories, low intensity wars in Afghanistan and Iraq are continuing in full blaze.

The recent 34-day war in Lebanon and the ongoing campaign in Gaza demonstrate the limits of Israel's military power. Used to decisive victories in less than 10 days, Israeli Defence Forces (IDF) were badgered by Hassan Nasrallah's jihadi militia. Reliance on air power, tanks and guns in Lebanon as substitute for ground troops-infantry-was motivated by casualty aversion. We too have to be sensitive to casualties.

The wars in Lebanon, Iraq and Afghanistan spurred by the growing cult of Osama bin Laden and Hassan Nasrallah require a redefinition of the concept of power and military success. Success would necessarily be an inclusive military victory encompassing post-conflict stability and reconstruction. For this we need Infantry.

The Indian Army should not get overly seduced by high-sounding warfare like 'netcentric' that the West is being diverted into. This is not to suggest we ignore the strides in high-tech warfare. But as a former US NATO Commander noted recently: "This netcentric stuff is great but our men in Baghdad are being blown up with their Humvees by IEDs." He suggested that we address the battle we are fighting before switching to the one we will fight in the future.

India's supreme operational challenge is and will be the maintenance of internal security. Just last month, Prime Minister Manmohan Singh stated this ground reality. The Infantry is at the heart of counterinsurgency and counter-terrorism operations and may well get sucked into anti-Naxal operations as well. Keeping the Army operationally ready for both conventional and unconventional missions is imperative but the emphasis has to be on the business of the day: CI and CT.

The Indian Infantry is belatedly embarking on a modernisation programme to enhance its combat skills through increased lethality, communications, surveillance, mobility and suvivability. These force multipliers will enable the soldier to fight all-weather, 24x7 and on any terrain in the right battle-configuration albeit with the accent on LIC. The GSQR for the Future-Infantry-Soldier-As a System (F-INSAS) must empower not encumber the soldier. DRDO must compete with domestic and international industry. DRDO has one more chance to make amends for its omissions and commissions. F-INSAS must strike the right balance between the surge of technology and sensibility of the soldier keeping the battle of the future in mind. Defence Minister AK Antony should accord F-INSAS the highest strategic priority.

ARMY MODERNIZATION: ENHANCING CAPABILITIES WITHOUT REDUCING MANPOWER

With personnel strength of 1.1 million soldiers (6 regional commands, a training command, 13 corps, and 38 divisions), the Indian Army has kept the nation together through various crises, including four wars since independence, Pakistan's "proxy war" in J&K since 1989–90, and insurgencies in many of the northeastern states. Given its large-scale operational commitments on border management and counterinsurgency, the army cannot afford to reduce its manpower numbers until these challenges are overcome. Many of its weapons and equipment are bordering on obsolescence and need to be replaced. The next step would be to move gradually toward acquiring network-centric capabilities for effects-based operations so as to optimize the army's full combat potential for defensive and offensive operations. The army is also preparing to join the navy and the air force in launching intervention operations in India's area of strategic interest when called on to do so in the future.

Lieutenant General J.P. Singh (retired), former deputy chief of the army staff (planning and systems), stated in an interview with the *CLAWS Journal* that "the critical capabilities that are being enhanced to meet challenges across the spectrum include battlefield transparency, battlefield management systems, night-fighting capability, enhanced firepower, including terminally guided munitions, integrated maneuver capability to include self-propelled artillery, quick reaction surface-to-air missiles, the latest assault engineer equipment, tactical control systems, integral combat aviation support and network centricity." The army's mechanized forces are still mostly "night blind." Its artillery lacks towed and self-propelled 155-mm howitzers for the plains and the mountains and has little capability by way of multi-barrel rocket launchers and surface-to-surface missiles. Infantry battalions urgently need to acquire modern weapons and equipment for counterinsurgency and counterterrorism operations to increase operational effectiveness and lower casualties.

Main battle tanks (MBT) and infantry combat vehicles (ICV) are the driving forces of India's conventional deterrence in the plains. This fleet is being modernized gradually by inducting two regiments of the indigenously developed Arjun MBT and importing 310 T-90S MBTs from Russia. A contract has also been signed for 347 additional T-90S tanks to be assembled in India. The BMP-1 and BMP-2 Russian ICVs, which have long been the mainstay of the mechanized infantry battalions, need to be replaced as well. The new ICVs must be capable of performing internal security duties and counterinsurgency operations in addition to their primary role in conventional conflicts.

Artillery modernization plans include the acquisition of towed, wheeled, and self-propelled 155-mm guns and howitzers for the plains and the mountains through import as well as indigenous development. The Corps of Army Air Defence is also faced with problems of obsolescence. The vintage L-70 40-mm air defense (AD) gun system, the four-barreled ZSU-23-4 Schilka (SP) AD gun system, the SAM-6 (Kvadrat), and the SAM-8 OSA-AK, among others, need to be replaced by more responsive modern AD systems that are capable of defeating current and future threats.

The modernization of India's infantry battalions is moving forward but at a similarly slow pace. This initiative is aimed at enhancing the battalions' capability for surveillance and target acquisition at night and boosting their firepower for precise retaliation against infiltrating columns and terrorists hiding in built-up areas.

These plans include the acquisition of shoulder-fired missiles, hand-held battlefield surveillance radars, and hand-held thermal imaging devices for observation at night. A system called F-INSAS (future infantry soldier as a system) is also under development. One infantry division has been designated as a rapid reaction force for employment on land or in intervention operations and will have one amphibious brigade and two air assault brigades. Similarly, the Indian Army proposes to substantially enhance the operational capabilities of army aviation, engineers, signal communications, reconnaissance, surveillance, and target acquisition branches in order to improve the army's overall combat potential by an order of magnitude.

Modern strategic and tactical level command and control systems need to be acquired on priority for better synergies during conventional and sub-conventional conflict. Plans for the acquisition of a mobile corps-to-battalion tactical communications system and a battalion-level battlefield management system likewise need to be hastened.

Despite being the largest user of space, the army does not yet have a dedicated military satellite for its space surveillance needs. Cyberwarfare capabilities are also at a nascent stage. The emphasis thus far has been on developing protective capabilities to safeguard Indian networks and C4I2SR (command, control, communications, computers, intelligence, information, surveillance, and reconnaissance) from cyberattack. Offensive capabilities have yet to be adequately developed. All these capabilities will make it easier for the army to undertake joint operations with multinational forces when the need arises and the government approves such a policy option.

NAVAL MODERNIZATION: MAJOR FLEET EXPANSION

The Indian Navy's ambitious Maritime Capabilities Perspective Plan seeks to dominate the Indian Ocean region by acquiring blue water operational capability while effectively countering current and emerging threats closer to the coastline. There is a perceptible shift in emphasis from an increase in the number of platforms to the enhancement of capabilities. According to a report tabled in the Indian Parliament in the last week of April 2012 by the Standing Committee on Defence, the navy's modernization plan seeks to achieve the following objectives:

- Augment airborne maritime surveillance, strike, anti-submarine warfare [ASW] and air defence capability through induction of shore-based aircraft, integral helos, carrier based aircraft, space based [assets] and UAVs [unmanned aerial vehicles], along with suitable weapons and sensors.

- Develop ASW capability through induction of suitable platforms, weapons and sensors.
- Build adequate stand off capability for sea lift and expeditionary operations to achieve desired power projection force levels, influence events ashore and undertake military operations other than war.
- Induct assets and develop suitable infrastructure to augment forces available for low intensity maritime operations (LIMO), protection of off-shore assets and [for] coastal security.
- Induct force multipliers like satellite based global communications, reconnaissance and network enabled platforms to achieve battle-space dominance capability and perform network centric operations.
- Induct state-of-the-art equipment and specialized platforms for special forces to enhance niche capabilities to conduct maritime intervention operations and other envisaged roles.
- Develop support infrastructure in island territories to support the planned force levels as well as support infrastructure for ships/submarines/aircrafts at ports and airbases.

According to Admiral Arun Prakash (retired), former chief of naval staff, India's naval modernization plans are designed to meet the following aims:

- Acquiring a capability for maritime domain awareness in the area of responsibility, including space-based surveillance, maritime reconnaissance, airborne early warning and control (AEW&C), and UAVs
- Developing the capability for expeditionary and joint warfare, supported by special operations
- Acquiring reach and sustainability through long endurance, tankers, turnaround facilities in friendly foreign ports, and longer intervals between maintenance cycles
- Acquiring modern capabilities in fields of tactical aviation,

ASW, anti-air/anti-missile, land-attack, mine countermeasures, and electronic warfare
- Networking ships, submarines, and airborne platforms via satellite
- Committing to self-reliance and indigenization, with the objective of harnessing national strengths in shipbuilding, engineering, electronics, and IT

The Indian Navy has two operational fleets—the Eastern Naval Command and Western Naval Command—and has proposed to center both fleets around an aircraft carrier. Eventually the navy plans to graduate to three carrier battle groups. The INS *Chakra,* a nuclear-powered submarine leased from Russia, will join the fleet later in 2012, while the INS *Arihant,* the first of three to four indigenously designed and developed nuclear-armed submarines, is expected to become fully operational by late 2014. India has also begun to induct Russian Nerpa-class submarines, which will give the navy a much needed fillip to the submarine fleet and considerably enhance sea-denial capabilities. Three stealth frigates have only recently been added to the fleet.

The Indian Navy's modernization plans, though much delayed, have thus finally begun to pick up steam. Pointing out the navy's role as a key facilitator in promoting peace and stability in the Indian Ocean region, Defence Minister Antony observed while commissioning a stealth frigate in July 2012 that the present operating environment of the Indian Navy "dictates that we balance our resources with a strategy that is responsive across the full range of blue and brown water operations....The maintenance of a strong and credible navy and strengthening cooperation and friendship with other countries to promote regional and global stability is the need of the hour."

The navy plans to expand to a fleet of 150 ships in the next ten to fifteen years, with 50 warships now under construction and 100 new vessels in the acquisition pipeline. The navy is also engaged in setting up operational turnaround bases, forward-operating bases, and naval air enclaves with a view to enhancing India's surveillance efforts in the Indian Ocean region. Plans for accretions to the naval aviation fleet are likewise progressing smoothly: Boeing

737 P-8I maritime reconnaissance aircraft have begun to be inducted, and 5 additional Kamov Ka-31 AEW helicopters will be added to the existing fleet of 11 helicopters. Further, the navy's amphibious landing capability has been enhanced considerably by the acquisition of the INS *Jalashwa* (ex–USS Trenton) and other landing ships, and additional capabilities for amphibious warfare are being rapidly developed.

As a result of these efforts, the Indian Navy is on the cusp of acquiring the capabilities necessary to join key strategic partners such as the U.S. Navy in safeguarding the sea lanes of communication in the northern Indian Ocean and ensuring unfettered freedom of the seas for TRADE and commerce.

AIR FORCE MODERNIZATION: AIR DOMINANCE AND FORCE PROJECTION

Until recently, India's traditional strategic sphere lay between the Gulf of Aden and the Strait of Malacca; but with India's global footprint expanding, the Indian Air Force should be ready to serve wherever the country's future strategic interests lie. The air force is gearing up to provide the strategic outreach that India needs as a growing regional power and to project power where necessary in order to defend vital national interests. According to Kapil Kak, a retired air vice marshal and senior defense analyst, although there is a gap between vision and capability with regard to shaping India's strategic neighborhood, forward movement is now visible. In his view, the modernization plans of the air force are aimed at achieving the following objectives:

- Air dominance and control of the air
- Deterrence, by both denial and punishment
- Long-range offensive reach—penetration, precision, persistence, and parallelity—in simultaneous operations at the tactical, operational, and strategic levels
- Strategic air-lift capability for power projection through both hard and soft power, such as humanitarian assistance and disaster relief operations and diaspora evacuation
- Build-up of capability for coercion

- Acquisition of force enablers and multipliers and related combat-support systems, including networking for tri-service command and control
- Capability of conducting cyberspace and information operations
- Indigenization of future capabilities for design and development.

From a sanctioned strength of 39 squadrons, the Indian Air Force is down to 34 squadrons at present, due to decades of neglect, but hopes to enhance its strength to 42 squadrons by 2022. Yet plans to acquire 126 multi-mission, medium-range combat aircraft—in order to maintain an edge over the regional air forces—are stuck in the procurement quagmire. Tejas, the indigenously designed light combat aircraft, which is expected to replace the obsolescent Mig-21, is still a few years away from becoming fully operational. India is also developing a fifth-generation fighter jointly with Russia and aims to fly it in 2015. New fighter bombers include a fleet of 272 Sukhoi-30 MKIs, half of which have already been built. AEW aircraft are being acquired from Israel as well as being developed indigenously. India has also acquired 6 C-130J Super Hercules aircraft for its special forces and will likely order 6 more from the United States. C-17 Globemaster heavy-lift aircraft are also likely to be acquired shortly, which will take India's defense cooperation with the United States to a new level. Although a contract has been signed with a Swiss firm for 75 Pilatus PC-7 basic trainer aircraft, India's fleet of jet trainers continues to be deficient. In the rotary-wing category, the indigenously manufactured Dhruv utility helicopter has entered service. The air force is also in the process of acquiring medium-lift transport helicopters and attack helicopters.

In keeping with developments in the region, India's strategic forces are also modernizing at a steady pace. The Agni-I and Agni-II missiles are now fully operational. Immediate requirements include the Agni-V intermediate-range ballistic missile, which has a 5,000-km range, and nuclear-powered submarines with suitable ballistic missiles to provide genuine second-strike capability. As noted above, the INS *Arihant*, India's first indigenously built nuclear submarine, will likely become fully operational by late 2014. While India's emphasis is on mobile missile launchers, a small number of hardened silos are also being constructed. The armed forces do not currently have a truly integrated tri-service C4I2SR system suitable for network-centric warfare, which would allow them to optimize their individual capabilities; however, plans have been made to develop such a system in the next five to ten years. In fact, all new weapons and equipment acquisitions are now being planned on a tri-service basis to ensure interoperability.

INDIA'S QUEST FOR STRATEGIC OUTREACH

Given its growing power and responsibilities, India has been steadily enhancing its expeditionary and military intervention capabilities, which have been amply demonstrated in recent times. During the 1991 Gulf War, India airlifted 150,000 civilian workers, who had been forced to leave Iraq, from the airfield at Amman, Jordan, over a period of 30 days. This was the largest airlift since the Berlin airlift at the end of World War II. During the 2004 tsunami, the Indian armed forces were at the forefront of rescue and relief operations. Over 70 Indian Navy ships transported rescue teams and relief material to disaster zones in less than 72 hours, even though the country's eastern seaboard had itself suffered considerable casualties and damage. Likewise, Indian Navy ships on a goodwill visit to European countries during the Lebanon war in 2006 lifted and brought back 5,000 Indian civilian refugees.

From the ongoing modernization plans described above, it is evident that India is preparing to join the world's major powers in terms of the ability to undertake out-of-area contingency operations. Further, the acquisition of SU-30 MKI long-range fighter bombers with air-to-air refuelling capability, C-130J Hercules transport aircraft, and airborne-warning-and-control-system and maritime-surveillance capabilities over the next five to ten years will give India considerable strategic outreach. New Delhi has consistently favored military interventions only under a UN umbrella. Though that position is unlikely to change in the near term, India is likely to join future coalitions of the willing even without UN approval when vital national interests are threatened and need to be defended. Shiv Shankar Menon, India's national security adviser, stated in a speech in August 2011: "As a nation state India has consistently shown tactical caution and strategic initiative, sometimes simultaneously. But equally, initiative and risk-taking must be strategic, not tactical, if we are to avoid the fate of becoming a rentier state." He went on to mention that India was cooperating extensively with other militaries to fight piracy off the Horn of Africa. Such cooperation will increase in the future as India adds to its intervention capabilities.

Given that India faces complex strategic scenarios and is located in an increasingly unstable neighborhood, it is in New Delhi's interest to encourage a cooperative model of regional security and work with all friendly countries toward that end. At the same time, New Delhi finds it pragmatic to hedge just in case worst-case scenarios—such as the collapse of China or China's use of military force for territorial gains—begin to unfold and threaten India's economic development or territorial integrity. The increasing emphasis on maritime cooperation, particularly with the United States, is part of India's continuing efforts to fulfill growing obligations and responsibilities as a regional power. New Delhi is now working to cooperate with all the major Asian powers in order to maintain peace and stability in the Indian Ocean and the Asia-Pacific more generally, though without aligning militarily with any one power. Toward this end, the armed forces are working together to achieve joint warfare capabilities for intervention operations in India's area of strategic interest. In sum, a rising India will soon become a net contributor to security in the Indian Ocean region, together with strategic partners such as the United States.

Nonetheless, India's modernization plans are moving ahead at a very slow pace. Policy paralysis in New Delhi due to the vagaries of coalition politics in a parliamentary democracy, along with the reduction in the defense budget as a share of India's GDP due to sluggish growth in the economy, has further exacerbated the difficulties in increasing the pace of modernization. However, the process is certainly underway, and there is hope that it will receive bipartisan support across the political spectrum because of the realization that no alternative exists for addressing emerging threats and challenges but for India to quickly modernize its armed forces.

India's military modernization, however slow it might be, will lead to a qualitative increase in defense cooperation with the United States and other strategic partners by enhancing the capabilities of the Indian armed forces for joint coalition operations, if they are in India's national interest. Overall, India will gradually acquire the capability to act as a net provider of security in South Asia and the Indian Ocean region. This positive development will allow strategic partners like the United States to reduce their military commitments to the region to a limited extent. Hence, India's modernization efforts will enhance and further cement U.S.-India relations.

3

China's South Asia Policy-Implications for India

PRESIDENT XI JINPING'S SOUTH ASIA POLICY

China's leader Xi Jinping seems to have shifted the focus of his regime's foreign policy including that towards South Asia from core interests to economic interests. Xi's statement that China is prepared to sign friendship treaties with the country's neighbours and the PRC's willingness to adopt a 'trilateral' (i.e China, India and the concerned South Asian country) approach towards tackling issues in South Asia, signal Beijing's new conciliatory thinking. Nonetheless, in terms of strategy, China under Xi Jinping shows no sign of any change – balancing India by supporting Pakistan appears to be the corner stone of Xi's regional policy; suggesting it, is the China-Pakistan agreement on the need to have a 'strategic balance' in South Asia. In a broader sense, through his regional initiatives, Xi seems to be conveying a firm message to Asian nations-China will use its increasing power to create an Asian order which is favorable to it.

To understand the latest position with regard to South Asia policy of the People's Republic of China (PRC) under President Xi Jinping, one has to pay close attention to what the leader has said on the subject during his visits to New Delhi (September 2014) and Islamabad (April 2015). In New Delhi, Xi, referring to South Asia's probable emergence as the new growth pole powering the economy in Asia and even the world, stated that "a peaceful, stable and prosperous South Asia conforms to China's interests. China is willing to align its development strategies with those of South Asian countries to achieve mutually beneficial development and common prosperity". He considered China's " one belt and one road " proposal as one in joint interests of the PRC and South Asian nations and expressed the hope that the proposal would lead to boosting the interconnectivity of countries along the traditional land and maritime Silk road, making their economies prosperous and trade complementary. Xi added that China will cooperate with South Asian nations in lifting the two-way trade to US$ 150 billion in the next five years and that the PRC will invest US$ 30 billion in South Asia, along with preferential loans of US$ 20 billion to the region.

Xi's remarks on South Asia in Islamabad have almost been identical with what he stated in New Delhi. He reiterated that a peaceful, stable and prosperous South Asia conforms to China's interests and that China is willing to align its development strategies with those of South Asian countries to achieve mutually beneficial development and common prosperity. New however has been Xi's observations on the occasion that "the Chinese side is willing to, within the framework of South-South cooperation, offer assistance and support to South Asian countries within its own capacity and that China-Pakistan economic corridor project will bring prosperity in all parts of Pakistan and the region, The Silk route project is a significant move on the part of China to fully open up".

Evident from the above is China's shift of focus at this juncture to economic interests as it conducts relations with South Asia nations. (In fact, judging from the overall picture, it is clear that the shift encompasses the entire gamut of China's Asia ties). In the region, the shift is getting manifested in Xi's efforts to establish economic connectivity with the countries in the region particularly through implementing schemes like the Silk Road Economic Belt (SREB) that would be established along the Eurasian land corridor from the Pacific coast to the Baltic Sea, and the 21st century Maritime Silk Road (MSR) connecting Asia and Europe through sea route. These schemes will facilitate China's gaining of direct access to the Indian Ocean and beyond, besides helping it in boosting its influence over South Asia and Central Asia. Outside support to the two schemes and membership in the China-proposed

Asian Infrastructure and Investment Bank (AIIB) which will finance infrastructure projects in the Asia region, have become critical for the PRC under Xi. China is to invest US$ 46 billion in various projects in Pakistan involving construction of roads, railways, pipelines, fibre optic cables, power facilities and economic development zones. In scale, such investment eclipses the US spending in Pakistan over last decade or so.

While it can be seen that Xi Jinping's pronouncements do not answer the question as to how his government is viewing ties with South Asia in strategic terms, some of the statements coming from senior officials in his government, appear to have dealt with this issue.. For e.g, the visiting Chinese foreign minister Wang Yi and the Adviser to Pakistan's Prime Minister on National Security and Foreign Affairs Sartaj Aziz, while taking stock of regional developments, agreed (Islamabad, 14.2.2015) on the need for maintaining strategic balance in South Asia. Going by the definition of the term "strategic balance", it means the relative capabilities of Pakistan and other regional powers, especially the rival India, to achieve their respective strategic objectives in relation to the other. Pakistan's key concern is over its lack of ability to establish strategic stability in South Asia which it believes is due to challenges from the conventional and nuclear imbalances between India and Pakistan. It hopes that not only USA but also other important members of the international community will support Pakistan's objective of regional balance and strategic stability in South Asia. Importantly, by implication, China seems to have extended such support to Pakistan through Wang Yi. In fact, the support had already manifested in the China-Pakistan Treaty of Friendship, Cooperation and Good-neighborly Relations, signed and ratified by both the sides on April 5, 2005 and January 4, 2006 respectively.

Wang Yi's support to Pakistan vis-à-vis India, as mentioned above, raises questions as to whether China will continue to follow its 'balanced' South Asia policy, which began in end seventies, in pursuance of the conceived pre-requisite for the country to have a 'peaceful periphery' conducive to its modernization. Under it, the PRC had modified its pro-Pakistan stand so far kept on Kashmir issue, with the state-controlled media dropping references to 'India-occupied Kashmir' and using instead the terms 'India-controlled Kashmir' and 'Pakistan-controlled Kashmir'. In December 1996, the then Chinese President Jiang Zemin favoured New Delhi – Islamabad 'consultations and negotiations' on Kashmir issue, during his speech to the Pakistan Senate. During the Kargil conflict in 1999, China refrained from taking sides and adopted a neutral position. China's oft-repeated stand since this time had been that the Kashmir issue is one 'left over by history' and that 'India and Pakistan should properly solve the problem through dialogue and negotiations.' Beijing no longer makes references to 'self-determination' for the Kashmiri people and does not consider the 'Kashmiri people' as a third party to the dispute.

Casting a shadow on China's 'balanced' South Asia policy is the emerging military relationship between Beijing and Islamabad. China's missile technology support to Pakistan still seems to continue. Prior to Xi Jinping's visit to Pakistan, reports appeared on the proposed sale of eight type 039A submarines by China to Pakistan. With the eight, Pakistan's such submarines will be more than doubled. India, according to reports, only has 13 aging conventional subs. It is generally believed that Pakistan, with China's help, would equip these 039A subs with nuclear tipped missiles.India still has no such subs with nuclear tipped missiles; though it has conducted trials for nuclear powered ballistic missile subs. India may therefore feel more and more anxious to fill this gap. India-China arms race is thus most likely to be the consequence. Another point relates to China's investments in Gwadar port (Pakistan), Hambantota port (Sri Lanka), Chittagong (Bangladesh) container facility and Kyaukpyu port (Myanmar). These, along with China's plan now to supply Pakistan the 039 A missiles, are likely to lead to a rise in India-China geopolitical rivalry in the Indian Ocean region. Such a situation may not be beneficial to India-China bilateral times particularly at a time when Indian Prime Minister is to visit China in May 2015.

Also worrisome to India is that Xi is vigorously pursuing the SREB and MSR initiatives known as "One Belt and One Road" project, of which the proposal of 'China-Pakistan Economic Corridor' is part. The corridor passes through Pakistan Occupied Kashmir. Backed by an extensive China-led funding infrastructure, the project, as being assessed, could shift the center of geo-economic power towards Eurasia, and undermine the "Asia Pivot" of the United States and its allies, widely perceived by China as the central plank to contain it. The Chinese expectations from the MSR has come clearly in a document released at the Bo Ao Forum conference (March 2015) which said that creation of maritime facilities with the PRC's assistance will have an obligation for the host country to serve Chinese interests including strategic interests. It is very likely that China will develop albeit in a slow manner an increased military presence primarily along the Indian Ocean portions of the MSR. In sum, the project conveys a firm message to Asian nations-China will use its growing power to reshape economic and security arrangements in the region. India for valid reasons may feel concerned with this. To be noted in this context, is India's policy against giving any blanket endorsement to China's two silk road initiatives and cooperating wherever Indian interests converge with those of China (Indian Foreign Minister Sushma Swaraj, Beijing, February 2015).

Raising questions for China's 'balanced' approach towards South Asia are railway projects falling under "One Belt and One Road" initiative, designed to link Pakistan and China via Pakistan Occupied Kashmir (POK) where Chinese troops are reportedly deployed ostensibly for construction work. The reported infrastructure projects undertaken by the Chinese military and nuclear establishments in Pakistan Occupied Gilgit-Baltistan region, may become strategically important to the Chinese army in the event of another conflict with India; especially, the Karakorum Highway could be useful for China as an overland route for moving missiles and spare parts to Pakistan. Also, there appears to be a deeper meaning to the continuing issue of stapled visas by Beijing to Indians from Kashmir. This may mark a nuanced Chinese position on Kashmir implying a dilution of China's past stand of accepting Kashmir as a de-facto part of India, while at the same time treating POK including Gilgit-Baltistan region as de-facto and de-jure parts of Pakistan. Is China's stand a quid pro quo for Pakistan's help to Beijing in fighting against Uighur separatism in Xinjiang? Is Beijing developing future options for questioning India's locus standi to negotiate with China on the territory in Ladakh ceded by Pakistan to the PRC? The remarks of the then Indian Prime Minister that China "could use India's soft underbelly of Kashmir to keep India in low level equilibrium",demonstrate how serious these questions are.

Xi Jinping's South Asia policy needs a study in a historical context. Since late Chairman Mao Zedong proclaimed founding of the PRC in October 1949, saying that 'China has stood up', a tradition always prevailed to develop an overall strategic vision for the country at different stages and link it with the direction of its external course. In the Mao Zedong era (1949-76), the strategic vision was consolidation of socialism in China; the matching domestic goals were 'self-reliant development' and the external line was 'leaning to one side', in other words getting the support of socialist allies, for consolidating the Communist party rule at home. Internal priorities underwent a major change in the post-1978 period, with veteran leader Deng Xiaoping made building of 'Socialism with Chinese Characteristics' as strategic vision ; he made reforms and modernization of the country as domestic goals and chose an open door external line to achieve it.

In the post-Deng period, the then Chinese President Jiang Zemin formulated national policies centering round his theory of "Three Represents", with the objective of making the Chinese Communist Party (CCP) a representative of majority of the people and codified 'three major historic tasks' for China – Modernization, National Reunification and Safeguarding World Peace and Common Development. To accomplish these tasks, he chose an 'Independent Foreign Policy of Peace'. Jiang's successor Hu Jintao brought forth a domestic development model marking a shift in emphasis – from GDP centric growth to 'balanced development'; to be backed by his own theoretical concept of " Scientific Outlook of Development", of which creation at home of a 'Harmonious Socialist Society' and 'Sustainable development' constituted main elements. Correspondingly, Hu put in place an external strategy based on the idea of a "Harmonious World" aimed at realizing a 'win-win' solution in international relations'. The then PRC Premier Wen Jiabao, tracing the links between his country's domestic goals and foreign policy objectives stated, "What China needs for its development first and foremost is an international environment of long term stability and a stable surrounding environment."

For the PRC under President Xi Jinping, 'national rejuvenation' is the strategic vision. For realizing it, Xi has set "double century" national goals – (i) building of "moderately prosperous society in all respects" by 2020, the year around 100th anniversary of the CCP's founding, when in all provinces, the average income of the middle class, will reach international standards, China's GDP of 2000 will be quadrupled to approximately $4 trillion with a per capita level of some $3,000. Military mechanization and major progress in informatisation will be achieved by this time, and (ii) establishment of an "affluent, strong, civilized, harmonious, socialist modern country" by 2050, the year around the PRC's 100th anniversary, when the annual per capita GDP can reach US$ 40,000, making China one among top 40 countries in the world'. Full military modernization will also get completed by that time.

In order to achieve the "double century " goals, Xi has chosen a foreign policy course with two pillars – striving for a win-win relationship with external powers and at the same time not compromising on issues concerning territorial sovereignty. The course, with assertiveness as dominant element, actually began in the middle of 2008; before that Beijing's emphasis in international relations was on 'hiding one's capacities and biding one's time' (veteran leader Deng Xiaoping's famous 24-character maxim of tao guang yang hui). It is an outcome of China's confidence gained through its ability to achieve a sustained growth; also due to its conviction that the country's 'comprehensive national strength' has grown and hence in proportion to that, it should increase its influence over the world. The course is leading to China's display of assertiveness externally, giving rise to fears among neighbours having territorial disputes with the PRC.

Adding further to such fears is China's military modernization. China's fundamental policy direction is that national defence building should be in the 'service of and subordinated to the country's overall development'. In other words, economic development and military modernization are to progress hand in hand. China's defence budget for 2014 was to the tune of US$ 132 billion, an increase of 12.2% over previous year. Its military expenditure has had a rapid rise in the past 20 years. The central point is that the development of modernization in China since 80s of land, air, naval and missile forces has led to a remarkable expansion in the capabilities of the People's Liberation Army (PLA) for not only defending the country form its soil, but also for operating well beyond its borders to protect PRC's growing global economic and security interests.

To understand the foreign policy of Xi Jinping, especially his approach to neighbours. It would be necessary to look into the reasons behind the PRC's decision, taken at the Central Work Conference on Foreign Relations of the CCP, held in November 2014 to accord top position to relations with neighbours with ties with 'Great Powers' and 'Developing countries' ranking second and third respectively. The move reflected the PRC's recognition that the periphery including South Asia is becoming increasingly vital to China's economy, trade and security. Notable in this regard is Xi's stress on the occasion about a Chinese proverb that "close neighbours are better than distant relatives".

Also significant is the concept of *"Community of Shared Destiny"*, highlighted by Xi at the same conference; it stipulated that "such a community will be based on deep economic integration, but going beyond trade. It will be a vision of a political and security community in which economically integrated countries in the region support and defend one another from outside threats and intruders, as well as manage internal threats together through collaborative and cooperative mechanisms". Xi spoke again on the concept at the Bo Ao Forum (Hainan, 28.3.2015) adding that China, jointly with Asian nations, would build a regional order that is more favorable to Asia and the world. He avoided saying that China would lead such order; but on the other hand his remarks that "given China's size, it will naturally play a larger role, but without seeking greater monopoly over regional and world affairs", convey a definite meaning.

Xi's observations at the forum that the PRC is ready to sign friendship treaties with neighboring countries to build trust are significant. They taken together with his readiness for China-

India-Sri Lanka trilateral cooperation to address security concerns in the Indian Ocean region (Xi, Colombo, September 2014) and the PRC's willingness for China-Nepal-India trilateral cooperation (Chinese Foreign Minister Wang Yi, Kathmandu, September 2014) reflect China's new thinking on relations with South Asian nations. In this regard also looking important is Xi's call for promoting "common, comprehensive, cooperative and sustainable security in Asia", and setting up" open and inclusive new security architecture in Asia", made at the summit of the Conference on Interaction and Confidence-Building Measures in Asia (CICA), held in Shanghai, in May 2014.

Why Xi Jinping now tends to give prominence to economic interests in its foreign policy? According to known Sinologists, it is due to the perception among the leaders that economic recession is a bigger challenge than external threats. They reveal that a consensus has been reached by the Xi administration on what should be the theoretical foundation of the current major contradictions in the Chinese society. Identifying the "Four Comprehensives" concept introduced by Xi Jinping in December 2014 ("comprehensively, build a moderately prosperous society, strengthen reforms, establish rule of law and enforce party discipline") as such foundation, they have observed that the leader, unlike his predecessors, seems to have realized that the central task of development can be achieved only if changes could be brought into the structure of international economic and political order. Also according to them, President Xi JInping has redefined and expanded the function of Chinese diplomacy and that he will attempt to alter some of the foreign policy processes and power relationship that have defined the political, military, and economic environment in the Asia-Pacific region. One has however to watch for future developments to confirm the trend in China towards according priority to economic interests.

There are also other determinants of Xi Jinping's South Asia policy. They include neutralizing the perceived US strategy to contain China with support of regional nations, developing economies of China's border areas, cooperating with South Asian countries in exploitation of much needed energy resources, protecting oil transport security in the Indian Ocean, getting support to 'One China' policy and last but not least securing cooperation from the nations in the region in the matter of meeting terrorism threat to China's South West border coming from outside.

What has been said above shows that the Xi Jinping regime in China, despite putting economic interests first in its foreign policy including on South Asia, may not give up its assertiveness on key issues – Sino-Indian border, Tibet and China-Pakistan nexus. The PRC is becoming more vociferous in claiming India's Arunachal Pradesh as part of its 'Southern Tibet' for e.g its objection to Indian Prime Minister's visit to Arunachal Pradesh. It is suspecting India's position on the Dalai Lama in spite of New Delhi's assurances on this count and keeping the talks between Dharamsala and Beijing deadlocked. It is further strengthening strategic ties with Pakistan. Both China and Pakistan are repeatedly laying stress to the relevance to bilateral ties of their peace treaty signed in 2005, unique in South Asia, providing for mutual support in protecting each other's national sovereignty and integrity; this treaty is being mentioned in several China-Pakistan joint statements. For China, the vital sea route for its energy import from the Middle East has become more important from the point of view of South Asian situation.. It is natural for India to watch for the strategic significance of China's naval modernization and its increasing focus on the Indian Ocean. Indian fears over the future military potentials of China's port projects in India's neighborhood, like Gwadar (Pakistan), Hambantota (Sri Lanka), Sittwe (Myanmar) and Chittagong (Bangladesh) seem justified.

Xi Jinping administration is projecting China's economic power into countries in India's neighborhood and thereby gaining capabilities to influence the latter strategically. This is putting India under compulsion to suitably challenge China. China has become the largest investor in Sri Lanka. During Xi's recent visit to Colombo, Sri Lanka and China reached 27 agreements, including one to start negotiations on a free-trade agreement.[1] China has several large-scale, ongoing projects in Bangladesh which include deep seaports in Chittagong and Sonadia Island. China also has plans to build a road and rail link through Myanmar to connect the Chinese city of Kunming to Chittagong. China has invested heavily in the Nepalese energy and transportation sectors, including a US$ 1.6 billion hydropower plant and a US$1.9 billion railroad project to connect Lhasa to Kathmandu. Other transportation projects include the Pokhara Regional International Airport, a number of roads, bridges and container depots. China has pledged to vastly increase its investment in Pakistan's economy and infrastructure sector. Among other initiatives, China has been helping develop Pakistan's infrastructure sector, details of which have already been mentioned above.

India may have to deal with the Chinese enthusiasm to enter South Asian Association for Regional Cooperation (SAARC) on the basis of mutual advantage. Chinese scholars believe that combined, the economic integration of the PRC and SAARC will create a huge market with 2.8 billion people, which will bring new force for economic development to China, South Asia and the whole world. The PRC wants to establish a China-SAARC free trade area. The scholars also think that India pays close attention to China's economic relations with other South Asian countries under the belief that they are aimed at China encircling India. They accuse India as interfering in other South Asian countries' economic agreements with China, both openly and covertly. India's contradictions with other South Asian countries will not disappear overnight, unless India abandons its ambition to play the role of "big brother" in South Asia. Furthermore, India's economic development over the past two decades has not produced substantial spillover effects for its neighbours. The scholars further say that SAARC is now in need of external forces to help drive its development and integration. Whether India likes it or not, it will be unable to prevent other SAARC countries from turning to China for financial support.

India under Modi, will have both opportunities and challenges in the South Asia policy of China under Xi Jinping. India can work towards capitalizing on the economic opportunities which may arise in South Asia as Xi promotes his 'shared destiny' concept to connect the region, especially through channeling funds through the AIIB, of which India is already a member. In a strategic sense, however, India should be prepared to face challenges as Xi's policy appears to aim at establishing a new Asian order in which China will play a big, if not leading, role. Hypothetically speaking, the neighbours of the PRC including India who want to benefit from close economic ties with China, but at the same time feel compulsions to worry about Beijing's aggressive push of its territorial claims, will feel relieved if Xi Jinping's China, under its economic interests-driven foreign policy, tones down its assertiveness abroad at action levels. In reality however the situation is different; consider creation of artificial islands in South China by sea by China with an eye on gaining strategic superiority vis-à-vis other claimants. This being so, undoubtedly one has to wait further for a full picture ; much would depend on the nature of future domestic and foreign policy developments in China. China's readiness to sign friendship treaties with its neighbours has been a notable development with major implications for future prospects for the regional geopolitics. In such circumstances, it would be beneficial for India to probe the Chinese new foreign policy thinking including on South Asia, utilizing the opportunity of the impending visit to Beijing by its Prime Minister.

In a nutshell, the main motivating factor for Xi Jinping's South Asia policy firmly appears to be the requirement for China to establish economic connectivity with the region arising from the country's need for natural resources and safe transit routes. The second requirement is the increasing compulsions on the leader to curb support to terrorism in Xinjiang, coming from across the borders. Looking from a strategic view point, however, it can be said that for the Xi regime, the South Asia policy determinants remain without change ever since the end of cold war; balancing against India by supporting Pakistan seem to continue as Xi's principal aim.

INDIA-CHINA BORDER ENGAGEMENT

After decades of pursuing Pakistan-centric war planning, the Indian Army and the Indian Air Force are recalibrating their sights towards the hitherto neglected northern frontiers with China, giving a hard push to improving its war-fighting capabilities against its more powerful neighbor and at the same time, increasing on-the-ground interaction with the People's Liberation Army (PLA).

This two-track policy, outcome of the experience of the past five years, is aimed at preventing any unnecessary flare ups along the Line of Actual Control (LAC), as the contested border between the two countries is known.

In July 2014, this writer has had the opportunity to undertake a rare tour of the border areas in Ladakh, a high mountainous desert that abuts the Tibet Autonomous Region (TAR). This remote region, rendered inaccessible by road for seven months a year because the passes leading to it are snow bound, is buzzing with an unprecedented military buildup. Consider this:

- A new Air Force Station to base fighter jets is coming up just 25 km from the Line of Actual Control
- For the first time since India's independence in 1947, a full-fledged armored brigade of T-72 tanks will now be based in Ladakh.
- One more infantry brigade (3000 plus troops) is now moving closer to a crucial area where Chinese troops had intruded and stayed put for over three weeks in 2013.
- Work has been accelerated on at least 13 strategically important road projects in this region.

But Ladakh is not alone in getting the attention of military planners. Across the 4,000-plus km of Himalayan frontier that stretches from Ladakh in the northwest to Arunachal Pradesh in the east, India is aggressively pushing for the development of its border areas. In Sikkim and in Arunachal Pradesh – like Ladakh – more troops have been pumped in, equipped with armored regiments and artillery support, more fighter aircraft like the Su-30 are based closer to the contentious borders, and more roads are being built right up to the border, following the reversal of an earlier policy of not developing the border areas.

In effect, India is playing catch up with China. But it will take almost a decade for India to come anywhere near the infrastructure that the Chinese have built in TAR. Since the 1990s, China has built a network of roads, airports and railway in the sparsely populated TAR which gives the PLA a distinct advantage when it comes to mobilizing its forces if needed in double quick time. The Qinghai-Tibet Railway that connects Lhasa to mainland China is set to come closer to the Indian border at Xigatse (near Sikkim) at the end of August. By 2020, a rail link to Nepal's capital Kathmandu is also planned. According to an Indian assessment, there are 15 airfields in the TAR, 12 of them meant exclusively for military purposes. The Indian military on the other hand, is still dependent on old airstrips and a couple of airfields built in the 1960s.

Aware of these shortcomings, Indian policymakers have decided to build military infrastructure but also to simultaneously engage the PLA more frequently across the border. Earlier this year, New Delhi and Beijing earmarked four locations along their contested border in Ladakh for holding emergency meetings to quickly resolve possible standoffs.

The locations, mostly in areas that witness frequent face-offs, were finalized when a Chinese PLA delegation led by one of its most senior military leaders, the deputy chief of general staff (operations) Lieutenant General Qi Jianguo, held day-long talks with an Indian Army team led by then vice Chief of Army Staff, Lieutenant General Dalbir Singh. Singh has since been elevated to the post of India's Army Chief.

In addition to the four flag meeting points, the two countries have also decided to open two more locations for holding scheduled annual meetings between senior field officers. To date these annual conferences, known as Border Personnel Meetings, have taken place at Bumla in Arunachal Pradesh, Nathula in Sikkim, and Chushul in Ladakh. From now on, troops across the long LAC will have two more venues – Kibithoo in Eastern Arunachal Pradesh and Mana Pass in Uttarakhand – to meet at least four times a year, on the occasion of each others' national days. During the talks in Delhi the two sides also decided to establish a hotline between the Indian Army's Director General of Military Operations and an equivalent officer in the PLA HQ in Beijing. All of these decisions are part of the Confidence Building Measures (CBMs) that New Delhi and Beijing have decided to pursue after the signing of the Border Defense Cooperation Agreement signed by the two countries in October 2013.

India's aggressive push along the border seems to have raised curiosity if not alarm in Beijing, at least sufficient for top-ranking Chinese generals and party officials to step up the frequency of their visits to cantonments bordering Ladakh and Sikkim.

Ananth Krishnan, *The Hindu's* Beijing correspondent, reported that a top ranking general of the PLA carried out a rare inspection visit to the disputed western section of the border with India, including stops to inspect troops at two sites that have been at the center of recent differences over incursion incidents — near the Karakoram Pass and the contested Pangong Tso lake. General Xu Qiliang, who is one of two vice-chairmen of the Central Military Commission headed by President Xi Jinping – the highest-ranking position in the Chinese military – made the visit last month to inspect frontier troops in Xinjiang and Tibet, including a stop in the Aksai Chin region claimed by India.

Other newspaper reports in China have indicated that a senior Communist Party of China official spent unusually long time in Western Tibet in areas bordering Ladakh and Sikkim. They reported that Deng Xiaogang, Deputy Party Secretary of the Tibetan Autonomous Region, responsible for the law and order, security and police, took considerable time "to inspect the border security and the People's Liberation Army bases."

On June 20 for instance, an article in *The Tibet Daily* notes that "Deng Xiaogang inspected Rutok, the border county." Rudok is located near Pangong Tso stretching between India and China. It is where Chinese "water" incursions often occur. Addressing the border guards, Deng Xiaogang stressed: "Tibet is very special strategic location; it is an important barrier for the national security; development and stability in these border areas is an important part of the region's overall situation."

But the Chinese need not worry for at least another decade. Much remains to be done in Ladakh, Sikkim and Arunachal Pradesh. Building roads in the high altitude areas and equipping a highly capable Mountain Strike Corps – India has decided to raise a 30,000-strongspecialized offensive force for the mountains – will take some doing. Until then, New Delhi is likely to follow a dictum China's strongman of the 1970s, Deng Xiaoping prescribed for his own country: "Hide your strength, bide your time."

IMPACT OF INDIA-CHINA BORDER ISSUE ON SOUTH ASIA

The issue of boundary demarcation between India and China together with the developments in Tibet not only affected the bilateral relationship but also completely changed the geopolitical situation of the entire South Asian region. The strained relations between China and the Soviet Union starting from 1957 on the one hand and the perceived Indo-Soviet closed relationship on the other compelled China to foster a strategic friendship with Pakistan based on common animosity towards India.

There were no cultural, historical, political and ideological commonalities or mutual economic interests between the two to come closure. The urgency to set up strategic relationship was evident from the fact that the two governments concluded the boundary negotiations just in seventy five days. This agreement suddenly pushed the Sino-Pakistan relationship to a higher level. The defence cooperation and nuclear and missile technology support that followed in next four decades between two countries speak volume about the closeness of the relationship.

The Chinese assistance to Pakistan in 1965 and 1971 Indo-Pakistan wars and support to Pakistan in past on Kashmir dispute are linked to China-India border dispute and Tibet issue. Further China's defence cooperation with India's neighbours like Bangla Desh and Myanmar and its support to insurgents in India's north eastern region till 1970s, were cause of concern for India.

NEW APPROACH TO BORDER SETTLEMENT

India and China have held fifteen rounds of talks at official level to resolve the border issue since mid 1980s with little progress. Clarification of the line of actual control has not been yet been completed. Only the maps in respect of the middle sector, which is least disputed, could be exchanged so far in about twenty years since the talks started.

The change in international situation, globalization of economy and national aspirations of the people of the two countries compelled the two states to reassess the over all bilateral relationship in the new situation. After recognizing the security and economic imperatives of each others the two states decided to develop a cooperative relationship for mutual benefit in a realistic way. Under this new approach the two countries, in 2003, separated the issue of border demarcation from the question of overall development of bilateral relations and assigned it priority by appointing Special Representatives to explore the settlement from the political perspective of the overall bilateral relationship.

The special representatives after holding several rounds of dialogues concluded an agreement on the 'Parameters and Guiding Principles for the Settlement of the India-China Boundary Question' in April 2005. This agreement provides that the two sides would abide by and implement the agreement on the maintenance of peace and tranquility along the Line of Actual Control in the India-China border areas, signed in 1993 and 1996 and seek a fair, reasonable and mutually acceptable solution of the boundary issue through peaceful and friendly consultations taking into account, *inter alia,* historical evidence, national sentiments, practical difficulties and reasonable concerns and sensitivities of both sides, and the actual state of border areas.

Important aspect of the agreement is that in reaching a boundary settlement, the two sides shall safeguard due interests of their settled populations in the border areas, which implies that no population transfer would take place. At the same time India and China have affirmed that the two countries are not threat to each other and neither side shall use or threaten to use force against the other in an endeavor to create a better friendly environment.

BORDER TRADE

The regular border trade between the two countries joined by a common landmass, particularly countries of the continental sizes like India and China, indicates respect for the sensitivities of each other. The border trade between India and China had completely stopped after the border conflict in 1962. It was resumed on a very limited scale after the agreements of 1991 and 1992 through Lepulekh (Uttranchal) and Shipkila (Himachal Pradesh) passes.

These two passes are located in remote mountain areas and remain open only for few months. In the absence of infrastructure facilities like motorable roads, the volume of the trade is insignificant, less than four million US dollar per annum. The Chinese government is extremely interested to start new trade routes to open up Tibet to south Asia and give impetus to the development of its land locked southwest region. Tibet region of China needs not only economic development but also an outlet to India and Indian Ocean like eastern provinces. Therefore, the agreement signed in 2003 to conduct border trade through Nathula pass is very significant.

First it was a traditional trading route which can be converted into a container route and is nearest to Lhasa and also to the Indian port city of Kolkata. Second, this route falls in Sikkim state of India which China had not recognized as a part of India since 1975 when it was merged into Indian union. China has recognized Sikkim as a state of India in 2005 when Chinese premier Wen Jiabao presented a revised map with Sikkim as part of India to the Indian Prime Minister. The trade through this route is likely to start from mid 2006. The opening of this trade route would impact tremendously on the political and economic situation in this region. China, as regional economic power, would like to maximize the benefit of the border trade with all its neighbours, which will ensure peace, stability and development. This initiative can be a major confidence building measure in future.

The 1726 km long Stilwell road, which was constructed in 1945 during the World War II for supplies from Ledo (India) to Kunming via Myanmar, remained in use only briefly till Japan surrendered. Two four-inch oil pipe lines were also laid along this road from Assam. 61 km long stretch of this road lies in India, 1,033 km in Myanmar and 632 km in China. At present, trade between Yunnan and India has to follow a convoluted route from Kunming to Zhanjiang port in Guangdong Province, then to be loaded onto ships bound for the Malacca Straits and India - a total of 6,000 km. The opening of this road has the potential to generate tremendous business opportunities. Negotiations on opening of this trade route are still in the initial stages at non governmental level.

SINO-INDIAN BORDER DISPUTE

Sovereignty over two large and various smaller separated pieces of territory are contested between China and India. The westernmost, Aksai Chin, is claimed by India as part of the state of Jammu and Kashmir and region of Ladakh but is controlled and administered as part of the Chinese autonomous region of Xinjiang. It is a virtually uninhabited high altitude wasteland crossed by the Xinjiang-Tibet Highway. The other large disputed territory, the easternmost, lies south of the McMahon Line. It was formerly referred to as the North East Frontier Agency, and is now called Arunachal Pradesh. The McMahon Line was part of the 1914 Simla Convention between British India and Tibet, an agreement rejected by China. The 1962 Sino-Indian War was fought in both of these areas. An agreement to resolve the dispute was concluded in 1996, including "confidence-building measures" and a mutually agreed Line of Actual Control. In 2006, the Chinese ambassador to India claimed that all of Arunachal Pradesh is Chinese territory amidst a military build up. At the time, both countries claimed incursions as much as a kilometre at the northern tip of Sikkim. In 2009, India announced it would deploy additional military forces along the border.

Aksai Chin

From the area's lowest point (on the Karakash River at about 14,000 feet (4,300 m) to the glaciated peaks up to 22,500 feet (6,900 m) above sea level, this is a desolate, largely uninhabited area. It covers an area of about 37,244 square kilometres (14,380 sq mi). The desolation of Aksai Chin meant that it had no significant human importance other than ancient trade routes crossing it, providing brief passage during summer for caravans of yaks from Xinjiang and Tibet.

One of the earliest treaties regarding the boundaries in the western sector was issued in 1842. The Sikh Confederacy of the Punjab region in India had annexed Ladakh into the state of Jammu in 1834. In 1841, they invaded Tibet with an army. Chinese forces defeated the Sikh army and in turn entered Ladakh and besieged Leh. After being checked by the Sikh forces, the Chinese and the Sikhs signed a treaty in September 1842, which stipulated no transgressions or interference in the other country's frontiers. The British defeat of the Sikhs in 1846 resulted in transfer of sovereignty over Ladakh to the British, and British commissioners attempted to meet with Chinese officials to discuss the border they now shared. However, both sides were apparently sufficiently satisfied that a traditional border was recognised and defined by natural elements, and the border was not demarcated. The boundaries at the two extremities, Pangong Lakeand Karakoram Pass, were reasonably well-defined, but the Aksai Chin area in between lay largely undefined.

The Johnson Line

W. H. Johnson, a civil servant with the Survey of India proposed the "Johnson Line" in 1865, which put Aksai Chin in Jammu and Kashmir. This was the time of the Dungan revolt, when China did not control Xinjiang, so this line was never presented to the Chinese. Johnson presented this line to the Maharaja of Jammu and Kashmir, who then claimed the 18,000 square kilometres contained within his territory and by some accounts he claimed territory further north as far as the Sanju Pass in the Kun Lun Mountains.

Johnson's work was severely criticised for gross inaccuracies, with description of his boundary as "patently absurd", and he was reprimanded by the British Government and resigned from the Survey. The Maharajah of Jammu and Kashmir apparently sent a few soldiers to man the abandoned fort at Shahidulla (modern-day Xaidulla) at one point, by the time most sources placed Shahidulla and the upper Karakash River firmly within the territory of Xinjiang (see accompanying map). According toFrancis Younghusband, who explored the region in the late 1880s, there was only an abandoned fort and not one inhabited house at Shahidulla when he was there – it was just a convenient staging post and a convenient headquarters for the nomadic Kirghiz. The abandoned fort had apparently been built a few years earlier by the Dogras. In 1878 the Chinese had reconquered Xinjiang, and by 1890 they already had Shahidulla before the issue was decided. By 1892, China had erected boundary markers at Karakoram Pass.

In 1897 a British military officer, Sir John Ardagh, proposed a boundary line along the crest of the Kun Lun Mountainsnorth of the Yarkand River. At the time Britain was concerned at the danger of Russian expansion as China weakened, and Ardagh argued that his line was more defensible. The Ardagh line was effectively a modification of the Johnson line, and became known as the "Johnson-Ardagh Line".

The Macartney-Macdonald Line

In 1893, Hung Ta-chen, a senior Chinese official at Kashgar, handed a map of the boundary proposed by China toGeorge Macartney, the British consul-general at Kashgar. This boundary placed the Lingzi Tang plains, which are south of the Laktsang range, in India, and Aksai Chin proper, which is north of the Laktsang range, in China. Macartney agreed with the proposal and forwarded it to the British Indian government. This border, along theKarakoram Mountains, was proposed and supported by British officials for a number of reasons. The Karakoram Mountains formed a natural boundary, which would set the British borders up to the Indus River watershed while leaving the Tarim River watershed in Chinese control, and Chinese control of this tract would present a further obstacle to Russian advance in Central Asia. The British presented this line, known as the Macartney-MacDonald Line, to the Chinese in 1899 in a note by Sir Claude MacDonald. The Qing government did not respond to the note, and the British took that as Chinese acquiescence. Although no official boundary had ever been negotiated, China believed that this had been the accepted boundary.

1899 to 1947

Both the Johnson-Ardagh and the Macartney-MacDonald lines were used on British maps of India. Until at least 1908, the British took the Macdonald line to be the boundary, but in 1911, the Xinhai Revolution resulted in the collapse of central power in China, and by the end of World War I, the British officially used the Johnson Line. However they took no steps to establish outposts or assert actual control on the ground. In 1927, the line was adjusted again as the government of British India abandoned the

Johnson line in favour of a line along the Karakoram range further south. However, the maps were not updated and still showed the Johnson Line.

From 1917 to 1933, the "Postal Atlas of China", published by the Government of China in Peking had shown the boundary in Aksai Chin as per the Johnson line, which runs along the Kunlun mountains. When British officials learned of Soviet officials surveying the Aksai Chin for Sheng Shicai, warlord of Xinjiang in 1940–1941, they again advocated the Johnson Line. At this point the British had still made no attempts to establish outposts or control over the Aksai Chin, nor was the issue ever discussed with the governments of China or Tibet, and the boundary remained undemarcated at India's independence.

Since 1947

Upon independence in 1947, the government of India used the Johnson Line as the basis for its official boundary in the west, encompassing Aksai Chin. However, India did not claim the northern areas nearShahidulla and Khotan, for including which in Indian territory, among other things, Johnson had been criticised. From the Karakoram Pass (which is not under dispute), the Indian claim line extends northeast of the Karakoram Mountains north of the salt flats of the Aksai Chin, to set a boundary at the Kunlun Mountains, and incorporating part of the Karakash River and Yarkand River watersheds. From there, it runs east along the Kunlun Mountains, before turning southwest through the Aksai Chin salt flats, through the Karakoram Mountains, and then to Pangong Lake.

On 1 July 1954 Prime Minister Nehru wrote a memo directing that the maps of India be revised to show definite boundaries on all frontiers. Up to this point, the boundary in the Aksai Chin sector, based on the Johnson Line, had been described as "undemarcated."

During the 1950s, the People's Republic of China built a 1,200 kilometres (750 mi) road connecting Xinjiang and western Tibet, of which 179 kilometres (111 mi) ran south of the Johnson Line through the Aksai Chin region claimed by India. Aksai Chin was easily accessible from China, but was more difficult for the Indians on the other side of the Karakorams to reach. The Indians did not learn of the existence of the road until 1957, which was confirmed when the road was shown in Chinese maps published in 1958.

The Indian position, as stated by prime minister Jawaharlal Nehru, was that the Aksai Chin was "part of the Ladakh region of India for centuries" and that this northern border was a "firm and definite one which was not open to discussion with anybody".

The Chinese minister, Zhou Enlai argued that the western border had never been delimited, that the Macartney-MacDonald Line, which left the Aksai Chin within Chinese borders was the only line ever proposed to a Chinese government, and that the Aksai Chin was already under Chinese jurisdiction, and that negotiations should take into account the status quo.

In April 2013 India claimed, referencing their own perception of the Line of Actual Control (LAC) location, that Chinese troops hadestablished a camp in the Daulat Beg Oldi sector, 10 km on their side of the Line of Actual Control. This figure was later revised to a 19 km claim. According to Indian media, the incursion included Chinese military helicopters entering Indian airspace to drop supplies to the troops. However, Chinese officials denied any trespassing having taken place. Soldiers from both countries briefly set up camps on the ill-defined frontier facing each other, but the tension was defused when both sides pulled back soldiers in early May.

Trans Karakoram Tract

The Johnson Line is not used west of the Karakoram Pass, where China adjoins Pakistan-administered Gilgit–Baltistan. On 13 October 1962, China and Pakistan began negotiations over the boundary west of the Karakoram Pass. In 1963, the two countries settled their boundaries largely on the basis of the Macartney-MacDonald Line, which left the Trans Karakoram Tract in China, although the agreement provided for renegotiation in the event of a settlement of the Kashmir dispute. India does not recognise that Pakistan and China have a common border, and claims the tract as part of the domains of the pre-1947 state of Kashmir and Jammu. However, India's claim line in that area does not extend as far north of the Karakoram Mountains as the Johnson Line

The McMahon Line

British India and China gained a common border in 1826, with British annexation of Assam in the Treaty of Yandabo at the conclusion of the First Anglo-Burmese War (1824–1826). Subsequent annexations in further Anglo-Burmese Wars expanded China's borders with British India eastwards, to include the border with what is now Myanmar.

In 1913–14, representatives of Britain, China, and Tibet attended a conference in Simla, India and drew up an agreement concerning Tibet's status and borders. The McMahon Line, a proposed boundary between Tibet and India for the eastern sector, was drawn by British negotiator Henry McMahon on a map attached to the agreement. All three representatives initiated the agreement, but Beijing soon objected to the proposed Sino-Tibet boundary and repudiated the agreement, refusing to sign the final, more detailed map. After approving a note which stated that China could not enjoy rights under the agreement unless she ratified it, the British and Tibetan negotiators signed the Simla Convention and more detailed map as a bilateral accord. Neville Maxwell states that McMahon had been instructed not to sign bilaterally with Tibetans if China refused, but he did so without the Chinese representative present and then kept the declaration secret.

V.K. Singh argues that the basis of these boundaries, accepted by British India and Tibet, were that the historical boundaries of India were the Himalayas and the areas south of the Himalayas were traditionally Indian and associated with India. The high watershed of the Himalayas was proposed as the border between India and its northern neighbours. India's government held the view that the Himalayas were the ancient boundaries of the Indian subcontinent and thus should be the modern boundaries of British India and later the Republic of India.

Chinese boundary markers, including one set up by the newly created Chinese Republic, stood near Walong until January 1914, when T. O'Callaghan, an assistant administrator of North East Frontier Agency (NEFA)'s eastern sector, relocated them north to locations closer to the McMahon Line (albeit still South of the Line). He then went to Rima, met with Tibetan officials, and saw no Chinese influence in the area. By signing the Simla Agreement with Tibet, the British had violated the Anglo-Russian Convention of 1907, in which both parties were not to negotiate with Tibet, "except through the intermediary of the Chinese Government", as well as the Anglo-Chinese Convention of 1906, which bound the British government "not to annex Tibetan territory."

Because of doubts concerning the legal status of the accord, the British did not put the McMahon Line on their maps until 1937, nor did they publish the Simla Convention in the treaty record until 1938. Rejecting Tibet's 1913 declaration of independence, China argued that the Simla Convention and McMahon Line were illegal and that Tibetan government was merely a local government without treaty-making powers. In 1947, Tibet requested that India recognise Tibetan authority in the trading town of Tawang, south of the McMahon Line. Tibet did not object to any other portion of the McMahon line. In reply, the Indians asked Tibet to continue the relationship on the basis of the previous British Government.

Tibetan officials continued to administer Tawang and refused to concede territory during negotiations in 1938. The governor of Assam asserted that Tawang was "undoubtedly British" but noted that it was "controlled by Tibet, and none of its inhabitants have any idea that they are not Tibetan." During World War II, with India's east threatened by Japanese troops and with the threat of Chinese expansionism, British troops secured Tawang for extra defence.

China's claim on areas south of the McMahon Line, encompassed in the NEFA, were based on the traditional boundaries. India believes that the boundaries China proposed in Ladakh and Arunachal Pradesh have no written basis and no documentation of acceptance by anyone apart from China. Indians argue that China claims the territory on the basis that it was under Chinese imperial control in the past, while Chinese argue that India claims the territory on the basis that it was under British imperial control in the past. The last Qing emperor's 1912 edict of abdication authorised its succeeding republican government to form a union of "five peoples, namely, Manchus, Han Chinese,Mongols, Muslims, and Tibetans *together with their territory in its integrity"* However, V.K. Singh cites the presence of the Mauryan Empire and Chola Dynasty in regions India does not place a claim to but which were heavily influenced by Indian culture.

India's claim line in the eastern sector follows the McMahon Line. The line drawn by McMahon on the detailed 24–25 March 1914 Simla Treaty maps clearly starts at 27°45'40"N, a trijunction between Bhutan, China, and India, and from there, extends eastwards. Most of the fighting in the eastern sector before the start of the war would take place immediately north of this line. However, India claimed that the *intent* of the treaty was to follow the main watershed ridge divide of the Himalayas based on memos from McMahon and the fact that over 90% of the McMahon Line does in fact follow the main watershed ridge divide of the Himalayas. They claimed that territory south of the high ridges here near Bhutan (as elsewhere along most of the McMahon Line) should be Indian territory and north of the high ridges should be Chinese territory. In the Indian claim, the two armies would be separated from each other by the highest mountains in the world.

During and after the 1950s, when India began patrolling this area and mapping in greater detail, they confirmed what the 1914 Simla agreement map depicted: six river crossings that interrupted the main Himalayan watershed ridge. At the westernmost location near Bhutan north of Tawang, they modified their maps to extend their claim line northwards to include features such as Thag La ridge, Longju, and Khinzemane as Indian territory. Thus, the Indian version of the McMahon Line moves the Bhutan-China-India trijunction north to 27°51'30"N. India would claim that the treaty map ran along features such as Thag La ridge, though the actual treaty map itself is topographically vague (as the treaty was not accompanied with demarcation) in places, shows a straight line (not a watershed ridge) near Bhutan and near Thag La, and the treaty includes no verbal description of geographic features nor description of the highest ridges.

Sikkim

India's annexation of Sikkim in 1975 was rejected by China at the time. The Sino-Indian Memorandum of 2003 was hailed as a *de facto* Chinese acceptance of the annexation. China published a map showing Sikkim as a part of India and the Foreign Ministry deleted it from the list of China's "countries and regions". However, the Sikkim-China border's northernmost point, "The Finger", continues to be the subject of dispute and military activity.

CHINA-SOUTH ASIA POLITICAL RELATIONS: A VIEW FROM NEPAL

"Peaceful co-existence" is the main principle in China-South Asia relations. The fundamentals of this principles are i) mutual equality, ii) non-interference in each other's internal affairs, iii) mutual respect to territorial integrity, iv) cooperation against hegemonism and power politics, and v) mutual accommodation and benefit (Wang Hongwei, 2005). In view of the colonial and feudal background, the main principle and fundamentals of China-South Asia ties are progressive. If one closely examines the natural and spiritual realities that persist between China and South Asia, the main principle and fundamentals of their ties can not truly be more than egalitarian.

China and South Asia are linked by land and water, mountains and rivers. Unlike East Asia and South East Asia and China, Chinese and most of South Asian ties are contiguous, more natural and comprehensive. Mountains pass through and major rivers flow down to China and South Asia from the Tibet Autonomous Region (TAR) of China. Now, it is science and technology that is poised to harness snow and water for larger benefits of the people. In China and South Asia, it has yet remained a geo-political as well as ecological truism that link maintained by mountains and rivers are more stable than opportunistic alliances offered by nuclear power.

Another basic articulation of China-South Asia relations is Buddhism. Gautam Buddha, who was born and had acquired knowledge about the ultimate truth in South Asia, very much lives life-size every where in China. The civilization of China and South Asia thus holds common source of inspiration with a profound degree of continuity. As Buddhism does not stand as an anti-thesis for any other religion, it helps to create an internal capacity to absorb, acculturate and assimilate in both China and South Asia. In short, geo-politically charged neighborhood in an intense natural and spiritual sense is what stands out in China-South Asia relations.

China's politics till the recent past was concentrated on its east coast of the Taiwan Straits. Asia as a whole ranked relatively low in its security agenda since creation of the People's Republic of China. But the Cold War era did not leave China untouched. Tibet in particular conditioned China in formulation of its South Asia policy and to the stability in its frontier regions. The tenets of this policy were: Peace at the south-west border region of China. Efficient signing of border treaty with the neighboring countries was part of this policy to ensure peace along China's long border.

The Tibetan question. This question raised by the external forces had made China acutely sensitive of its national integration and domestic stability. Chinese policy recognized Tibetan separatism as having serious implications for the national integration and domestic stability. It also recognized that the forces supporting the Tibetan separatism were working by proxy, and many aspects of the separatist moves were utterly non-transparent. So trying its best to correctly understand the external as well as internal features of Tibetan question, and appreciating highly those neighboring countries and organizations who did not allow Tibetan separatists to engage in activities and also did not permit outside powers to support such activities on their soil, China's South Asia Policy tried proactively hard to work at the two inter-related fronts at the same time-discouraging the separatist elements and, praising and encouraging those countries and organizations who did not support and did not provide any ground to support the Tibetan separatism.

Independent relations with South Asian states. China was aware of the unequal interstate relations that do not allow development of cordial and trustily ties between them. Difference in size, power and interpretation of agreements had affected relations between states in South Asia. During the Cold War years, the dominating trend in the interstate relations was exploitation and gains at the cost of other, and a tendency to have "sphere of influence." Exchange and cooperation between China and a number of small South Asian states was not liked by India. But China continued to cultivate ties with small South Asian countries independently. It supported independence of these countries, and their independent decision making. After 1962 border war with India, the importance of independence of the countries in South Asia-particularly of those small and non-nuclear power countries-had increased for China. China realized that only unilaterally wishing for cooperation might not be wise and realistic.

Therefore in view of a Chinese analyst, "It is undeniable, ...after the 1962 border war, China's policy toward Nepal might have reflected, to some extent, a strategy in which China supported Nepal, along with other small countries in South Asia, to check India's influence" (Hua Han, 2005). Despite so, China provided unflinching support to late King Birendra's proposal to declare Nepal a "Zone of Peace" in mid 1970s. It was indicative of China's firmer conviction that the indigenous will and ability of neighboring small states in South Asia to independently conduct their foreign and defence affairs together with its independent foreign policy and self-defence strategy was more important and conducive for peace and stability of China's frontier regions than mere lonely Chinese efforts directed at the same. It was this sense of working together which had been the driving force for China to reciprocally commit to the independence of the small South Asian states. Whatever financial, material and military assistance China has provided to these countries were corollary of the said policy.

The United States of America (the US) has ever been at the centre stage whether it was the end of the bi-polar Cold War, 9/11 terrorist attacks and the subsequent US campaign against terrorism, and now the US campaign for democracy. It is the only power which could put troops in Iraq and Afghanistan at the same time and spend enough money to rebuild the economies. Indeed, despite the euphoria for multi-lateralism after the end of Cold War, the South Asian countries were "gravely relying on the assistance and loans provided by the World Bank and developed countries, which in turn resulted in the heavy burden of foreign debts and shortage of foreign exchange reserves and investment capital.

After 9/11, the new strategic development (beginning of the US offensive in Afghanistan) changed the security environment in Asia. US military presence in Uzbekistan and Afghanistan and the new military relationship of the US with Pakistan and India completed the US military involvement in the whole of the Asian continent. Until then South Asia was a gap between the US involvement in West Asia and East Asia. After the US completed its Asian military expansion by filling the gaps left by collapse of Soviet Union under its "war against terror" planning, it felt a need to address another gap which its own larger military involvement had created. The felt US need was primarily due to genuine domestic concerns. The felt need this time was democracy.

For China and the US "the week that changed the world" in February, 1972 when President Nixon visited China had a clear American objective, and that was "to transform the two-power world of the Cold War into a triangle then to manage the triangle in such a way that we would be closer to each of the contenders than they were to each other, thereby maximizing our options". With the disappearance of the Soviet Union, one of the two-power world, despite the initial instability and uncertainty, the US and China appear to move into a maturing stage, and carry out responsibilities particularly in Asia-Pacific region. The following statements of President Bush and Premier Wen confirm how they viewed their role in relation to each other.

Welcoming Chinese Premier Wen Jiabao at the White House on December 9, 2003, President George Bush of the United States of America described the US and China as "partners in diplomacy working to meet the dangers of 21st century."

He further added: "As our two nations work constructively across areas of common interest, we are candid about our disagreements. The growing strength and maturity of our relationship allows us to discuss our differences, whether over economic issues, Taiwan, Tibet, or human rights and religious freedom, in a spirit of mutual understanding and respect."

Replying to President Bush on the occasion, Chinese Premier Wen said, "Our cooperation in a wide range of areas such as counterterrorism, economy, trade and international and regional issues has effectively safeguarded our mutual interests and promoted peace, stability and prosperity in the Asia Pacific region and the world at large."

The key policy statements above from President Bush and Premier Wen, beyond any doubt, eloquently establishes the importance of Sino-US relationship for the Asia-Pacific region and the world at large over and above the bilateral ties existing between the two great countries. In the period ahead where agenda for democracy is pushed to the front, China-US ties may loose glitters; and China may face all the blames for being a "communist" state. And specifically in the context of South Asia, where the majority belongs to the poor and level of interstate cooperation is low, it is for the people and states of the South Asia to decide either for China-inspired peace with independence and self-governed development or for the US-inspired peace with global democracy and development. Whatever the choice the people and states of South Asia make, the decision of Thirteenth Dhaka SAARC summit to associate China and Japan with SAARC was indeed a very welcome unprecedented geopolitical development. The constructive role played by the small SAARC members in this decision making will certainly help fruitfully maximize comparative advantage of SAARC member's vis-à-vis the new partners (China and Japan).

South Asian states are poor. One major reason for such a condition is they do not have an effective good neighborly policy between themselves. At times certain state's behaviour suggests that it wants to live without neighbours. Mahatma Gandhi has provided an example of a good neighborly policy. In his words of wisdom, "One who serves his neighbours serves all the world."

Since 1978 when the modernization and reform process started, economic growth in China has averaged 9.5 percent per year which remains a truly astounding rate. Similarly, foreign trade has expanded at an annual rate of 15 percent over the same period. As for foreign investment China was able to attract $53.2 billion in 2002 as against $52.7 billion for the United States of America. Indeed, the economic transformation has been so rapid that even renowned investment banking firms like Golsdman Sachs predict that China could be the world's largest economy by 2050 with a GDP of $44.4 trillion ahead of the US GDP of $35 trillion and India's GDP of $27 trillion in the same period.

To correct some of the economic divide of a market based economy so that no part of the country remains left out in the great process of economic transformation, the Chinese government is allocating increasing resources including new investment funds from better off provinces in building new physical and social infrastructure and new industrial establishments in the western region. As a part of this strategy the Qinghai-Tibet railway is completed at a cost of $3.16 billion. Similarly, road network in Tibet is being expanded and improved with links to important cities in other provinces.

China's rapid economic growth has its neighbours change their perception on China. The shift from a "China threat" to "China opportunity" theory opens the alternative to explore the benefits that can be draw from the gigantic China's market-leading to deeper and inner natural and spiritual bonds with China. As the immediate neighbours, as many South Asian scholars and experts have wisely suggested, the SAARC members states should take full advantage of China's achievement, especially China's "western development program," which can facilitate a closer economic and trade interaction specially between Tibet, Xingjian, Sichuan and Yunnan and neighboring South Asian states. Opening of new transport and trade routes and just completed railway line over "the roof of the world" will provide China's western parts with efficient access to neighboring countries leading to a change in geo-political outlook.

The ultimate test of the South Asian ability will lie with its leaders' determination to practically conduct the principle of peaceful co-existence along with its fundamentals in relationship with China. Hopefully the Himalayan twins as if representing north face and south face of Kailash-China and South Asia-cherish more a vision of working together than a division of sphere of influence.

It was this spirit of working together that had inspired the press release that was issued after the international seminar on

SAARC and China. China Study Centre, Nepal organized this seminar on 23 December, 2002 in Kathmandu, the venue of SAARC Secretariat.

The press release stated: "Based on the papers presented and comments and observations made during the discussion, the participants of the seminar on SAARC and China ...have come to the following consensus." There is a need for institutionalized dialogue mechanism between SAARC and China. The imperative for good neighbourhood and challenges and opportunities of the 21st century in regard to peace, cooperation and development dictate the needs for bold and speedy action to move forward in this direction. In this connection it is necessary to hold follow-up seminar focusing on the specific of the institutionalized dialogue mechanism between SAARC and China.

The SAARC member states may try to expand and intensify their social and economic interaction with China at sub-regional level. The Track II initiative prepares ground for promoting and complementing official level discussion. It is gratifying to note that Thirteenth SAARC summit at Dhaka in November last has gloriously taken initiative for establishing institutionalized dialogue mechanism between SAARC and China. The SAARC member leaders should be commended for their bold and glorious initiative. It is hoped that they will also ensure speedy actions regarding the paraphernalia of China's institutionalized association with SAARC.

What is expected are upcoming SAARC official meetings at various levels will prepare grounds for the SAARC member states to expand and intensify their social and economic interaction with China at sub-regional level. Various sub-regional groupings within SAARC may find, for example, i) eastern Himalayan resource, ii) western Himalayan resources, iii) transportation links and networks, iv) nature tourism and v) spiritual tourism as important themes for sustainable cooperation to the various sub-regional groups within SAARC. It has been learned that attempts have been made to organize seminars on China and South Asian Relations in Colombo. Such activities are encouraging as they promote and compliment official level discussion on inter-regional collaborative dialogue between China and South Asian states.

It will be extremely good if the SAARC member states attempts to expand and intensify their social and economic interaction with China at sub-regional level. A sub-region (based on sub-geographical level-for example, eastern South Asia, western South Asia, and/or function-for example, culture, natural sources or infrastructure) is recognized as a practical mechanism to promote and strengthen SAARC's over all link with China. As more effective, immediate and direct geo-political link between China and South Asia will be through sub-regional grouping of South Asia; members of the South Asian sub-regional grouping will be more dependent on each other to realize the purpose. Whereas for China, this sort of cooperative arrangement will ensure required stability and peace in the frontier regions, for each South Asian sub-region value will be added to tourism, culture, and physical development which will enhance overall quality of life of its people.

4

Strategic Road-Building along the India-China Border

One of the most strategic landscapes for India is the northeast of India. The region shares a 4,500 km international border with Bangladesh, Bhutan, China and Myanmar.

The 1,080 km border with China across the state of Arunachal Pradesh in the northeast is disputed, a dispute that led to a war between India and China in 1962. While the 1962 war did not escalate beyond a border war, the cause of the war, a disputed border, has not been resolved as yet.

Besides a disputed border, China also claims 90,000 square kms of territory in the northeast; which includes the entire state of Arunachal Pradesh. To China, the state of Arunachal Pradesh is significant for two strategic reasons. First, Arunachal Pradesh borders Tibet.

Tibet is one of the most uncomfortable political issues for China given the continuous Tibetan and international questioning of its legitimacy there. China fears that the Tibetan-government-in exile in India could use Arunachal Pradesh as a base to provide external support to the Tibetans in Tibet to resist the Chinese occupation. Secondly, Arunachal Pradesh is home to the second most important monastery of Tibetan Buddhism after Lhasa: the Tawang Monastery. The strong Tibetan Buddhist culture along the border districts of Arunachal Pradesh like Tawang and Upper Siang could provide the vital link to Tibetans inside Tibet looking for outside support. The presence of the Dalai Lama in India and his visits to the Tawang monastery for religious purposes further creates anxieties for China in this regard.

To bolster its territorial claim and keep Tibet under its control, China has built up its military presence in Tibet with about 300,000 People's Liberation Army (PLA) troops coupled with six Rapid Reaction Forces (RPFs) at Chengdu with the ability to reach the India-China border in 48 hours. Several airfields have also been established in Tibet, namely Hoping, Pangta and Kong Ka. Added to this is the massive road building projects undertaken by China in both Tibet and Yunnan right up to the India-China border with an approximate budget of $ 325 billion. Of critical value to China's troop movement into Tibet is the 2000 km Qinghai-Tibet railway.

Responding to the urgent need to build strategic roads along the India-China border, the Ministry of Home sanctioned Rs.1,934 crore on 4 June 2012 for strategic road projects of about 804 kms in order to support the operational movement of the Indo-Tibetan Border Police (ITBP) along the India-China border, both in the eastern and the western sector. This includes the territory from the Karakoram Pass in Ladakh to Jachep La in Arunachal Pradesh covering about 3,488 kms of border. The task of building these roads have been given to the Border Roads Organisation (BRO), the Central Public Works Department (CPWD), and the National Projects Construction Corporation. Significantly, the *Arunachal Pradesh 2005 Human Development Report* identified infrastructure development as one of the key concerns of the state. This was followed up with Prime Minister Manmohan Singh's package of Rs. 24,000 crore in 2009 for building the 1,500 kms Trans-Arunachal Pradesh highway.

One of the biggest obstacles to road-building in Arunachal Pradesh has been the Indian strategic mindset which viewed the lack of roads in the state as a defence mechanism to stop Chinese troop movement into India's heartland if China did a repeat of 1962. This mindset continued to influence New Delhi's policy towards Arunachal Pradesh right up to mid-2000. However, a more confident India with a strong economy could ill afford to neglect the aspirations of the people of Arunachal Pradesh for better infrastructure. There has been growing demand within

Arunachal Pradesh for better roads, more robust Indian defence mechanisms, and better institutional structures. The first sign of a shift in the Indian defensive thinking about strategic roads came about in May 2006 when the Cabinet Committee on Economic Affairs (CCEA) cleared the construction of strategic roads in Arunachal Pradesh. This reversed the 1962 mindset. Moreover, India was also forced to respond to the rapid Chinese road building activities in bordering countries like Myanmar, Nepal and Pakistan. China established vital road-links with Nepal via the Kodari highway, which connects Lhasa and Kathmandu. With Pakistan, China is connected through the Karakoram highway. The Chinese presence in Myanmar is enabled by an open border in Yunnan. Roads have benefited Chinese economic activity in these countries and have also enhanced China's influence in these states that are located along India's borders. One must note that it is within the Chinese grand strategic matrix to rapidly increase economic ties in South Asia, an effort in which it has been successful.

Besides, one of the biggest complaints of the 120,000 Indian troops stationed in the eastern sector is the lack of road infrastructure in Arunachal Pradesh. In that light, the recent announcement of the road package by the MHA is a welcome sign. It now remains to be seen as to how fast the project gets executed. For instance, in 2006-2007, out of Rs.10 crore sanctioned for building border roads, only Rs. 1 crore was spent. In 2008-2009, the allocation of resources went up to Rs. 50 crore but only Rs. 9.1 crore was spent. The utilisation of FUNDS has improved since 2009-2010 with the Rs. 334 crore sanctioned fully utilised that year. Despite that, the BRO, the main strategic road building organisation, indicated to this author during a field visit in 2011 to Arunachal Pradesh that it is an arduous task to build two-lane highways in such hilly and inaccessible terrain. Also, to get the necessary permissions to move the huge dozers for road-building to the interior mountainous areas by helicopter takes a long time. Moreover, the release of FUNDS allocated for border roads takes more than two years to reach its destination, thereby affecting the morale and efficiency of the BRO. Inclement weather also creates havoc, with roads to the India-China border closing down due to landslides during the monsoon season.

Despite all these obstacles, the roads have to be built given the criticality of defending the India-China border. One of the success stories in this regard has been the completion and inauguration of the longest bridge in Arunachal, the 720 metre Digaru Bridge linking Lohit and Dibang valley districts, on April 10 this year. Constructed by the BRO, this bridge will help both locals and the army to move faster.

Strategic roads in Arunachal Pradesh will also play a critical role in defending the border against any future Chinese attack. If at all the Chinese escalate their posture, it will, at best, be a combined RRF and aerial move. Hence, India's air defence structure must be robust and fully prepared taking into account Chinese capabilities and alternative war strategies. Given the present road conditions in Arunachal Pradesh, the physical movement of Indian troops to the border areas takes more than five to seven days. This aspect can be improved with the time taken reduced once the several announced road projects sees the light of day in the near future.

CHINA'S INDIA-POLICY: DECIPHERING CHINA'S LONG RANGE INTENTIONS

China's India-policy formulations and China's long range intentions need to be deciphered in view of Indian PM Modi's visit to China next month. China's long range intentions pertaining to India are neither benign nor friendly and this must never be lost sight of.

China's India-policy seems to be premised on the following conclusions which India itself has not taken any deliberate steps to disabuse China's mind-sets on India: (1) India's political leaders lack the will to stand upto Chinese provocations and brinkmanship on the Himalayan borders (2) India's lack of strategic and military infrastructure in the border regions and incomplete Indian military inventories limit strong responses from India, even if political will was there (3) India's successive policy establishments avoid taking hard decisions against China and seek 'soft solutions' in crisis situations, and (4) India lacks the political will and strategic audacity to stand upto China 'alone' and stand strategically tall.

Contextually, in light of the above Chinese perceptions of India, it is hoped that PM Narendra Modi during his forthcoming visit to China would set right these flawed Chinese misperceptions of India otherwise and stand tall, bold and even audacious in his dealings with China. China respects boldness and audacity and it is fervently hoped that India under the stewardship of PM Modi would not be found wanting.

Indian PM Modi's arrival in China is a month hence and China's pronouncements at different levels and forums are already divergent from India's expectations and defensive on the border and territorial disputes.

China's differences on strategic and political issues with India are widely divergent. The Indian Prime Minister is looking forward to make gains in the economic relations by attracting Chinese FDI in India's infrastructure sector in the absence of any headway on the border and territorial disputes.

Indian strategy seems to be to put aside strategic and political divergences aside and concentrate only on economic gains, presumably where there are no disputes other than trade imbalances in China's favour.

Media reports suggest that China is not receptive to this Indian approach and insist that any momentum in China-India relations can only be made by intertwining both political and economic issues. So that is a brake on India's economic expectations from China.

Further latest reports from China suggest that China is not willing to make any commitments on Chinese investments in India until China has studied and feels assured that Indian laws are not restrictive if trade disputes boil down to arbitration.. In other words China is not willing to press on the accelerator to at least impart momentum in the economic and trade spheres.

China's current India-policy stands fixated on keeping India off-balance strategically, politically and militarily. There are no optimistic indicators hovering on the horizon of China-India relations which suggest otherwise.

China's strategy to keep India off-balance is through the instrument of keeping alive the issue of disputed borders and illegal claims to large tracts of Indian Territory extending from Aksai Chin region in the North and the whole of Arunachal Pradesh in the East.

Chia is unlikely to discard this strategy or arrive at compromises which will rob China of a potent coercive weapon against India.

Regrettably, when Indian political leaders and their security advisers talk of an 'orbital jump' in China-India relations or 'out-of-box' solutions on long-shelved territorial disputes by China, both entities seem oblivious to China's long range intentions pertaining to India.

To those in India who constantly harp on peaceful relations with China, one can only point out, that such assertions are admirable at seminars but when measured against China's intentions as manifested on the borders with Tibet, such assertions do not pass the test of credibility.

To these China-apologists I would like to point out that the onus of 'Orbital Leaps' and 'Out-of Box' solutions to resolve China-India border issues lies squarely on the shoulders of China. It was China which needlessly generated border and territorial disputes after brutal military occupation of Tibet and it devolves on China to offer comprises which accommodate India's security concerns.

At first instance, deciphering China's long range intentions would require a credible answer as to whether China is ready or even remotely inclined to change its existing formulations or demands on the India-Tibet border issues and her other legally untenable demands to Indian Territory under Chinese occupation or her new-found claims to whole of Arunachal Pradesh.

China has no intention at all to arrive at any compromises or adjustments of the Indian borders with Tibet. Barring an economic upheaval in China, its Comprehensive National Power is increasing by the day. This would make China even more militarily intransigent with India on the border and territorial issues. India therefore should give up all optimism on arriving at solutions on border and territorial issue, and concentrate on improving its defensive postures on its borders with Tibet. The acid test of China's good intentions as a first step towards normalisation of relations with India would be to agree to demarcate the Line of Actual Control on the ground along the entire length of India's borders with Tibet. This could help greatly in reducing border tensions and likelihood of limited armed conflict due to Chinese military intrusions which has become an irritable regular feature.

China neither currently nor in the long range future would ever agree to a physical demarcation on the ground of the Line of Actual Control between India and Tibet. Any Chinese agreement to do so would rob China of the tactical advantage of shifting constantly the Line of Actual Control into Indian Territory to China's advantage by military intrusions.. It would also rob China of her political and military coercive power against India. Perceptional interpretations on where the un-demarcated Line of Actual Control stands, offers a plausible exit to China to get away with its military transgressions/intrusions in Indian Territory.

Besides he border and territorial issues that have escalated into unbridgeable disputes, the next weapon that China employs to keep India of-balance strategically and militarily is China's unholy alliance with Pakistan. The sole motive of China here is two-fold. China with its massive infusion of military aid, equipment and nuclear weapons and missile technologies to Pakistan has created Pakistan as the regional spoiler state and Chinese proxy in South Asia to checkmate India.

Militarily, China has enlisted Pakistan to jointly pose a "two-front threat "to India with all its attendant security complications. Can India expect that in the overall ambit of normalisation of China-India relations and as a long range intention, would China give up its strategic stranglehold over Pakistan in which it has invested so heavily as a regional spoiler state to checkmate India albeit even with diminishing returns?

China-Pakistan relations are entering a testing phase where Pakistan with diminishing support from United States and Saudi Arabia would have to rely heavily on China. Similarly, China would seek added reliance on Pakistan in view of being strategically cornered in East Asia. Therefore the strategic marriage of convenience between China and Pakistan portends greater strengthening and reinforcement. China in no case is likely to dilute its heavily strategic relationship with Pakistan. That is a "given' which Indian policy establishment has to accept and factor-in in its policy approaches to China. India needs to draw firm 'Red Lines' here.

The last issue which I would like to dwell on is the issue of Tibet. China has declared Tibet as a "Core National Interest" to be defended by military might, if required. It is also forgotten in India, thanks to Nehruvian mind-sets that "Tibet is also India's Core National Interest" and no scope exists for India to keep on acquiescing to a historical distortion that Tibet is a part of China. PM Narendra Modi would be well advised not to reiterate this as past Indian Prime Ministers have been parroting it on their visits to Beijing.

China's borders would never have rested on India's borders with Tibet, had India under Nehru as Prime Minister not meekly surrendered its inalienable rights in Tibet as the successor state of British India. Tibet lies at the core of competing and adversarial relations between China and India. Is China capable of any 'out-of-box" solution over Tibet's future in the interests of long-term betterment of China-India relations?

Short of massive political upheaval in Tibet, China is unlikely to give up its colonial stranglehold over Tibet. Over-militarisation of the Tibetan Plateau and merging greater parts of Tibet in China Proper highlights China's intentions. China indulged in forcible military occupation of Tibet to push China's borders to "Strategic Frontiers" rather than adhering to centuries-old and historical borders. India has to live with the stark reality that China will continue to be an overbearing and adversarial neighbour of India.

Tibet as a 'Core Issue' for both China and India has generated an arms race in which both China and India are presently engaged which has both Asian security and global security implications.

The last issue that needs to be addressed in terms of China's long-range intentions in terms of China's India-policy is the wide chasm of "Strategic Distrust" between the two countries as the spillover of China's perfidious 1962 military aggression against India. Reflected in my earlier SAAG Paper was the reality of the psyche of the Indian public opinion being deeply scarred by China stabbing India in the back, despite, India in the face of international opinion, espousing China be accepted in international forums. Reflected therein was also the assertion that China would really have to make more than magnanimous amends to the Indian nation to get over the 1962 scars. Is China capable of such a magnanimous initiative?

China in her present heady ascendant power trajectories would not be inclined to attempt any initiatives that could dilute the "Strategic Distrust" that pervades heavily in China-India relations. Nor would China plagued by its self-perceptions as a superpower stoop to offer any magnanimous gestures to soothe the Indian psyche over 1962.

So what is PM Narendra Modi and his advisers left with during the China visit in May 2015? China would throw some economic sops to India at the Beijing meet and the Indian policy establishment would gloat over it seconded by the Indian electronic media in the absence of any other substantial outcome from the Beijing Meet.

The above analysis does not imply that China should not be engaged by India. India must engage in dialogues with China but not let China dictate terms in such dialogues.

Endless rounds of dialogues at various levels and with regular frequency have yielded no results for over half a century. No indicators exist to suggest that this will be otherwise in the China-India Summit Meet in May 2015. The Indian disappointment in strategic dialogues with China came out starkly during photo-ops in the recent exchange in New Delhi. The Chinese State Councillor was definitely beaming with smiles whereas the Indian National Security Adviser appeared decidedly glum and disappointed. It presents a most truthful representation of prevailing realities of China's India-policy.

Concluding, while one concedes that the show with China must keep going-on, but with the caveat, that Indian political leaders and their advisers must never lose sight of the reality that China and India seem pre-destined to an uneasy "Cold War" or "Cold Peace" state of strategic environment in their relations, even in the long term perspective.

China's overall strategic postures towards India and China's intentions are not benign and politically mature. India needs to factor-in this strategic reality in its own China-policy responses.

INDIA IS PLANNING A NEW ROAD NEAR THE CHINA BORDER

The road will connect sparsely populated and poorly-connected hill communities living in four large frontier districts of Arunachal Pradesh.

It will also help farmers in the mountainous region to transport their organic crops and medicinal herbs to low-lying and busy markets in neighbouring Assam state.

"This road will not boost our defences but help connect far flung communities for economic development denied to them for so long," says India's junior home minister Khiren Rijiju, himself a resident of Arunachal Pradesh.

But Indian military officials say the road will help consolidate Indian defences.

This represents a change in Indian military thinking that has so far opposed developing roads near the border, in case it is used by the Chinese during a conflict for speedy movement inside Indian territory.

The road, however, could could ignite fresh tensions between India and China.

The world's two most populous countries disagree over the demarcation of several Himalayan border areas and fought a brief war in 1962.

'Colonial legacy'

Chinese foreign office spokesperson Hong Lei has said India's plan may "complicate" the boundary dispute which he described as a "colonial legacy".

"Before a final settlement is reached, we hope that India will not take any actions that may further complicate the situation. We should jointly safeguard the peace and tranquillity of the border area and create favourable conditions for the final settlement of the border issue," he told reporters in Beijing.

Chinese officials say it is not fair of India to undertake such a huge road building project in an area which is still in dispute.

"Once the dispute is resolved and the boundary is clearly demarcated, India can build such roads in its territory, but it would be unfair to build a road in a disputed territory," says Kong Can of the Yunnan Development Research Institute.

He says India should agree to develop the BCIM (Bangladesh-China-India-Myanmar) highway and economic corridor from Calcutta in India's West Bengal state to Kunming in China's Yunnan province cutting through Bangladesh, India's north-eastern states of Assam and Manipur and Myanmar's northern provinces.

"This highway and economic corridor will help integrate our economies and open huge opportunities for developing our under-developed frontier provinces and create a climate of trust that will help resolve the border dispute," Kong Can said.

India is going slow on the project, so far just agreeing to "explore" its possibilities.

Indian Prime Minister Narendra Modi has responded to demands from his security establishment to develop its defences against China, which has reportedly beefed up its military infrastructure in Tibet with a string of new railway lines, roads and at least five new airports.

Also, the rail route to Lhasa is likely to be extended to Nyingchu, close to the Arunachal Pradesh border, Indian military officials say.

"China has vastly beefed up its military infrastructure in Tibet and we are only catching up. Unless we do that, China will always arm-twist us on the border and try to impose a solution on its terms," says Lt Gen JR Mukherjee, former chief of staff in India's eastern army.

Last month India and China pulled back troops after a two-week stand-off near their de facto border in Ladakh. Chinese President Xi Jinping was visiting India when India accused his country of the fresh territorial incursion.

Many believe that has added to Indian apprehensions and could have influenced the decision to build the long border road that now upsets China.

CHINA WARNS INDIA AGAINST PAVING BORDER ROAD

China has sharply reacted to India's plans to construct a road network along the McMohan line in Arunachal Pradesh and expressed hope that India will not take any action which may complicate the situation before a final settlement is reached to end the boundary dispute.

"We still need to verify the specifics. The boundary issue between China and India is left by colonial past. We need to deal with this issue properly," Foreign Ministry Spokesman Hong Lie told a media briefing in Beijing.

He was reacting to comments by Union Minister of State for Home Affairs Kiren Rijiju stating that plans are afoot to construct a road network along the international boundary from Mago-Thingbu in Tawang to Vijaynagar in Changlang district of Arunachal Pradesh to match the China's infrastructure development.

"There is a dispute about the eastern part of the China-India border. Before final settlement is reached we hope that India will not take any action that may further complicate the situation," Hong said. "We should jointly safeguard the peace and tranquillity of the border area and create favourable conditions for the final settlement of the border issue," he said.

India's concerns arise out of extensive road, rail air network developed by China in Tibet which could play pivotal in moving the troops and equipment at a greater speed in the rugged Himalayan region.

Besides extensive highways, China's rail network came close to Sikkim border and Beijing has announced plans to build a new rail network up to Nyingchi which is close to the border of Arunachal Pradesh.

China has build about five airports in the Tibet region.

Beijing asserts that the infrastructure development is part of efforts to develop remote parts of Tibet.

China claims Arunachal Pradesh as a part of Southern Tibet and disputes McMohan line.

Chinese position is that the border dispute is confined to 2,000 kms mostly on Arunachal Pradesh where as India asserts that the dispute covered the western side of the border spanning to about 4,000 km.

The two countries have held 17 rounds of Special Representative talks so far to resolve the boundary dispute. The issue also figured during last month's talks between Prime Minister Narendra Modi and Chinese President Xi Jinping during his visit to India. The two leaders agreed to make efforts to resolve the border dispute at the earliest.

INDIA-PAK MUST SHOW RESTRAINT, STOP FIRING ALONG LOC

China also called on India and Pakistan to show restraint, stopTRADING fire along the Line of Control and resolve their issues through dialogue. "China is highly attentive to the situation. As a neighbour and friend of both Pakistan and India we hope the two sides can exercise restraint and stopTRADING fire and stick to dialogue and consultation, keep the situation in check and properly deal with the issues," Hong said.

"They should work together to jointly safeguard the peace, stability and development of South Asia," he said.

CHINA OPENS NEW HIGHWAY NEAR ARUNACHAL PRADESH BORDER

China on Thursday opened a new highway that links what the government has described as Tibet's "last isolated county" – located near the border with Arunachal Pradesh – with the rest of the country and will now provide all-weather access to the strategically-important region.

Chinese state media have hailed the opening of the highway to Medog – which lies close to the disputed eastern section of the border with India – as a technological breakthrough, with the project finally coming to fruition after seven failed attempts over the past fifty years.

China first started attempting to build the highway to Medog – a landlocked county in Tibet's Nyingchi prefecture – in the

1960s, according to State media reports, in the aftermath of the 1962 war with India.

With Thursday's opening of the road, every county in Tibet is now linked through the highway network, underlining the widening infrastructure gulf across the disputed border, even as India belatedly pushes forward an upgrading of border roads in more difficult terrain.

The official Xinhua News Agency on Thursday described Medog as "the last roadless county in China". Before this week, Medog was the only one of China's 2,100 counties to remain isolated from the highway network, according to State broadcaster *China Central Television* (CCTV).

What the project will do

State media reports have focused on the development benefits that the project would bring and have sought to play down the strategic dimensions. Local officials said the road's opening will bring down commodity prices and widen access to healthcare.

The road will also provide access to the border county for nine months of the year. That the government was willing to spend as much as 950 million Yuan – or $ 155 million – on a 117-km highway, with ostensibly few economic returns expected, has underscored the project's importance to State planners.

Local officials said prior to the opening of the highway, reaching Medog required traversing the treacherous Galung La and Doxong La mountains at an altitude of 4,000 metres. With frequent landslides, the road was often rendered impassable.

Now, the road will be accessible for "8 to 9 months per year, barring major natural disasters", Ge Yutao, Communist Party head of the transportation department for the Tibet Autonomous Region (TAR), told Xinhua.

Work on the 117-km road began in 2009, a year after the project was given the green light by the State Council, or Cabinet.

Renewed attention on infrastructure projects

The opening of the road comes at a time when there has been renewed attention on infrastructure projects in border areas in India and China.

Last week, both countries signed a Border Defence Cooperation Agreement (BDCA) during Prime Minister Manmohan Singh's visit to Beijing, aimed at expanding confidence-building measures. The agreement calls for setting up channels of communication between military commands, increasing the number of border personnel meetings, and formalising rules such as no tailing of patrols, to built trust and avoid incidents.

The agreement does not specify or limit either country's plans to boost infrastructure – an issue that, analysts say, has in the past triggered tensions along the disputed Line of Actual Control (LAC), most notably in April when a Chinese incursion sparked a three-week-long stand-off in Depsang, Ladakh.

Han Hua, a South Asia scholar at Peking University, suggested in a recent interview that the "basic reason" for the incident was "too much construction" along the border. The Chinese side, she acknowledged, did not have to build closer to the disputed LAC because their infrastructure, as well as more favourable terrain enabled quicker mobilisation.

"If we don't have the overall collaboration of the military, policy-makers and decision-makers on both sides," she said, "it will be difficult to avoid such incidents".

'India's plans will not be limited'

The BDCA, Indian officials said, will not limit India's plans to upgrade infrastructure. It recognises the principle of equal and mutual security, which allows either side to pursue its security in its own way. At the same time, officials say the BDCA will still help "regulate activity" along the border by opening up new channels of communication, even as the border continues to remain a matter of dispute.

On Thursday, Chinese Defence Ministry spokesperson Yang Yujun told a regular press conference that military personnel would hold "regular meetings" and "make joint efforts" to maintain peace in border areas, following the signing of the BDCA. The agreement, he said according to a Xinhua report, "summarised good practices and experiences on the management of differences in China-India border areas".

CHINA'S BORDER SPAT WITH INDIA

The recent meeting between India's National Security Adviser MK Narayanan and China's Vice-Foreign Minister Dai Banggio at Coonoor in Tamil Nadu was the continuation of a series of such meetings in the context of the border dispute between the two countries. While this is a good thing to go by, the main point is: what has been the actual progress in the matter?

After every meeting, a standard joint communiqué is issued to the effect that the téte-a-téte was fruitful and the dialogue is being maintained in an atmosphere of friendship and mutual cooperation. Diplomatic jargon cannot be limitless; it must end somewhere. Again, from time to time one hears of Chinese intrusion into Arunachal Pradesh, especially in the area of Sumdorong Chu Valley and the northern range of the Mishmi Hills. There is also the occasional media report that China claims this North-eastern state of ours on the grounds of a combination of history as well as geography.

India's drawback is that our foreign policy has always been linked to the vote bank. In fact it was a vote bank issue that created the border dispute with China in the first place way back in the late '50s and early '60s. The origin of this problem is worth discussing as this itself suggests the solution. Soon after China secured Tibet, Beijing sent a delegation to New Delhi under then Prime Minister Zhou en Lai with a proposal on Aksai Chin in northern Kashmir, adjacent to the Siachen Glacier. The delegation submitted to us that movement from Tibet to Sinkiang province was a huge problem because one had to traverse the inhospitable Kunlun Mountains en route. Hence it was suggested both countries could arrive at an understanding by which India could lease out Aksai Chin to China, as this would enable the latter to build an all-weather highway across this stretch of territory.

Thus movement from Tibet to Sinkiang would not then involve negotiating the Kunluns at all and India, too, could use this highway as a bonus. In any case, Aksai Chin was just an ice desert with an average height of 18,000-19,000 feet and nothing grew there, let alone having any human habitation. New Delhi reacted with its usual brash arrogance, thundering words to the effect that 'not an inch of our sacred motherland' would be given, et al. Zhou en Lai was shown the door gracelessly.

The Chinese delegation went back and decided to implement a tenet in Hindi conveying the meaning that if ghee cannot be taken out by a straight finger then a crooked finger would be used! China militarily attacked India and physically captured Aksai Chin by force in late 1962 and built the desired highway through it. China is still very much in occupation of this area, cocking a snook at India now and then! On our part we bemoaned our fate, blamed Beijing for gerrymandering into our territory and generally made a political nuisance of ourselves. Nothing helped, of course.

During its attack on India, China had also deeply transgressed into what was earlier known as the North East Frontier Agency that later became Arunachal Pradesh. However, after delivering a crushing military-cum-political defeat on India, China moved back to its own side of the border in this area. This apart, China disputes an area along the Uttarkhand-Tibet border named Barahoti. China has a strong army garrison in this area at a place called Taklakot that keeps a watching brief over Barahoti. India, therefore, has been well and truly boxed in by China, courtesy New Delhi's folly of riding the high horse with Zhou en Lai's delegation of yore. Diplomacy has never been a strong point with us and the country has suffered badly as a consequence. The science and art of statecraft continue to be subservient to the omnipotent vote bank as far as our leaders are concerned. New Delhi, for reasons best known to itself, brought out a Lok Sabha resolution in 1994 wherein it was categorically stated that we would retake Aksai Chin by force. Obviously this resolution was nothing but a vote bank gimmick that our näive citizens — including many members of our intelligentsia — swallowed all the way.While firmly occupying Aksai Chin, China periodically needles India over Arunachal Pradesh and Barahoti. Normally, Barahoti remains dormant but Arunachal Pradesh makes news, sometimes with alarm. This has been the state of affairs since 1962. No government at New Delhi since that year has tried to accept the reality and taken any pragmatic steps to reconcile the border situation with China, notwithstanding the fact that currently our relations with China are improving virtually by the day.

The question is, what needs to be done in order to resolve the ongoing impasse? There is only one solution: India must formally accept Zhou en Lai's suggestion of yesteryear but cede Aksai Chin to China. It is doubtful whether China will accept the lease aspect now. The Chinese are a very proud race and will never climb down. In any event, China holds the aces in this matter, never mind the McMahon Line's relevancy to us.

Truth to tell, this solution was hinted by China's previous regime under President Jiang Zemin through his then Foreign Minister Tang Jiaxuan during Prime Minister AB Vajpayee's tenure. While the Sikkim issue got reconciled, Aksai Chin could not be followed through due to the change of government in India in 2004.

China is not really interested in Barahoti and Arunachal Pradesh — Beijing uses these two as pressure points on New Delhi to see reason over the border dispute, a dispute that hinges purely on Aksai Chin. The sooner we come to terms with this, the better.

5

China's Infrastructure Development in Tibet

The People's Republic of China (PRC) has officially put forth the claim that Tibet belonged to China from the time of the Yuan Dynasty, if not earlier. Thereafter, the scenario changed with the Qing Dynasty (1644-1912), when Tibet was an integral part of a larger game being played between the Manchu, the Zunghar Mongols and the russians. For decades, the Manchu and Zunghars competed over control of Tibet. Tibet, which existed independently up to 1950, comprises approximately one-fourth of China's landmass today. Tibet, traditionally, encompassed the regions of the central plateau, kham and amdo after annexing Tibet, China separated amdo (the present Dalai Lama's birthplace) as the new Qinghai province, carved the central plateau and eastern kham into the Tibet autonomous region (Tar), and later merged the remaining parts of Tibet into the Chinese provinces of sichuan, Yunnan and Gansu. According to sinologist Mira sinha Bhattacharjea, as far back as the early 18th century, the Chinese placed boundary stones at points west of Batang, to claim the Yangtse as the watershed, east of which Tibet would exercise only nominal control. Batang is part of sichuan province at the border with the Tar what was then called eastern Tibet, it seems, was designed to be a buffer area between China and Tibet, under loose Chinese suzerainty.

If these areas were to be ceded to Tibet, the remaining part of the mainland would have been disproportionately reduced.

Batang seemed to be an important landmark east of the Yangtse river, which remained outside the *de facto* control of the Tibetans at the time of the Manchu empire from 1727-with the establishment of the People's republic, China had in place a government that, for the first time since the collapse of the Qing Dynasty — marshalled both the capability and the determination to assert its dominance over Tibet. For the leadership of the PrC, particularly the intellectual cadre, the vagaries of random conquests and submissions in the past no longer sufficed in making sense of history. Tibet's inclusion within the Chinese state was now something to be asserted, proven, and justified scientifically. The ideological imperative obliged the PRC to deal more specifically with the nature of Tibet's historical inclusion within the Chinese state. Out of this milieu evolved the interpretation that has been in place for several decades now – the affirmation that Tibet became an integral part of China during the period of the Mongol empire when the Mongol rulers of China united Tibet and China. It was in the 1950s that China coined what has become the present standard designation of Tibet: *Zhongguo de yi bufen* (one part of China), precise enough for the political purpose at hand and, thereby, affirming that Tibet was firmly within the PRC. Assuming vital importance by being a key element of China's nation-building process, the PrC, since 1949, appeared determined to end what they termed as "the century of humiliation" and consequently, established sovereignty over Tibet. Furthermore, the Tar was established in september 1965 with an area of 1.23 million sq miles as against 2.5 million sq miles of greater Tibet, large parts of which were merged with Qinghai, Gansu and sichuan provinces of China. Controlling the Tar remains crucial to China vis-à-vis enhancing its security on the western frontier.

The Hu Jintao Administration has significantly tightened its policy over Tibet in an apparent attempt to ensure the proverbial Chinese Communist Party's "long reign and perennial stability" in the restive region. More hardline cadres are being appointed to run the Tar while unprecedented aid has been pledged for the estimated 6.5 million Tibetans living in the Tar as well as the neighbouring provinces of sichuan, Gansu and Qinghai, the bulk of the new infrastructure projects also serve to speed up han Chinese migration.

The tough stance adopted by the Party and state apparatus towards the ethnic minorities was approved at the 08 January 2010 Politburo meeting that was devoted exclusively to the Tibetan issue. President hu Jintao, who was Party secretary of Tibet from 1988 to 1992, heralded two goals for the Tar in the coming decade during the course of deliberations at the meeting:

- seeking a breakthrough-style (economic) development; and
- Maintaining long-term stability.

In the Politburo meeting, President hu promised that the central government would help Tibet by boosting investment, transferring technology, and sending in more qualified officials as well as "experts and talents." Significantly, the region's GDP is set to grow by 12 percent this year, while fixed-assets investments are expected to grow by a whopping 18 percent. Under President hu's dictum of "going down the road of development with Chinese characteristics and Tibetan flavour" (*Zhongguo tese, xizang tedian*), additional input has been focused on areas including infrastructure, tourism, mining and manufacturing. However, President hu and his team have not mentioned what kind of 'experts' will be dispatched to Tibet. In the wake of ethnic violence in both Tibet and Xinjiang in 2008, more soldiers and officers of the paramilitary People's armed Police (PaP) have been stationed in the two regions.

In its latest 2010 *White Paper on National Defence* released in March 2011, the PrC categorically stated that "separatist forces and its activities are still the biggest obstacle and threat... working for Tibet independence have inflicted serious damage on national security and social stability." In fact, the issues of Taiwan, east Turkestan and Tibet should be read in correlation to the larger concept of Chinese national integration. China reiterated that its concepts of warfare and capability upgradation go well beyond meeting challenges in the form of Taiwan, Tibet and east Turkestan thus, explicitly implying that China's military capabilities shall continue to grow unabated, even as the Taiwan issue thaws; and that the Chinese national security strategy is set to be focused to look beyond Taiwan.

The Chinese military recognises the importance of build-up of logistics on the battlefield and is taking steps to maximise its logistics capabilities. It was not until 2002, when hu Jintao, then vice President of the PrC, issued an order to transform PLa logistics, that rapid renovation actually began. The PLa logistics doctrine in 2000 still depended heavily on the "people's war" concept and not particularly on military assets. A portion of this doctrine stipulated that an individual must carry his own support and sustainment packages while fighting the enemy on the front lines. The General Logistics Department (GLD) and the PLa gradually began linking civilian and military logistics to provide what former Chairman of the Central Military Commission, Jiang Zemin, called "precision logistics." According to the Us Department of Defence, the PLa is purchasing heavy lift assets from Russia to move their heavy Brigade Combat Teams (hBCTs) to outlying provinces, including Fuzhou. The significance of Fuzhou province lies in the fact that it is the gateway to Taiwan, and if Taiwan decides to declare independence from the PrC, the PLa is likely to use Fuzhou as a platform to launch an offensive against Taiwan nevertheless, the PLa units still lack high-mobility transportation assets, modular equipment, and automated tracking systems and have still not developed logistics packages that can support the hBCT concept. The PLa's current modernisation campaign will enable it to support future offensive operations outside of its mainland, given that the PLa's precision logistics is modernising rapidly. An ancient Chinese maxim states: "If you know your enemies and know yourself, you will win a hundred times in a hundred battles. If you only know yourself, but not your opponent, you will win one and lose the next. If you do not know yourself or your enemy, you will always lose."

EMPHASISING LOGISTICS DEVELOPMENT

While emphasizing logistics reform, the 2010 Defence white Paper focuses on enhancing logistical support capabilities for diversified military tasks. In fact, the PLa is working on a multilateral approach towards building a modern logistics system by speeding up the process of integrating systems, outsourcing services, informationising processes and managing its logistical support systems more scientifically. The White Paper also accepts completion of the PLa's three-year plan for integrated improvement of grassroot logistics systems for border and coastal defense units.

It should be recalled that a unified national logistics apparatus was not established until 1950, and even afterwards, logistical matters continued to be a low priority for the top brass. The first large-scale exercise to assess the readiness of logistics units to take part in mobile wars under high-technology conditions took place in 1996. This was a major logistics drill in southwest China that was designed to examine the rapid reaction and mobile capabilities of logistics units located in the Chengdu Mr, with the presence of GLD Director General, wang ke, underscoring the importance of the exercise. Portions of the drill included logistical support of joint land-air-sea operations. The PLa training exercises have increased in size, intensity and complexity since the early 1990s and logistics have been heavily involved in many of these drills, especially those that have focused on mobility and joint operations. The PLa is likely to retain a sprawling logistics apparatus, but with expanding pockets of excellence, in the form of emergency support units and other rapid reaction logistics forces to provide support for future mobile wars. The PLa will increasingly utilise rapidly expanding civilian transport and infrastructure capabilities to augment its own limited resources.

Logistics development has progressed upwards in China's military hierarchy, particularly since the PLa began in the early 1990s, to focus its attention on how to fight limited wars under high-technology conditions. Logistical support is at the heart of this new operational doctrine, especially the need for rapid mobility, intensive supply of materials and forward technical support. Consequently, logistics modernisation has become a high priority in the PLa's quest to build a 21st century fighting force. The enhanced status of the logistics apparatus was underlined by CMC Chairman and Party General secretary, Jiang Zemin, in 1991, when he included logistics support as one of his five major requirements for army building. He also pointed out that "there would be no high combat effectiveness without a strong logistics supply," the understanding being that the logistics system needed to be overhauled to enhance its ability to support a more mobile and better-equipped fighting force, as well as to cope with the challenges of economic liberalisation.

The general principles of the war-fighting doctrine involving limited high-technology wars, emphasise mobility, rapid response, intensive consumption of war materials and off-shore operations. without the logistical capabilities to meet such demands, the PLa would be unable to undertake military operations at, and above, the campaign level.

Moreover, a high-technology war is highly mobile and concentrated, where rapid tactical and strategic mobility would be essential. Contingency planning for the situation that the PLa may confront in the coming years, vis-à-vis Taiwan and the spratly Islands in the south China sea, includes operational concepts being worked out, dealing with sea and air blockades, landing operations, operations on coral reefs, mobile warfare, counter-attack in border areas, urban offensives, airborne operations and surgical counter-attacks. Logistics planners in China are conscious that existing logistics capabilities are woefully inadequate to be able to support these demanding missions. They point out that there are several key areas in which capabilities need to be significantly expanded:

- Strategic and Tactical Mobility*:* The PLa's transportation capabilities are limited, heavily reliant on ground assets, and primarily tactical in reach. rapid strategic and tactical mobility, especially coordinated joint-service operations, are critical in a high-technology war. Some logistics planners argue that at the campaign level, each war zone (equivalent to a Military region) should have the logistics capacity to support an amphibious landing of one infantry division.
- Emergency Support Forces*:* Quick reaction logistical support units are vital to provide immediate assistance for frontline rapid reaction forces. A network of such units at high levels of readiness should be established throughout the armed forces.
- Battlefield Repair and Support*:* The rapid repair of damaged weapons on, or in the vicinity of, the battlefield

is critical to maintaining combat effectiveness during war-time. This will become increasingly important as the PLa acquires new generations of advanced arms to replace its ageing arsenal of 1950s and 1960s-era weapons.

- Advanced Stockpiling of War Materials: Forward pre-positioning of large stockpiles of war materials is considered of vital importance because of the rapid and unexpected nature of how high-technology wars break out. The PLa's strategic war materials reserve system is concentrated in inland areas and needs to be extensively reorganised and relocated to coastal regions.
- Logistics Mobilisation and Reserve Forces: The mobilisation of reserve forces and civilian resources in war-time needs to be accelerated and significantly expanded because of the pressing time constraints of a high-technology war. This requires closer coordination between civilian and military authorities and the establishment and training of specialised logistical reserve support units. Logistics planners urge that each war zone should have two or three logistical reserve support brigades. Although reforms only began in the mid-1990s, the PLa is beginning to make progress in the upgrading of capabilities in these areas. Some of the major reforms that have taken place include the following:
- Creation of Emergency Support Units and Reserve Logistical Support Brigades: networks of small-scale emergency support units and depots have been established in all Military regions over the past few years. They are usually selected logistics units or depots that are tasked to provide rapid support in war-time, and many of them appear to be organised around logistics sub-units (*houqin fenbu*) attached to the Military region logistics departments. Reserve logistical support units have also begun to be set up in recent years to augment regular forces. The PLa's first reserve logistical support brigade was set up in 1996 in Liaoning province.
- Enhancing Strategic and Tactical Transport Capabilities:

hampered by limited funds, the PLa has been pursuing a double-pronged approach to the development of its transport capabilities.

The Tar's biggest logistics centre in southwest China was completed in June 2009. The logistics centre is located next to a railway station at an altitude of 4,500 metres (m) in the nagqu township of nagqu county, in northern Tibet. It is about 300 km northeast of the regional capital, Lhasa. The project is expected to further exploit the potential of the Qinghai-Tibet railway (QTr) and boost the region's economic development. Construction of the logistics centre stands at a cost of almost 1.5 billion yuan (Us $220 million). The centre is expected to handle 2.23 million tonnes of cargo by 2015 and 3.1 million tonnes by 2020.

The Chinese have always claimed that the primary aim of the logistics ramp up in the Tar is directed towards the economic prosperity of the region by providing more and more business opportunities. Tibet's economy has been growing at an annual rate of 12 percent or more over the past seven years, and the Qinghai-Tibet railway is believed to have played a great role in boosting the region's development. The consequent strategic challenges and their implications, however, continue to loom large, especially for India. The Chinese investment in infrastructure development in the border areas with India, coupled with a sustained double digit growth in its defence budget and the massive military modernisation undertaken by the PLa, are reasons enough for India to take cognisance of the above developments since they undoubtedly pose a security challenge to India.

The completion of the Golmud-Lhasa rail link is central to China's Great western Development Policy, aimed at promoting the cause of Chinese nationalism and 'great power status' by virtue of greater economic development of the country's under-developed western areas that are primarily populated by ethnic minorities. In fact, hu Jintao has long advocated a policy of generating economic prosperity so as to eradicate separatism in this part of China. Accentuating the potential of the Golmud-Lhasa rail link, work on Tibet's largest logistics centre to handle freight for the railway line was completed in June 2009. The nagqu

Logistics Centre comes up adjacent to a railway station at an altitude of 4,500 m in the nagqu township of nagqu county, northern Tibet, 300 km northeast of the region's capital, Lhasa. Covering an area of 533 hectares, the centre is expected to handle up to 4.07 million tonnes of freight by 2030, further exploiting the potential of the QTr and boosting the region's economic prospects.

ON ROAD TOWARDS ECONOMIC CONSOLIDATION

Like Deng Xiaoping, hu Jintao, too, advocated a policy of generating economic prosperity to eradicate separatism in Tibet and Xinjiang. Hailing the infrastructural development in the Tar as a national security strategy, hu stated, "rapid economic development is the fundamental condition for realizing the interests of all ethnic groups in Tibet and also the basic guarantee for greater ethnic unity and continued stability there."

In the last decade, Tibet has been the largest per capita recipient of subsidy and funding from the central government. On the Tar's 20th anniversary, the government spent 500 million yuan (Us $78.2 million) on 43 projects; on the Tar's 30th anniversary, it spent 4.6 billion yuan (Us $720.1 million) on 62 projects; and on the Tar's 40th anniversary, it spent 6.42 billion yuan (Us $1 billion) on 24 projects. Tar Chairman, Jampa Phuntsok stated that in 2004, over 16.6 billion yuan (Us $2 billion) was invested in building infrastructure. Most of the funds came from the central government under the "western Development Programme." As per the testimony of Tsering Dhondup (a nomad from kanlho County) to the Tibetan Centre for human rights and Democracy (TChrD), mismanagement and embezzlement of public funds are common at the local government levels.

Today, Tibet houses more than 300 moderately-sized modern industrial and mining enterprises, including key industries such as electric power, mining, building material, chemicals, textiles, tanning, printing and food processing but, hardly any of them seems to be defence-oriented. As per numerous reports, the Chinese government has planned to invest Us $3.8 billion to develop an additional 117 industries in the Tar. China also intends to make

Lhasa a special economic Zone (seZ). The status being conferred on the region will entail a host of incentives such as low tax rates (15 percent as compared to the usual 33 percent). Earlier experience has shown unprecedented growth rates in areas declared as seZs (up to 32 percent). The GDP of the Tar grew at 14 percent in 2007, much more than China's average. This rapid growth rate is attributed to readjustment of the existing, and introduction of new, industries; heavy investments by the central government in infrastructure; and reforms in state-owned enterprises and government organisations. To implement its development plans, the Chinese government has undertaken certain development projects like road, rail and air network, Fuel, Oil and Lubricants (FOL) pipelines and communications. It has announced a Us $40 million project for restoration of the sacred buildings in Tibet. Beijing has also announced plans to convert 50 counties of the Tar and two zones of sichuan and Yunnan into "shangri La Tourism economic Zones" for which Us $9.6 million has been allocated.

CHINA'S VULNERABILITIES INFRASTRUCTURE IN TIBET

Today, the Chinese economy is growing an average 10 per cent of it's Gross Domestic Product (GDP) since 2000. In 1978, when China opened to economic reform, the US economy was 31.5 times that of China. By 2001, the gap had closed to 7.5 times and in 2010 its GDP was a staggering 4.5 trillion dollars, just a third of the US and still growing. The foreign exchange reserves have exceeded $3200 billion and in 2009 it surpassed Japan as the second largest economy in the world. The official defence budget was $8 billion in 1995, $30 billion in 2005 and has gone up to over $106 billion in 2012.

Such figures lend credibility to China's growing economic and military power. As the growth figures began to ring alarm bells in capitals across the world, Chinese spin doctors coined the 'peaceful rise' theory. Zheng Bijian, a former Vice-President of CPC Central Party School and Hu Jintao`s diplomatic advisor, was cornered in 2003 to answer Western proponents of the 'China Threat Theory' who believed that China would challenge the international order and rise through territorial expansion and muscle power.

Zheng unveiled this theory to assuage the fears of the Western world stating that, 'China would integrate with the world order instead of challenging it' essentially to assuage the fears of the Western world.

Zheng assured the world that:

- The past 25 years have been quite extraordinary. Our biggest achievement is to have realised that peace and rise, which look quite contradictory, can actually be integrated. In the past, the rise of a big power often involved toppling the international order and a threat to peace. China breaks the rule.—Zheng Bijian, April 2004

But the 'peaceful theory' doesn't cut ice with China's post independence strategic culture. In fact, it has been somewhat of an enigma. To avenge its 'Century of Humiliation', China has not hesitated to go to war even when internally it has been relatively weak. In 1950, China went to the Korean Peninsula in support of the Communist regime in Korea; barely a year after Mao had overthrown the Nationalists and won the revolution in the country.

In fact, the Chinese Army had entered Tibet and Mao was on a campaign to integrate the minorities in Tibet and Mongolia while the war raged in Korea. In 1962, China attacked India immediately after the disastrous 'Great Leap Forward' (1958-61), which caused widespread famine and food shortages as Mao attempted to change China from an agrarian based economy to an industrial one with catastrophic consequences. Again in 1969, China confronted the USSR in the Ussuri River crisis, which snowballed into a near nuclear exchange, soon after the tumultuous and despised 'Cultural Revolution' (1966-69) in which Chinese society was deeply scarred by religious persecution, forced indoctrination and violence.

Even in 1979, China attacked Vietnam and suffered humiliation, despite having embarked on a policy of economic liberalisation and development, just a year earlier, in 1978. Scholars contend that, paradoxically, China seeks peace when it is strong and will go ahead with the 'reunification of lost territories'. As China developed 'peacefully', so did Tibet. But the development has been one sided, benefiting the state and not the Tibetan people. Most of the development has been focussed on creation of infrastructure to exploit Tibet's vast mineral resources and enable the PLA to use military force whenever China wants to use muscle to resolve the border issue with India. Tibet has been a major issue in India – China relations. Ever since Dalai Lama fled to India in 1959, China has looked at India with suspicion. Over the years, India's policy on Tibet has been unwavering. India recognises that Tibet is a part of China and that the Dalai Lama is a revered guest in India. India has assured China that it will not permit its land to be used for anti- China activities by the Tibetan people settled in India. Chinese policy on Tibet on the other hand has seen significant changes.

It has vacillated from being a geo-political security concern in the early 1950s to becoming an economic security concern post 2000. In the period between the World Wars, Tibet was a 'buffer' state separating the Great Powers, a pawn in the Great Game. Mao was convinced that Britain wanted to ultimately use Tibet as the base for conquest of China. Today, Tibet is a source of abound mineral wealth and water for the Chinese industrial complex and the millions of Chinese people that live along the banks of the rivers that flow out of Tibet towards coastal China. China and India have fought a bloody war over the border dispute concerning Tibet.

While India and China are talking on a peaceful resolution of the dispute, China has ramped up infrastructure, roads, railways, airports, logistics and communications in the Tibetan Autonomous Region (TAR). After 2006, China has raised the ante on Arunachal Pradesh (ALP), calling it "Southern Tibet" and escalated tension by raising pinpricks on the ALP issue; protesting against the visit of Indian Prime Minister to ALP or even the Dalai Lama to Tawang etc. The fact that China has resolved its land borders with 12 out of 14 neighbours is not lost to the Indian strategists.

Presently, China is focussed on 'unification of territories' at sea - Taiwan, South China Sea and Japan. The resolution of land borders is a matter of time. The implications on India are clear in the sense that it is prepared to face any eventuality in this region. The 'two front theory' is an outcome of the militarisation and internationalisation of the border dispute all along the Line of

Actual Control (LAC) and in particular, in ALP. The Sino-Indian discourse in recent years mainly centres on the rise of China and its explosive economic growth, its aggressive foreign policy and massive military modernisation. There is no dearth of research work on China's strength and power. However, there is little work on China's vulnerabilities. Tibet and the Tibetan people will play a key role in any Sino-Indian conflict in future.

HANISATION OF TIBET

The invasion of Tibet by the PLA which commenced in 1950, ostensibly to integrate Tibet with the mainland, culminated in violent attacks and rebellion in 1959. While no official Chinese records or documents are available for the loss of life, livestock and property, during this period, there is sufficient proof and evidence cited by emigrants of Tibet of terrible repression and savagery inflicted by the PLA on the Tibetan people.

Some term it as 'genocide'. The ingrained prejudice against the minorities is a historical truth and Han always treated the minorities with mistrust and disdain. The major policy that the Chinese pursued once Tibet was subjugated was to change its demography. Mao is quoted as saying, 'Tibet covers a large area but is thinly populated. Its population should be increased from the present two or three million to five or six million and then to over 10 million.' This was done by engineering large scale migration of Han Chinese into Tibet with the ultimate aim of reducing Tibetans to a minority in their own land. Clearly Mao wanted to 'Hanise' Tibet. Conflicting reports of population of TAR are available through a number of sources. Official Chinese Government figures are 2.62 million (2000 census) of Tibetans in TAR, but the Dalai Lama's office disputes the official figure and believes that 7.5 million Chinese live alongside six million Tibetans in TAR. The Dalai Lama's office figures seem exaggerated as they include the entire erstwhile state of Tibet. However, in Amdo (Qinghai) and Kham (Sichuan) the Han have already outstripped the locals. Asia Watch in its report in 1990 has disagreed with these figures of 7.5 million given by TGIE but agrees that the migration has been sizeable. Robert McCorquodale and Nicholas Orosz have in a report concluded that, 'a very significant transfer of Chinese to Tibet has taken place since 1949-59.' The report quotes Asia

Watch Report 1990 that, 'majority of population in Lhasa is clearly Chinese.'

The report adds, 'in essence, the authorities appear to be applying a discriminatory policy barring Tibetans from coming to Lhasa, while placing no restriction whatever on Chinese migration into the city......a professionally capable and strategically placed Chinese population seems to be the key element in the Chinese Government's plans for the integrated and military development in Tibet.' In June 1987, Deng-Xiaoping admitted that, the Chinese were being encouraged to move to Tibet as the regions two million population is inadequate to develop its resources. Venting his fears at the National People's Congress in 1987, the late Panchen Lama said, 'The expense of keeping one Chinese in Tibet is equal to that of four in China.

Why should Tibet spend its money to feed them?... Tibet has suffered greatly because of the policy of sending a large number of useless people. The Chinese population in Tibet started with a few thousand and today it has multiplied manifold.' So how has this 'demographic aggression' or 'Han migration' affected the average Tibetan in Tibet? To encourage migration from mainland China, the Chinese Government announced a slew of attractive benefits and concessions for its employees and settlers. According to Chinese economists, 'The personnel brought in from developed regions cannot be expected to live on the local fare of tsampi (roasted barley flour) and raw meat. They need good housing, hospitals, cinemas and schools for their children.' The benefits to migrant were: housing, health care, special leave to China, cultural and educational facilities, high altitude allowance; 87 per cent higher wages than in China, special tax exemptions and loans at low interest rates. Above all, the one child policy did not apply to Chinese settled in Tibet. However, to be fair to China's Tibet Policy, Tibet was given favourable treatment. Tibetan businesses enjoyed a preferential tax rate of three per cent lower than mainland China, farmers and herdsmen were exempted from taxes and administrative charges.

Banks have enjoyed a preferential interest rate of two points lower than the mainland as well as low rate on insurance premiums. All this has ensured a double digit growth for TAR for a decade.

Has this benefited the Tibetans? In one decade (2000-09) in Tibet, the average savings in rural China were pegged at 1160 Yuan. Yet for Tibet this is 1080 Yuan, well below the national average. Even in business, sales in state owned and individual (largely Han owned in cities) enterprises during the period 2000 to 2009 multiplied five times, but 'others'- smaller/household businesses owned by the common people just trebled over the same period. Large businesses like wholesale and retail, hotels, restaurants etc. multiplied four times over the last decade (2000-09) but 'others'- small business, largely household and small shops stagnated. It may be argued that overall Tibet has benefited but the fruits have not trickled down to 76.2 per cent of the population that is largely rural as per 2009 figures.

During his visit to Lhasa, Professor Dibyesh Anand observed that there were no Tibetan shop owners in Lhasa, only Han and Hui. The smiling and happy Tibetans holding latest mobile phones were only those seen on large posters in Lhasa. The modern Tibetan village was located behind those posters in Lhasa…and that is where Tibetans lived in extreme poverty. Natural growth rate has dropped by 40 per cent in Tibet over the period 1990-09, with birth rate also dropping by 40 per cent over the same period, indicating economic pressures are forcing people to have smaller families to earn a livelihood. There are reports that Tibetans have been relocated to higher reaches in Kham and Amdo areas leaving the fertile valleys for the Han. In 1959 the total area of TAR under farming was 0.2 per cent largely restricted to the river valleys. By 1991 it had increased to 0.3 per cent (almost 50 per cent) largely due to influx of migrants. However, increase in cultivable land was at the cost of pasture land forcing the nomads and the shepherds to look for pastures in higher reaches as also overuse the pastures upsetting the fragile ecology balance. More importantly, this has resulted in a drop in cropland per capita. In Ganze prefecture, for e.g, cropland increased by 4562 hectares while population increased by 255,293 thereby resulting in drop of per capita cropland from 0.17 hectares to 0.11 hectares.

In 2006, a relocation project moved 290,000 Tibetans into urban homes - almost 10 per cent of the whole Tibetan population. Critics of the location policy cited that, China had not researched its urbanisation policy and the effects it would have on employment, jobs and Tibetan culture.

VULNERABILITY IN LINES OF COMMUNICATION

Roads

Geographically, the Tibetan plateau is bound by the Kun Lun mountains in the north and the Himalayas in the south. Prior to the annexation of Tibet, access to Tibet from the Chinese side was much more difficult and restricted to just two routes; the South-Western through Sichuan and the North-Western through Xinjiang. By comparison, routes through Chumbi valley, (present day Sikkim) and Tawang through India were easier. In fact, even Chinese had accessed Lhasa from these Indian routes in the earlier years.

After 1950, China realised that, that access through India would become a major vulnerability as there was a growing belief in the Chinese polity, especially with Mao, that India was leaning to the West. The possibility of having a capitalist US ally on its southern borders forced China to embark on major road construction projects to access Tibet and reinforce its full control over the Tibetan plateau. In 1950, China commenced on the construction of four major strategic highways which linked Tibet to the main land. The northern and western highways, in particular, run just 35 kms parallel to the Himalayan borders are critical to more deployment and sustenance of troops in the forward areas.

Sichuan Tibet Highway

The Sichuan-Tibet Highway is a marvel of road construction. The Association for Safe International Road Travel (ASIRT) votes this highway on the list of 'World's 23 deadly roads'. The Chengdu-Lhasa route is divided into two: The northern route which is 2415 km long including 1304 km in Tibet, which was opened on December 25, 1954. Subsequently, the Dongerluo-Zhubalong-Bamda south section was commissioned in 1969 with 1285 kms length in Tibet. The southern route came up as an alternate route to the northern road which is vulnerable to vagaries of weather and geography. The routes are treacherous and pass through 14 mountain ranges and 10 rivers including Mekong and Salween and are known to be susceptible to frequent closure due to land slides and rock falls.

The road is a vital link for all formations and units of Chengdu Military Region which mobilise to Tibet, essentially the 13 Group Army's 37 Division, located at Chongqing, 300 km south east of Chengdu and 149 Mechanised Infantry Division located at Leshan, 120 kms south of Chengdu. With numerous bridges and long stretches of glaciated terrain, the highway is susceptible to attack by the Indian Air force (IAF) and assault by organised rioters. This highway passes through Sichuan province which has a very large population of Tibetans living outside present day TAR lending credibility to Chinese fears of being disrupted during critical periods. Realising this, perhaps redundancy was created by constructing the south section.

Qinghai - Tibet Highway

The Qinghai-Tibet Highway is one of the highest in the world starting from Xining in Qinghai Province to the city of Lhasa, a total of 1937 kms. It crosses four major mountain ranges, the highest point being Tangula (5150m), and three major rivers. First built in 1950, it was commissioned on December 25, 1954 to support the PLA march into Tibet. It is the main state secondary road, 10 metres wide, and has a speed limit of 60 km/hr and by far the shortest and the safest highway with best road conditions into Tibet. Short of Lhasa, it branches off due west towards Ngari through Nagqu- Nyime-Gerze and is the alternate route to the Xinjiang Highway. This highway is called 'Hei-A' Highway.

In the event of sabotage of the Sichuan-Tibet Highway, as was done by Khampa rebels in the 1950s, this highway is the alternate route to Tibet from the mainland. However, this highway too is unreliable especially in winter when snowfall makes it impassable. The other issue is the need for acclimatisation. In a high altitude area troops moving from the plains need to get used to the rarefied oxygen in the atmosphere as they climb to higher altitudes. There is a need for transit camps and medical facilities at regular intervals of distance to ensure acclimatisation process is facilitated. This has a bearing on the need for logistics all along the routes of induction of the troops. The road is vital for use of units of Lanzhou MR, essentially 61 Infantry Division from Tianshui and 12 Armoured Division from Zhangye both in Gansu Province.

Xinjiang - Tibet Highway

The Xinjiang -Tibet Highway starts from Yecheng county of Xinjiang and ends at Lhaze county of Shigatse Prefecture in Tibet, a distance of 1455 kms. Its construction commenced in 1951 and the road was commissioned in 1957. Crossing 10 mountain ranges, its average height is 4000-5000 metres reaching the highest elevation of 5433 metres. From Yecheng it goes on to Kargilik, an additional distance of 1288 km near the Tajikistan border, passing through the disputed territory of Akshai Chin, connecting Ngari to Kashgar. Near Shigatse the road branches into three; one continuing towards Xinjiang the second leads to the Nathula border with India, leading on to the trade route through the Chumbi valley: and the third to Kathmandu, also called the Sino-Friendship Highway. The road is likely to be used for units of Lanzhou Military Region inducting into TAR from 'Hei-A' Highway and Qinghai-Tibet Highway opposite the Ladakh and Central Sector of India.

The Yunan-Tibet Highway

The Yunnan-Tibet Highway is 800 km long starting from Dali (Yunan) to Markham (Tibet). It was constructed as an alternate route to Tibet from Yunnan due to unreliability of the Sichuan- Tibet Highway in 1974. Crossing peaks of 4300 metres height and the Jinsha and Lancang rivers, its importance lies in the fact that it skirts the entire state of Arunachal Pradesh and North Myanmar, enabling mobilisation of troops from Kunming to the India-Tibet border. Units of 14 Group Army, essentially 40 Motorised Infantry Division at Dali and 49 Motorised Infantry Division at Kaiyuan can quickly mobilise on this route.

Railways-QTR (Qinghai - Tibet Railway)

The inauguration of the Qinghai - Tibet Railway on 01 July 2006, was a major achievement in China's Great Western Development Policy which aims at economic development of West China and minorities in an attempt to reduce the East- West divide. Besides being an engineering feat, the QTR is also a symbol of China's power status and promotes the policy of 'Hanisation' of the West. It is 1956 km long, traversing over 550 km of permafrost and crosses heights of 5072 metres (Tangula pass). It also boasts of 675 bridges totalling 160 kms of length and the world's longest tunnel, Fenghuashan Tunnel, which is 4905 metres long.

The QTR is proposed to be extended to Nepal by 2013 as also to Nyingchi in East, Shigatse in the West and Yadong in the Chumbi valley by 2020 AD. The QTR is the core of Deng's minority policy which hinged on economic development of minorities as the best way to 'assimilate' them with the mainstream. The larger importance of the QTR is 'strategic'. The Qinghai Tibet plateau accounts for 10 per cent, 12 per cent and 26.7 per cent of the world's boron, lithium and caesium reserves respectively. This resource corridor has a potential value of $ 750 billion.

Tibetans believe the QTR has been made to facilitate exploitation of Tibet's vast resources generating resentment – large contracts will only benefit the Han and the mainland. The QTR has the capacity to transport an average of almost 70,000 passengers a month, thereby opening the TAR to Han migration, a policy long enunciated by the CPC. One of the key vehicles that have facilitated the migration process has been the QTR. Not only has it provided jobs, it has also opened Tibet to tourism, transportation and mining. The QTR facilitates movement of heavy equipment and stores in the event of mobilisation of the PLA.

A total of 361 high altitude passenger carriages were provided by Bombardier transportation, 53 of which are luxury sleeper carriages for tourist service. Thus, QTR will have 300 plus carriages for mobilisation of the military in the event of internal unrest or external aggression. Each carriage has a seating capacity of 98 and assuming one rake comprises of 20 carriages, QTR can transport approximately 2000 troops in one rake in one trip. The QTR line has a capacity of eight pairs of passenger trains. Thus, 16,000 troops can be moved every 48 hours along the QTR or one Division every two days.

The Yarlung Tsang Po or the Brahmaputra

Originating from the Tamlung Tso lake, south east of Mount Kailash, the Yarlung Tsang Po is the largest and the longest river in Tibet. Its general flow is from west to east dropping from 4500 metres in the west to 3000 metres in the east across 2900 kms of South Tibet. Its alignment flow meanders along the line Ngari-Shigatse-Lhasa-Nyingchi. The river is a major obstacle to all movement south of this line and can only be crossed at key bridges all along till it enters into India from the Great Bend near Namcha Barwa peak in East Tibet. There are a number of bridges of importance, *viz,* Paizhen Bridge on the Lhasa-Nyingchi road, Qushui Bridge on the Lhasa- Gonggar airport road- the lifeline to Lhasaalmost 300 metres long and 10 metres wide, Tsetang Bridge near Tsatang, Saga bridge to the west of Shigatse and Nyago Bridge. These bridges are vulnerable to interdiction by air and long range weapons. They affect movement of the PLA from their bases in the depth to the forward areas and forward positions on the Plateau. It would be reasonable to assume that all major depots and logistics nodes would also be north of the Tsang Po due to proximity to the Line of Actual Control (LAC) and would depend on the safety of these bridges for secure lines of communication.

Airlift

In terms of sheer numbers, the PLAAF is the third largest air force in the world after the US and Russia. The PLAAF's early years were under the shadows of the PLA Army and therefore was a lesser known service. In fact, it went unrepresented at the CMC till as recent as 2004. PLAAF's chain of command is organised into four levels with Headquarters Air Force (HQAF) with a Commander Air force at the apex level directly under the CMC and now a member of the CMC; 7 Military Region Air Force (MRAF) Headquarters at the MR level; Air Divisions with the Group Armies; and Air Regiments and operational units which function under the Air Divisions. While the overall responsibility of operations in a MR remains that of the PLA Military Region Commander, the Air Force commander is the Deputy Commander of the MR, subordinated to the PLA commander. In the Indian context, only two of the seven MRs are opposite India - Lanzhou, opposite the Ladakh region and Chengdu, facing the Central and North Eastern India.

Very few active units of the PLA of Lanzhou and Chengdu MRs are permanently based in Tibet. The borders are normally looked after by the Region Military District (Tibet and Xinjiang) and troops of the PAP. In the event of hostilities, the active units are required to be mobilised into Tibet by road and by air. The Chengdu MR maintains 149 Mechanised Infantry Division as the Military Region Rapid Reaction Unit, which is expected to be the first to be mobilised for operations in Tibet. During the March 2008 Tibetan uprising, 149 Mechanised Infantry Division was identified as the formation which mobilised and was responsible to quell the riots that broke out in and around Lhasa.

There are 14 airbases from where PLAAF can launch operations. Of these, five are on the plateau and the rest at comparatively lower altitudes and plains. The five on the plateau are at 4500 metres height and have a runway length of 4000 metres, which can take most wide bodied aircrafts. Due to altitude, capability of the aircraft is reduced, requiring additional runway length and restricting its capability to carry cargo and passengers. The capability is severely degraded when taking off from these airfields due to altitude and climatic conditions. Fighter aircraft taking off from these high altitude airfields can barely operate with full operational loads and depend entirely on air-to-air refuelling to execute missions deep into enemy territory which in any case is a serious limitation on its inventory.

This raises the vulnerability of fuel tankers in proximity of the borders. Alternatively, the PLAAF will have to use airfields in the plains which have the inherent limitation of reduced radius of action and operational depth into Indian Territory. In the case of a civilian aircraft like the Airbus 319, for *e.g.*, its load carrying capacity is reduced by 20-25 per cent when it takes off from the plains and lands at an airfield at 11,500 feet. On its return, depending on time of the day, weather and conditions it may take off with almost negligible load. Therefore, the capability to airlift troops, their subsequent sustenance, and replenishment of supplies, fuel and war like material is degraded. China possesses just 14 per cent and 6 per cent of the heavy strategic lift capability that Russia and the US possess respectively. This is a critical vulnerability of conducting operations in Tibet. China's National Defence White

Paper 2008 has included one additional mission to the PLAAF; 'Strategic projection'. While China aspires to achieve such a capability and recent acquisitions indicate a number of indigenous and import projects to procure heavy lift aircraft are in the pipeline, yet, the PLAAF's progress in this area over the past decade has been modest.

The transport fleet of the PLAAF in TAR is based on the following units:

- 4 Transport Division (Chengdu MR) based at Kionglai with one Regiment of Y7 Transport aircraft and one Regiment of MI-17V Helicopters.
- Two Transport Regiments of Y5/Y7 Aircraft at Lanzhou. While there are reports of ongoing modernisation of the PLAAF's Transport Fleet, it is noteworthy that none of these are based in TAR. Out of the total Transport Fleet of 600 Aircraft on their inventory, the only modern Aircraft are approximately 50 IL76 and 48 AN12 (Y8) Aircraft. Of these, the contract of 50 IL 76 is unlikely to have materialised. Instead, the AVIC project, an indigenous transport aircraft, is still a few years from fructification.

The carriage capacity of the Y8 is at best 20 tons or one main battle tank or 96 soldiers. One Chinese Brigade comprising of 3000-4000 troops can be airlifted in 60-80 Y8 aircraft or 13-17 IL76 aircraft. According to Fravel, China has a fraction of the strategic airlift capabilities limited to just one fully equipped Light Mechanised Infantry Brigade.

Thus, a Rapid Reaction Division like the 149 Mechanised Infantry Divisions or the 15th Airborne Corps, the strategic reserve of the PLAAF with three Airborne Divisions (43rd, 44th, 45th), each with 10,000 troops is restricted in its timely deployment due to limitation of strategic mobility and restrictions imposed by high altitude airfields.

Heavy vehicles and heavy equipment of these formations will have to be moved by road or prepositioned. It has been assessed that the overall capability of the PLA is to air transport about a Division plus (13,000 troops) in a single evolution or airdrop a regiment worth 3000 troops in a single airlift.

This capability was on display during 'Stride 2009' and Exercise 'Airborne Movement 2009' (Kongjiang Jidong) in which 15 Airborne Corps inducted a 20 day large scale, multi modal transportation, trans-regional exercise with 13,000 troops and heavy equipment. The other major limitation is the heavy lift helicopter capability. Once men, material stores and equipment are landed at airfields, they need to be transported to far-flung posts at extreme high altitudes. Helicopters are the mainstay of maintenance and replenishment operations at those altitudes.

A Mi-17, which can lift 3000 kgs at sea level, would lift a mere few hundred kgs at altitudes in excess of three kms. Contingency of an heli-borne assault in this region has a remote chance of success. The PLAAF has just 20 Mi-17V heavy lift helicopters and a few variants of the Z9 with limited cargo carrying capacity on its inventory. These were found to be grossly inadequate during the Sichuan earthquake in 2008, when in the absence of heavy-lift helicopters the PLA was unable to ferry relief supplies and heavy equipment to the interior areas which were affected by the earthquake. Even in winter months and during inclement weather, when the roads are cut off, the helicopter supply chain remains the only reliable means of relief and communication.

CHINA'S DEVELOPMENT STRATEGY IN TIBET

In 1950, Mao Zedong sent PLA soldiers to "liberate" Tibet from the oppression of feudalism; however, "liberation" resulted in the occupation and colonization of Tibet. Ever since the occupation of Tibet, the PRC's most credible claim cited as justification for its presence in Tibet is to promote development and to rescue Tibetans from the clutches of "backwardness and medievalism". The Chinese government claims that it is empowering and helping its 'Xizang brothers' [Tibetan brothers] the way in which Tibet has been transformed reflects a stark contrast between official rhetoric and the situation on the ground.

In the last decade we have seen radical urbanization in Tibet. Urban enclaves and towns have mushroomed everywhere. The changing face of Tibet's old cities like Lhasa has never been dramatic and radical the way it has been transformed since the coming of

Chinese. In the wake of China's miraculous economic growth and rapid rise of stature in the international and diplomatic arena, Beijing has sought to earn international credibility by investing millions of dollars in massive state-sponsored infrastructure developments and projects in Tibet.

However, in an economic era of globalization and consumerism, the term 'd*evelopment' is a loaded term. It cannot be viewed in 'isolation'. Development* includes education, culture and traditions, Aids and investment, employment, agriculture, science and mining, healthcare, environment, Tibetan medicine, tourism and nomadic life style of Tibetans.

In the age of neo-global diplomacy, political opportunism and national-interest-come-first, advocacy for human rights of Tibetans in Tibet, particularly the rights to development of the Tibetan people presents daunting challenges for many of countries who has close trade ties with China. 'Human Rights Commission' and 'Human Rights Council' are a mere change of words.

There is far more to China's development campaign in Tibet than a mere effort to project a new modernized and prosperous Tibet. Moreover, because China is a reclusive State, it remains a mountainous task to overcome the lack of access, obstacles and hurdles to carrying out investigative research into the nature of 'development' in Tibet. 'Developmental scientists' like Andrew Fischer and others based much of their research papers and assessments on facts and figures released by the State as attempts to carry out field research met with difficulties due to the secretive nature of the Chinese State and political sensitivity attached to the Tibetan issue. It is therefore difficult to reach to a precise and accurate understanding of 'development' is a challenge faced by researchers and monitoring agents.

In backdrop of 'development' inside Tibet, the report attempts to give an overview of the situation of 'development' inside Tibet. This report tackles two main issues related to 'development' in Tibet. First, it addresses China's 'd*evelopment strategy', analyzing whether China fulfilled its stated objectives.* The report highlights the flaws of the Chinese government's 'flawed *development strategy and model implementing in Tibet'. Secondly, the report* uncovers the application of China's 'development strategy' in Tibet and how far it goes out to achieve development in Tibet as stated by the Chinese government.

The report unravels the nature of the dual economies currently functioning in Tibet, the rapid development and creation of urban enclaves and the existence of neglected rural hinterland where more than 80 percent of Tibetan population live. The report also uncovers the fact how China's development strategy in Tibet failed by breaking Tibet's economy into three sectors.

DEVELOPMENT AS OWNERSHIP

It is to be noted that China has been a great success in creating vibrant urban centres and bringing superficial infrastructure changes to Tibet. Not so surprisingly, many visitors to Tibet are shocked because reality differs drastically with the images of Tibet they gained from books. Lhasa City epitomizes an old Tibet that is hardly visible today. Today, Lhasa contains modern buildings, shopping malls, bars, broad boulevards, discotheques, hotels and traffic. However, the picture of modern Lhasa City, as well as that of other Tibetan towns and cities, can be very deceptive. China intends that they prove its claims of 'development' in Tibet after fifty years of Chinese rule. However, Tibet's development cannot be gauged from superficial images.

The true yardstick to measure development is the ownership of development from the first stage of formulating policy, to implementation and finally to the reaping of benefits from development. Throughout these processes, the interest and benefit of Tibetan people must remain at the center and not on the periphery. China's development in Tibet over the past years has failed to benefit Tibetans because it excludes the agrarian Tibetan community, which composes more than 80 percent of the Tibetan population.

Although every year the central Chinese government pours billions of yuan into Tibet, underdevelopment in rural areas persists. In the last decade Tibet has been the largest per capita recipient of subsidy and funding from the central government. On the Tibetan Autonomous Region's (TAR) 20th anniversary, the government spent 500 million yuan on 43 projects; on TAR's 30th anniversary, it spent 4.6 billion yuan on 62 projects; and on TAR's 40th anniversary, it spent 6.42 billion yuan on 24 projects. TAR Chairman Jampa Phuntsok said that in 2004 over 16.6 billion yuan (US$ 2 billion) was invested in building infrastructure. Most of the funds came

from the central government under the "Western Development Program." Tsering Dhondup a nomad from Kanlho County testified to TCHRD that mismanagement and embezzlement of public funds are common practice at local government levels.

LOCAL GOVERNMENTS' MISUSE OF POWER

In the same county of Kanlho, the local authorities mismanaged the nomad's fund. In 2001, a Chinese entrepreneur collected money from Tibetan nomads, however, with the involvement of local authorities, the money collected disappeared without a trace. The nomads forwarded a petition to the local authorities but received no response.

In 2005, a peaceful protest against the local authorities was held, however, a local Tibetan official, Tsering Dhondup; Huis Chinese officials; and PAP soldiers suppressed the protest and issued a terse warning that such protest would amount to counter revolutionary activities with dire consequences.

Later, after a change in government officials, new local officials solved the case by stating that this was a case of "corruption and misuse of public funds". Each family had invested 100 Yuan in the enterprise and there were 2,200 families.

The authorities at all levels-County, Township and Prefecture-took money rightfully owned by the Tibetans. So far, the authorities have not reimbursed the local Tibetans.

However, the monetary and political energy has been focused on the urban sector. This indicates the absence of a 'human face' to a planned economic policy. One of the most viable and reliable means to uncover what obstructs the development of Tibetan people is to study the nature of three sectors of Tibetan economy i.e. primary, secondary and the tertiary.

In the case of land and housing rights, China's constitution provides, "land is owned by the State...can be requestioned for public purposes." The Tibetan people in Tibet today face ownership crisis of their ancestral lands and housing rights through forced eviction, displacement, confiscation of private properties, and the practice of population transfer.

Development in three sectors of Tibet

The true form of development promoted by social scientists for Tibetans is 'human capital formation' and implementation of the 'right to development' and right to self-determination. It is only on these grounds that true development of Tibet can be accessed and examined. In order to assess Tibetans' development, we must look at the primary, secondary and tertiary sectors of the Tibetan economy. The monetary investments and infrastructure projects in Tibet do not represent an accurate picture of growth.

Comparison among three sectors:

The breakdown of Gross Domestic Product (GDP) in the TAR, Qinghai and China as a whole reflects unfair growth. Furthermore, the entire GDP picture of Tibet also reflects the false growth figure. The GDP of Tibet in 1998 was 9.118 billion yuan, 10.561 billion yuan in 1999, 11.746 billion yuan in 2000 and 13.873 billion yuan in 2001. Therefore, the GDP growth of entire Tibet reflects is 10 percent annually.

The GDP of primary sector was 3.131 in 1998, 3.419 billion yuan in 1999, 3.632 billion yuan in 2000 and 3.747 billion yuan in 2001. This shows growth in the primary sector was roughly 2 percent yearly. In the secondary sector, the GDP was 20.24 percent in 1998, 24 percent in 1999, 27.21 percent in 2000 and 32.18 percent in 2001.

Here, the growth was 4 percent annually in the secondary sector with growth picking up from 2000 onwards, indicating that the sector enjoyed growth due to the economic boom in coastal China. In comparison, the growth in the secondary sector doubled that of the primary sector, which has only 2 percent annual growth. This demonstrates that 87 percent of the agrarian Tibetan community in the primary sector's derived growth of only one half of the growth enjoyed by the secondary sector, which is overwhelmingly non-Tibetans or migrant workers.

In the tertiary sector the GDP was 39.63 percent in 1998, 47.42 percent in 1999, 53.93 percent in 2000 and 69.08 perent in 2001. In this sector the growth was 6 percent annually, highest of the three sectors. Only middle-class Tibetans has a robust share in the tertiary sector in areas of administration and clerical works. The 6 percent annual growth demonstrates the overriding political emphasis and weight.

Based on these statistics, GDP growth in Tibet as well as in China was 10 percent. However, further analysis reveals that the urban enclaves grew disproportionately. While in the primary sector, the majority of Tibetan population, growth increased a meager 2 percent. Only the 13 percent of Tibetan population living in urban enclaves enjoyed the benefit of significant growth while 90 percent of those living in urban centers are Chinese.

In the Qinghai region, where the secondary sector dominates, statistics demonstrate considerable growth; however, closer study reveals a similar trend. The benefits and prosperity go to Chinese migrants to the exclusion of Qinghai nomads and semi nomads. The GDP of entire Qinghai was 220.16 million yuan in 1998, 238.39 million yuan in 1999,263.59 million yuan in 2000 and 300.95 million yuan in 2001.

Based on these figures, the GDP was 12.2 percent annually in the Qinghai region. Judging from the overall picture, there was growth, but a closer look reveals further discrepancies. In the primary sector, the GDP growth *was 41.63 percent in 1998, 40.54 percent in 1999, 38.53 percent in 2000 and 42.79 percent in 2001.*

The annual growth was 1.16 percent, which is slightly lower than the TAR. This lower growth could be because of the fact that the TAR is the favourite destination of central funding because of the political sensitivity attached to the region. In Qinghai the Chinese migrants are mostly concentrated in the secondary sector unlike the tertiary sector in the TAR.

The secondary sector shows strong growth of 88.42 percent in 1998, 97.88 percent in 1999, 114 percent in 2000 and 132.18 percent in 2001.

This is 16.5 percent growth. Such growth may have resulted from the area's proximity to China as well as from its other economic and logistics advantages. Regardless, the projection overstates the development of the Tibetan people involved in the secondary sector, who are a minority in any case. Moreover, the growth in the tertiary sector was lower than in the secondary; however, it was high compared to China's overall growth standard. The GDP in the tertiary sector was 90.11 percent in 1998, 99.97 percent in 1999, 111.06 in 2000 and 125.98 percent in 2001.

The growth rate in the region is 13.3 percent annually. In order for Tibetans to compete in the tertiary sector in the Qinghai region, they need both competitive and comparative advantages to compete with their Chinese counterparts in the secondary sector.

In the Qinghai region, the Tibetan population has a largely rural nomadic background. Hence, the players in this sector are predominantly Chinese migrants. In the secondary sector, Chinese shop owners, entrepreneurs, skilled workers and semiskilled workers working in the large construction projects, mining and industry in the Qinghai belt occupy this sector. The massive role of the secondary and tertiary sectors almost entirely nullifies any trickle down growth for ordinary Tibetans.

The government expenditure in the TAR, the Qinghai region and entire China in 2001 gives us a clear picture of China's preference and emphasis on infrastructure and fixed asset growth over human capital formation.

In the year 2001, the investment in infrastructure development in China was roughly 12.5 percent while in the TAR it was a massive 33 percent and a relatively high figure of 26 percent in the Qinghai region. This illustrates that investment in infrastructure development in the TAR was three times more than in China while investment in infrastructure development in the Qinghai region was two times more than in China. In this regard, China's investors in state projects, both skilled and semi-skilled migrants workers, businessmen and contractors from the western regions of China benefited most from the massive infrastructure in the TAR and the Qinghai region considering that the majority of the agrarian Tibetan population have no direct and indirect role in this investment sector. Out of the overall government investment in China in 2001, the TAR eclipses both China and Qinghai, which were 13 percent and 8 percent, respectively. The statistics show that China has the highest expenditure in education of 15 percent while the TAR has the lowest of 8 percent and the Qinghai region a higher rate of 10 percent. This affirms and illustrates what many international experts and social scientists argue for the social and human development of Tibetan people. In the health sector, all three regions have relatively low rates of 4 percent in China, 3 percent in the TAR and 4 percent in Qinghai. Again the TAR scores the lowest investment in health sector amongst the three regions.

Amongst all the regions of China, Tibet lags in terms of human development. Today Tibet remains one of the poorest regions in China. In terms of education, in 2001 China had an illiteracy rate of 9.1 percent with 22.9 percent below the age of 14.

With this high ratio of illiteracy not many Tibetans can reach the secondary sector, a thoroughly skill-based sector of the economy. In the TAR, the illiteracy rate was a staggering 47.3 percent, more than five times the national average, and 31.2 percent of children below the age of 14 are illiterate. In other words, three in every ten children in Tibet below the age of 14 don't know how to read and write.

The Qinghai region had a slightly lower illiteracy rate of 25.4 percent when compared to the TAR, which is almost three times the national average, with 26.9 percent of children below the age of 14 illiterate. The Sichuan region has a 9.9 percent illiteracy rate, which is far lower than the TAR and negligibly higher than the national average. 22.6 percent of children below the age of 14 are illiterate, which remains a concern. It means that out of 100 hundred illiterate people in the region, 22 of them are children below the age of 14. This is the overall bleak picture of the level of education and literacy for Tibetans in Tibet.

Poverty in the TAR and rural Tibet results from apathy and China's leaders self-interest. While agriculture comprises the background of the economy of rural Tibetans in the TAR, it has the lowest investment of 2 percent. China and Qinghai have investment of just over 2.5 percent. The President of the World

Bank said on 18 October 2005 that China has 150 million people living in acute poverty. Excluding Tibetans was the chief factor for the lack of development and progress in Tibet. In order for leaders in Beijing to achieve meaningful results, they need to rethink their agriculture policies. This sector desperately needs a human face in its development pursuits.

The Primary Sector

The primary sector forms the basic subsistence economy of Tibetans involved in first level economic activities such as agriculture and animal husbandry. Since over 80 percent of the Tibetan population lives in rural regions, the primary sector of the economy forms the backbone of the Tibetan economy till today. The TAR is the most agrarian region of Tibet followed by Qinghai. The economic growth in all of China is divided into three growth rates i.e. 'fast growth' in the coastal Chinese cities where it has experienced phenomenal economic growth for at least a decade and the interior and non-TAR regions of Tibet where the secondary sector of the economy is strong and therefore categorized under 'moderate growth'. However in the TAR, where currently two forms of economy are functional, the traditional agrarian and rural economy and the urban model economy are heading in opposite directions.

By and large, the living patterns in rural Tibet, as indicated from the testimonies, is still much the same as that of the living patterns that existed during pre-1959 Tibet. The yields from the farm provide rural Tibetans with a staple diet and grains throughout the year, and animal husbandry provides them with meat and dairy. In this way the Tibetan people subsist on a basic self-sufficient economy. Animal products such as milk, butter, wool, hide and most importantly the ready supply of meat, serve Tibetans' daily needs. So far all the investment and subsidies in the TAR have primarily concentrated on the urban enclave with massive infrastructure development and investments with little focus and emphasis on the traditional Tibetan economy. Hence, Andrew Fischer described it as 'highly polarized growth'.

Exile returnee Lobsang Choedor testifies to TCHRD about the presence of widespread poverty in rural Tibet.

POVERTY WIDESPREAD IN RURAL TIBET

An exile returnee, Lobsang Choedor, 32, from Samdup village, Chukhog township, Ngari county, "Tibet Autonomous Region" ("TAR") gave testimony to TCHRD at Kathmandu Refugee Reception Centre on 6 May 2006 in relation to widespread poverty in his native hometown in Tibet, to which he returned after an absence of 7 years.

Lobsang Choedor sought exile India in 1999. He became monk and joined Drepung Monastery in South India. 7 years later, he returned to his native hometown in Tibet. He said: I really wanted to know the true situation in my home town. But to my disappointment, nothing had really changed in all those years. Instead, the Chinese are more cautious and wary of exile returnees, particularly monks and nuns.

Lobsang Choedor recounted: To my disbelief, no positive changes were visible. In the name of development, the local government constructed one stone house, but there was nothing of practical assistance to the local Tibetans. In the past, the Chinese government had distributed two and half kilograms of wheat flour and three and half kilograms of rice to the locals. The event was widely publicized and broadcast in the State media.

In truth, the local Tibetans are mostly farmers and they live in abject poverty. The village still has no electricity. The Chinese government has completely neglected the locals because of their remoteness and lack of political significance. Villagers of all ages seek jobs in the nearby township and county city and work on construction sites. There is no school and all the locals in village are illiterate.

For the ethnic Chinese, however, the situation is different. Huis Chinese and Han Chinese who have settled in the region in last decade today dominate business in the area and the local economy. They are far wealthier than Tibetans, owning restaurants and hotels.

They have more political clout and influence. Tibetans are reduced to a minority community, alienated from the new Chinese settlers. As Choedor concluded, "It is sad and pitiable to see the situation in which Tibetans live. The widespread poverty and their plight are very visible".

In the primary sector the 'trickle down of benefits' for Tibetans is minute since economic policy is focused on the creation of urban enclaves and much of the resources are being spent for administration, maintaining security and the large presence of military forces in the TAR. Administrative and security requirements consume most of the central funds, leaving little to trickle down to ordinary Tibetans.

Tashi Tsering, a native from Nyingtri Prefecture reported to TCHRD about the ecological and environment destruction in Tibet.

Curbs and livelihood restrictions for Tibetans in countryside

Tashi Tsering, aged 18 from Dromo Township, Gyamda County, Nyingtri Prefecture, gave testimony to TCHRD at Kathmandu Refugee Reception Centre on 17 October 2006 in relation to ongoing environmental and ecological destruction in his native hometown.

According to Tashi Tsering, China is continuing its' immense destruction of the Kongpo forest in Tibet with no regard to ecological considerations. The famed Kongpo forest was a region of dense forest prior to the Chinese occupation and even before the Cultural Revolution. Today, however, a major part of the forest cover has disappeared, leaving behind barren valleys and hills after years of unchecked deforestation and logging. Many of the species of the region have also vanished according to local people.

Ironically, the Chinese government issued strict orders restricting the collection of firewood by local Tibetans, explaining to villagers the harmful consequences of ecological and environmental destruction caused by cutting down trees. The local and central governments initiated campaigns calling on local people not to cause damage to the environment and ecology. Villagers were mobilized to plant and grow trees. The local authorities, in close collaboration with central government, then resorted to rampant and reckless deforestation and logging to sell and trade timber to companies outside of the region. Tashi Tsering recounted, "It was a regular sight to see huge convoys of trucks transporting timber and wood to Lhasa and to other provinces in China. Strangely, not a single piece of wood or log reaches ordinary Tibetans".

It is now rare to see species which inhabited Kongpo forest and were previously prevalent, including bears, mountain sheep and musk deer. Of late, the Chinese government has banned Tibetans from poaching; however, there is a growing number of Chinese settlers in the Kongpo region, many of whom make their living by poaching and hunting.

The key reason why the traditional Tibetan economy remained on the periphery for so long seems to have been the nature of economy in the first place. The nature of traditional Tibetan economy is subsistence, based on agriculture, which normally does not generate surpluses of income. In other parts of the world, even the rich and developed countries of the European Union, give high subsidies to their farming communities. It naturally would not attract private investors and migrant Chinese entrepreneurs because of the absence of comparative and competitive advantages in this sector.

The core objective of China's economic plans in Tibet seems to be a rapid and fast track creation of urban enclaves and industrial regions so as to achieve a great economic take-off as has been experienced in coastal China. However, the Chinese seem to have over-looked the fundamental factors that triggered the economic take-off in China's coastal regions. There are (a) huge untapped markets, (b) absence of bureaucratic interferences, (c) a supply of cheap labour, (d) ready availability of cheap raw materials, (e) intensive farm production, (f) and rural township enterprises adding value to farm products.

If the absence of the above favourable conditions have kept private investors away from Tibet, then the only valid argument would be the Chinese leaders have neglected the real needs and interests of Tibetan farmers and nomads, whether deliberately or not. Instead, Beijing has crafted the Tibetan political issue in its favour. Tibet's current economic blueprint has tremendous potential to attract and drive in floods of migrant workers and immigrants from China. If the leadership in Beijing wants to disprove such criticism, then it should rethink and reprioritize the economic policies currently in place in Tibet.

The regular influx of Chinese migrant workers to Tibet suggests that China has almost exclusively relied on manpower and expertise imported from China rather than recruiting and training local Tibetans. Tibet has unique ethnic and ethnographic characteristics, and any developmental program must focus on long-term development and genuine growth for Tibetans. In his review of Andrew Fischer's work, Bill Hillman stated, More controversially, Mr. Fischer denies that poverty in Tibet is entirely a result of ecological factors (altitude, harsh climate, low soil fertility) on the high plateau. He argues that impoverishment emerges from the very process of state-led modernization as Tibetans become less able to participate in the economic opportunities available. The solution he proffers is a sensible one-the state should completely reprioritize its development strategies in the region and invest more in people, especially in basic social services such as education and health care. He also advocates a different strategy for economic growth, one that supports local economy activity, locally owned and controlled businesses and local capital accumulation.

However, it seems that better days lay ahead for the farming communities in rural areas of China and Tibet. According to the United Nations Development Progam (UNDP) report, the Chinese Government is going to take some bold and positive steps for the Chinese farmers such as abolishing the agriculture tax and relaxing the Hukou or residential permit which was long described as 'peasant apartheid'. As Khalid Malik states,

The Government is already taking concrete steps to address these human development inequities. By the end of this year, it will have completely abolished agriculture taxes across the country. To improve literacy rates in rural communities, the government is promoting compulsory education for the rural poor through renovation of primary and middle schools and providing free textbooks for 24 million students and poor families.

The Secondary Sector

The secondary sector forms the backbone of the Chinese economy in all the different provinces of China. In terms of income and wealth, this sector contributes far more to the national GDP than the primary and tertiary sectors. In the case of Tibet, the secondary sector prospers in the non-TAR regions, such as Qinghai and Sichuan. The Qinghai region has more industrial units and productive core regions than TAR. While in the TAR the tertiary sector dominates in terms of income and central funding, the primary sector is the largest sector with over 80 percent of the Tibetan population. The absence of a dominant role of the primary and tertiary sectors in the non-TAR regions allows the secondary sector to loom large.

Because the 2001 labour share show that 71.8 percent of the labour forces are concentrated in the primary sector, one could argue that the TAR is the most agrarian province in all of China. In sharp contrast to the trend in China, where the secondary sector is the highest contributor of income, this sector in the TAR contributes labour shares as low as 6.5 percent, which is roughly ten times lower than the primary sector. The labour shares reveal a grim tale. Over 90 percent of the Chinese population in the TAR, including military personnel, police forces, technicians, businessmen, prostitutes and skilled and semi skilled workers, lives in urban enclaves. On the other hand, the labour share in the tertiary sector is 21.7 percent because of the high presence of a service sector, such as administration, in the TAR which constitutes the largest component of the tertiary sector, followed by the booming tourism industry, prostitution, retailing, banking and transport.

In Qinghai the labour share is 60 percent in the primary sector, which includes Tibetan farmers and nomads. The labour shares in the secondary sector were 13.0 percent, twice as much as the TAR's 6.5 percent. Qinghai has some of the most productive industries and petrol chemical factories. Due to the region's proximity to China, Chinese migrant works fill most of the labour forces in these factories. In the case of the tertiary sector in Qinghai, more than 80 percent of the Tibetan population is involved in agriculture and animal husbandry. In addition to Chinese immigrants, ethnic Chinese who have lived in the region for years compose the labour force for the secondary sector in Qinghai.

Dhondup Tsering testified to TCHRD about economic disadvantages face by Tibetans as a minority in their own land.

MINORITY AND ECONOMIC DISADVANTAGES

Dhondup Tsering also gave testimony to TCHRD in relation to the economic disadvantages faced by Tibetans as a minority group.

There are many shops, restaurants and hotels owned by Huis Chinese in and around the Kokonor Basin. In the summer, and even in winter, Huis Chinese people catch fish from Kokonor Lake. Since they have become the dominant ethnic group in the area, they monopolize the fishing business in the area. Every year, thousands of Chinese tourists flock to the area in and around Kokonor Lake Basin and stay in hotels and guesthouses built by the Chinese government. These hotels and guesthouses are rented to the Huis Chinese, who run them, keeping a share of the profits and giving the rest to the government. Huis Chinese hoteliers charge around 6000 to 7000 Yuan per year. This is 7 times more than the annual per capita income of Tibetans in Tibet.

Huis Chinese businessmen are skilled and shrewd. Dhondup Tsering couldn't survive the competition and his business was no longer profitable. He reports that every month, hundreds of Huis Chinese move to the Kokonor Basin to begin new life. Owing to immense pressure, waste and drainage are heavily polluting the Kokonor Lake. In hope of finding a new life and hope for the future, Dhondup Tsering sought exile in India.

It would be interesting to know why Tibetans are excluded from the secondary sector, the largest contributor of income and wealth in China, as Tibetan exclusion has created such a disproportionate economic system in Tibet. The following statistic sheds some light on the ownership of labour share ratios of Tibetans in the TAR and Qinghai region in all the three sectors of economy. It would be interesting to know about the labour concentration of Tibetans, which casts China's development process a dubious shadow.

For now, the focus must concentrate on how much of the meager 6.5 percent of labour shares consist of Tibetan work forces.

The statistics demonstrate the prospect for job opportunities and employment prospects, and evidence the need for Tibetans to take direct participation in the development projects and processes. According to Andrew Fischer, out-of-province investors tend to invest in Mainland China while local investors tend to invest locally. Perhaps the biggest concern of this poor show of labour shares in the secondary sector is that if this trend continues, China would never produce skilled and semi skilled Tibetan work forces. The 2005 UNDP report expressed similar concern,

The authors highlight that improving the educational level of farmers plays an important role in raising their skills levels and ultimately their incomes. To make the curriculum and the education system more relevant to the demands of the labour market, the study recommends the establishment of community universities for vocational training to disadvantaged groups and enterprise training.

It is understandable that China's urbanization in Tibet will continue to gain momentum and support, but it is also critical to the Tibetan issue that skill and expertise stay in Tibet and subsequently benefit the local economy. In order to empower Tibetans, a sincere effort is needed from the Chinese Government in investing funds in social services such as education and training Tibetans in scientific know-how and other vocational training.

The Tertiary Sector

In the case of the tertiary sector, Tibetan society is predominantly concentrated in urban enclaves. Lhasa City is a classic example. The booming tourism industry, fast flourishing prostitution, ever expanding administration units, transport, retail, banking and finance constitute the main tertiary sector activities.

Of all the three sectors, the tertiary sector generates the most income and wealth in terms of salaries and other incentives in the administrative urban enclaves such as Lhasa City. In urban enclaves, administrative works absorbed a large chunk of funds meant for the TAR, i.e. constructing and renovating office buildings, staff, cadres, electricity, water and other security purposes. Although central government funds may appear huge, the money simply evaporates when it goes down the administrative apparatus. In terms of economic productiveness, the administrative projects greatly drain money and resources because they don't generate profit and income. As a result, the billions of yuan from Beijing fail to trickle down to the needy and actual targets of the government's development efforts. While middle class Tibetans in the urban areas benefit in the administrative service of the tertiary sector, middle class Tibetans are negligible in number even though they represent a high proportion of the Tibetan population in the urban center.

This scenario reflects the troubling economic divide between rural hinterlands and urban enclaves, where mostly Chinese migrants live. According to Fischer, 160,000 Chinese, including military and migrants, lived in Lhasa City between September and April 2000. Almost 90 percent of Chinese migrants live in the urban enclaves, and they benefit most from the three service sectors. For instance, Chinese migrant entrepreneurs own most of the hotels, bars and shops, and most of the sex workers in Lhasa were Sichuanese Chinese. Thus, the Chinese and urban elites dominate the Tibetan economy's most profitable and booming industries.

Choepa Tso testified to TCHRD about how rural poverty and lack of economic opportunities forced young rural girls into prostitution.

Poverty and Prostitution

Choepa Tso, 25, from Nyagong village, Lhucho Township, Sangchu County, Qinghai Province, gave her testimony to TCHRD at Kathmandu Refugee Reception Centre on 23 June 2006 in relation to widespread poverty in her village and how young rural girls opt to work as sex workers in order to evade poverty. Choepa Tso said:

I was born to a poor semi-nomadic family in Amdo. In our family, we have six members. A poor agricultural yield and taxation by the local authority are common in our village. Poverty is widespread. I am illiterate; people in my village hardly go to school. When I was 20 years old, I developed a strong urge to support my family financially. I was forced to leave my home and lived in Lhasa working as dishwasher cum waitress in restaurants. I moved from one ill-paid job to another. Most of my masters were Huis Chinese Businessmen, very cruel and mean.

There are many Tibetans from rural Tibet who are willing to do any kind of work in order to escape poverty. They are not educated. They are illiterate and exploited on the streets of Lhasa and other big cities. There were 8 other girls working in Choepa Tso's restaurant. They were beaten, scolded, maltreated and threatened and had to work long shifts in unhygienic conditions. They were often coerced by the owners to sleep with clients with the promise of increased wages.

Choepa Tso said: Finally I landed in a well-paid job as a waitress in one of the gambling dens in Lhasa. The owner was a Tibetan; customers were Tibetans, Huis Chinese and Han Chinese. Waitresses in the gambling den smoke, drink alcohol and even sleep with clients to make easy and fast money. Sex workers charge 100 Yuan for a night. I have seen so many lives of young Tibetan girls ruined. Like me, more and more young Tibetan girls from rural areas are moving into cities in search of a better livelihood at an alarming rate. However, very often they end up working as prostitutes, as it is the only way to make fast and easy money. They belong to the most vulnerable portion of population.

Seeing nothing but a bleak future in Tibet, Choepa Tso fled Tibet and reached Kathmandu, Nepal on 21 July 2006. In the last decade, the tertiary sector enjoyed honeymoon status in receiving central funds. Throughout the years the percentage has jumped by leaps and bounds. In the TAR, there was a huge increase in funds from 1998 to a moderate increase in 1999 to a 5 percent increase in 2000.

In Qinghai, the increment grew from 12 percent to a massive 17.5 percent between the years 2000 and 2001. Under the Western Development Program the agriculture sector has grown slowly at a rate of 5 percent percent a year. In the tertiary sector too the trickle down of benefits is staggeringly low.

Out of the multiple billions of yuan that China pumps into Tibet every year, only 6.5 percent of labour shares involve the secondary sector which is completely dominated by Chinese migrant skilled workers, professionals, businessmen, investors, hotels and shops in Lhasa city.

At the macro level the concentration of wealth exists chiefly in the secondary and tertiary sectors where Han and other ethnic Chinese have the upper hand in generating income and wealth. Contrary to China's claims, the funds mostly reach the hands of non-Tibetans directly and indirectly.

The Tibetans do not benefit from the subsidies. 138 Human Rights Situation *in Tibet: Annual Report 2005 The United Nation's top staffer in China,* Khalid Malik10, commented at the release of China's Human Development Report 2005 that,

China's wealth gap between urban and rural communities is among the highest in the world, but according to a UNDP report released today, the government is coming to grips with the widening disparities that threaten the country's stability. China's Human Development Report 2005 is the first comprehensive study to offer a set of bold and practical policy recommendations to improve conditions for the rural poor, and bolster education, health care and the social security system.

Issues Tibetan People Face In Tibet

The key reasons why China had went wrong in their development of Tibet, particularly the agrarian and nomadic countryside where more than 80 percent of population live is precisely because of missing formalae on part of planners in Beijing.

Several decades of development pursuits and initiatives have shown consistently that the entire model of development implemented in the past and still implementing is a flawed strategy. The rapid industrialization of rural economy or to bring it to the market economy has proven ineffective in alleviating the poverty in the countryside. Beside the introduction of hardware and infrastructure has also proven ineffective to lift rural Tibet from poverty to age of prosperity and modernity. The inflow of skilled migrant workers and resources from China has in the past only produced a tiny class of neo-Chinese elites in Tibet. It failed in bringing modernization and development in rural Tibet. Even the industrialization in Tibet itself has failed miserably because they do not operate under fundamentals of economy or rate of return. So far the Industrialization of the secondary sector is driven by a political goal of achieving 'stability' inside Tibet. As a result, industries in Tibet are unproductive and inefficent. Over more than 90 percent of industries inside Tibet malfunction, however these have to be there in Tibet as a showpiece or a sign of Beijing's development activities inside Tibet. If the agrarian community has to usher into age of prosperity and modernization, then a straight jacket approach of bringing skilled technicians and forcefully implementing policies that goes against the interests of farmers and nomads must be put to hold. An overhaul of entire policy on farmers and nomads must be introduced and implemented in Tibet. However this has to be done after consulting the farmers and nomads.

A gradual and systemic strategy of introducing farmers and nomads is needed; first empowerment of farmers and nomads in field of modern education, health care, exposure to ideas and innovation, probably a University must be built and set up solely for the studies and research related to animal husbandry and farming in permafrost Tibetan tundra landscape. All these studies and research has to be done only the Tibetans farmers and nomads, if need be, foreign and Chinese agriculture scientists and experts may be invited but they role should only of a mere facilitator.

This empowerment of modern Tibetans farmers and nomads will take at least one generation if not more. The time it takes for transformation and growth, only Tibetans will take the entire charge and ownerships of affairs, ranging from making decisions, consultation and grass root democratic process. State's role should be the provider of resources and facilities not implementer.

Lobsang Choedrak from Toelung Dechen County told TCHRD about the lands being forcefully seized and grabbed from the local Tibetans in the name of development and progress.

LOGISTICS DEVELOPMENT IN TIBET

In the decades since the founding of the PrC, coastal China did, indeed, race ahead as far as development was concerned while western China stagnated. In fact, Deng Xiaoping, himself a son of the sichuan soil, told the people of western China, "Let them (coastal China) get rich first, you can get rich later." Once the economy of coastal China had acquired a self-sustaining momentum, policy-makers under President hu Jintao subsequently appear to have turned their attention to western China.

The justifications for the western development policy are economic, political and social. Beijing is increasingly concerned about the growing economic gap between east and west, which led to social unrest and riots in different areas during the 1990s. The "Go west" campaign, it is declared repeatedly, aims to make the west an "incubator for skilled manpower" and a "hotspot for foreign investments."

The PrC has been carrying out extensive infrastructure development in the Tar and areas close to its southern borders to include the development of road, rail and air networks, FOL pipeline, telecommunications and industrial base, besides giving a boost to the economy of the Tar. Such extensive development of logistics infrastructure in the Tar indicates the impetus being made available to the PLa's logistics capability which, in turn, will enhance its operational capability in the Tar. This dual objective was further underscored when it was reported that, "The infrastructure development is well beyond the genuine needs of Tibet."

The Chinese government's deliberate attempt of supporting an influx of the han population that is settling in these areas is changing the demographics of the region in favour of the han Chinese. A rising tide of han Chinese migrants is flooding into Tibet, diluting its character and taking away many of the available jobs. The hans constitute a major chunk of the population in Lhasa, increasing from approximately 4 percent in 1990 to 6 percent in 2000. It is believed that by 2015, there will be 20 million han Chinese in the Tar, subsequently shifting the cultural boundaries between the Tibetan people and the Han Chinese. The "Go West" campaign includes giving fiscal incentives and sending Chinese graduates to Tibet recently, the Chinese have instructed all conscripts posted in the Tar to apply for change of residential registration, which will facilitate the demobilised cadres to find employment in the Tar. Such a practice would, in the long run, change the demographic pattern of the Tar, as a large majority of the approximately 50,000 cadres demobilised every year is encouraged to settle in the Tar. A decision has been taken to make the Chinese language the medium of instruction in schools, which will necessitate more Chinese tutors to come from the mainland.

The improvement of rail infrastructure continues to remain a top priority. The demand for rail capacity is much greater than the supply; roughly 160,000 carloads per day are needed, but the railroads can only support 90,000 carloads per day. Also, China is making significant investments to improve its highways and is planning to build over 50,000 km (31,000 miles) of expressways over the next 15 years. The Chinese government has begun placing priority on infrastructure because it comprehends that the overall health and growth of the economy is increasingly dependent on logistical capabilities.

By virtue of initially launching unmanned trial operations, the Qinghai-Tibet railway (QTr) became functional on 01 May 2006, thus becoming Tibet's maiden railway line connecting and integrating the Tibetan plateau with the rest of China, at a staggering cost of Us $4.2 billion. The QTr is the latest manifestation of China's resolve to consolidate its hold on Tibet, along with other channels of logistics infrastructure build-up, given that it would ramp up induction timings while increasing build-up and logistics sustenance capability in the Tar up to major townships. Qinghai lies in the Tibetan highlands at an average elevation of 3,000 m (9,800 ft) and is mainly a high, desolate plateau. Opened to the public by Chinese President, hu Jintao, the 1,142-km Qinghai-Tibet railway line from Golmud in Qinghai province to Lhasa in Tibet became fully operational on 01 July 2006. Incidentally, the launch of the QTr coincided with the 85th anniversary of the founding of the CCP as well as the 10th anniversary of hong kong's handover from British rule to China.

In a televised address, President hu Jintao, who was present during the opening ceremony, alongside top Communist Party cadres, state news media, and 40 foreign journalists handpicked by officials to ride the first deluxe run, called the completion of the railroad "a magnificent feat." hailed as an "engineering marvel," the Chinese already see the railroad as an example of China's greatness in the new century and proof of its claim to be a "technological superpower." The completion of the railroad, however, would not have been possible without Us General electric's diesel engines, which maintain an average speed of 100 km per hour, even at altitudes of 4,000 m, where the thin air can have a halving effect; and Canada's Bombardier, which fulfilled a US $280 million contract to build carriages that can withstand the journey through Tibet's frozen mountains (some of these have deluxe sleeping compartments equipped with showers, glass-walled sides for a panoramic view, entertainment centres, gourmet dining areas, and toilets with sewage and waste-treatment systems).

The highest point of the QTr comes in at the 5,072 m (16,640 ft) Tanggula Pass in the kunlun mountain range. In addition, China has also unveiled plans to extend the Chinese national rail network to the border with India. The railway line would likely reach the Tibetan town of Dromo near nathu La and sikkim. Further, up to Us $1.2 billion is expected to be invested in building new rail lines in the Tibetan region in the coming decade, including a line extending west from Lhasa to shigatse and another heading east from Lhasa along the Yarlung Tsangpo river (Brahmaputra) to nyingchi (kongpo). The line to Dromo/Yatung will be an extension of the Lhasa-Shigatse line. Significantly, the double guaging of the railway line from Lanzhou to Golmud will extend to the Lanzhou Mr, greatly enhancing the Chinese operational logistic capacity. Besides, the korla-Lanzhou-Chengdu railway line is also likely to be converted into a double track. The eastern link from Chengdu to Lhasa via ngiti, Pangta and Markhan Dzong is slated to be completed by 2015. It has been widely reported that the QTr will facilitate an increase in the movement of products up to 45 times its current level and cut down transport costs for goods by 75 percent. China is likely to project Tibet as a major trade hub between China and south asia. It has built settlements every 60 km of this 1,118-km-long railway line. These settlements, primarily of han Chinese, are indicative of the growing han lifestyle in Lhasa.

The rapid build-up of China's national road and rail transport system has greatly enhanced the PLa's land-based transport capabilities. Many key civilian highway and railway projects, especially trunk rail lines and inter-provincial highways linking interior and coastal regions, have been constructed to military specifications and can be turned over to the PLA in the event of war. During the eighth Five-Year Plan, for example, more than 50 national highways were built or renovated to military standards, including three roads leading into Tibet.

China has developed a network of internal highways and subsidiary/feeder roads in the TAR to connect strategically significant border areas with India, Nepal, Bhutan and Pakistan by means of motorable roads. It has developed 58,000 km of road network in Tibet, including five major highways and a number of subsidiary roads. It is learnt that the PrC plans to build additional roads in the Tar to link 92 percent of the Tar's towns and 70 percent of its administrative villages. The PrC is expected to spend 20 billion yuan (Us $3.13 billion) in the coming years, mainly on the construction of 103 highway projects. Presently, 80 percent of Tibet's townships and nearly 20 percent of villages are accessible by highways. The western, Central and eastern highways have leveraged greater connectivity between western and mainland China.

Qinghai-Tibet Highway (Central Highway): running from Xining in Qinghai to Lhasa in Tibet, this highway is the most crucial and is often referred to as the 'lifeline' of the Tar. The 2,122-km highway carries more than 80 percent of cargo and 90 percent of passengers into or out of Tibet. It is paved with asphalt and crosses the kunlun and Tanggula mountain ranges. The entire stretch of the road is black-topped two-way, with proper highway markings wherein vehicles can travel at an average speed of 35-40 km per hour and cover a distance of approximately 200-250 km in a single day.

Lhasa-Kashgar/Aksai Chin/Xinjiang Highway (Western Highway): Connects Xinjiang to Tibet, by linking kashgar and Lhasa (3,105 km). From Quilanaldi, the road branches off to khunjerab Pass and, subsequently, becomes the karakoram highway right upto Gilgit. In addition, there are large numbers of lateral roads leading to the passes on the Indian borders. Sichuan-Tibet Highway (Eastern Highway): This highway between Chengdu (sichuan) and Linzhi (ngiti) is 1,715 km long (2,413 km up to Lhasa).

There has been a crucial upgradation of the 400-km stretch from Lhasa to ngiti (opposite central arunachal Pradesh). Black-topped and asphalt-surfaced, it is primarily aimed at improving lateral mobility between central and eastern Tar. The Chinese government had earmarked 5.3 billion yuan (Us $829.6 million) for improving the 573 km stretch of the sichuan-Tibet highway along with six regional highways and the 3,000 km road leading to local counties and villages, among other highway projects.

Yunnan-Tibet Highway: This 716-km-long highway branches off from the Eastern Highway and is four to five metres wide, prone to frequent landslides and disruptions during the winter and monsoon season. This highway holds special significance in military terms for India, owing to the build-up of the PLa opposite India's eastern theatre, given China's logistics capacity-building and accelerated facilitation of men and material in the critical sectors of the northern and eastern borders. A major infrastructure development project in the Tar, including two highway bridges over the Lhasa and Yarlung Tsangpo rivers, and a 2.4-km-long tunnel (total road length of 13.28 km) costing 650 million yuan, (Us $101.7 million) is underway, which will reduce the travelling distance between Lhasa to Gongar international airport from 98 to 53 km. with the opening of border trade via nathu La, additional border trade venues in Nepal (in addition to the existing two in central and western Nepal), and plans for border trade at Bumla, Demchok and the old stilvel route, the Tar appears poised for 'fast-track' holistic development. Moving of the logistics resources from townships to the place of application and sustenance of forces during road closure periods (when dumpling of additional safety stocks for the road closure period is required) will continue to be a criticality for the PLa.

Upgradation of Airfields

There are five operational airfields inside Tibet and as many as 15 surrounding it. The main airfields within the region include

Gongar, Hoping, Pangta, Linchi and Gar Gunsa. The Gongar and Pangta airfields are being upgraded to cater to 1.1 million and 1.0 million transients respectively, i.e., 2.1 million transients per year. Other additional airfields include Donshoon, Nagchuka and shiquanhe. In fact, Pangta is known to have the highest elevation in the world.

Further, ten new airports are planned to be constructed in the next five years. Construction of the nyingtri airport (Linzhi) located in southeastern Tar was one of the key projects completed in the Tenth Five-Year Plan and was made operational in July 2006. It is situated near nyingtri in the nyingchi Prefecture, which shares borders with India and Myanmar and is strategically significant to India. Another airfield in central TAR at Bayixincun is being pursued. China is also opening another airport at nyingchi, apart from modernising Lhasa's Gongar airport. There are 15 airfields in and around Tibet, of which only three are open for civilian activity. Further, su-27s have recently been deployed in the Chengdu Mr and they might, in the future, also be deployed in Tibet.

Significantly, the establishment of the TAR International Airline is presently under consideration in Tibet. Currently, the China southwest airline has 10 domestic air routes in Tibet, including those from Lhasa to Beijing, Chengdu, shanghai, Guangzhou, Chongqing, Xi'an and Xining, as well as one international air route from Lhasa to kathmandu. Such developments would progressively increase the air induction capability into the Tar. It needs to be mentioned here that owing to the critical high altitude of the airports in Tibet, the Chinese air Force encounters problems in terms of fuel, oxygen as well as the length of the runways. Owing to this, China has purchased an additional 18 IL-78 aircraft for developing the existing air-to-air refuelling capability, so that the aircraft can take off with added load and use less fuel and, subsequently, can be refuelled in the air to achieve greater endurance, which shall be crucial as far as the radius of action as well as payload of all aircraft is concerned.

Construction of new airfields and the upgradation of Advanced Landing Grounds (aLGs) and helipads in and around the Tar (coupled with acquisition of new transport aircraft) is likely to enhance China's strategic airlift capability. The Chinese will be able to induct/concentrate formations in comparatively shorter time-frames and, consequently, shorter warning periods. The functional international standard airfields in the TAR (Gongar, Pangta and nyngchi) would give the Chinese a considerable strategic airlift and logistics advantage. Further, the airfields on the periphery of the TAR can be activated to give additional logistic and operational support. The construction/upgradation of airfields/ ALGs closer to the borders enhances the PLaaF aircraft's striking range and provides the PLaaF the ability to strike/engage targets in India on a broad front and in depth.

Foremost among the infrastructure schemes mooted for the 12th Five-Year Plan period of 2011 to 2015 is what the official Chinese press bills "the world's highest airport." Construction of the 1.8 billion yuan (Us $263.5 million) airport in Tibet's nagqu prefecture, which has an elevation of 4,436 m (14,639 ft), will begin later this year. According to the local media, the nagqu airport would, together with ultra modern facilities such as the Qinghai-Tibet railway, "perfect a three-dimensional transport network that will envelop all Tibet."

Fibre Optic Communication (FOC)

Fifty-eight very small aperture Terminal (vsaT) satellite stations are reported to have been installed in the Tar. All PLaaF units and sub-units in the Tar have been connected by satellite communication. China is reported to have laid a fibre optic network in all the 55 counties, which includes Ali, and the border area of Chamdo; 1,100 km of Optical Fibre Cable (OFC) have been laid, connecting Lhasa with nyingchi and Qamdo counties in east Tar. The plan to connect all the cities and counties of the Tar by 2005 appears to have been successful. Another major development has been the inter-connecting of Chengdu and Lanzhou Mrs with one another, and both these Mrs to Beijing, through secure communications, ensuring secure and real-time communication. This aspect has further been emphasised during subsequent training. FOC is being steadily extended towards military installations along the borders. All Military supply Depots (MsDs) are connected to Lhasa by radio and OFC.

In 2006, Tibet invested 1.447 billion yuan (Us $226.5 million) for improvement of the telecommunications service in the farming and pastoral areas. Telephone lines now link 2,112 administrative villages, accounting for 35.59 percent of the total in Tibet. In 2006, 56,900 phone lines were added, bringing the total capacity to 394,400 lines. The number of additional fixed telephone subscribers was 156,700, bringing the total number to 682,200, including 649,700 urban subscribers and 32,500 rural ones. In all, 140,000-line mobile phone exchanges were added, bringing the total capacity to 800,000. There are 605,500 mobile users, 136,200 of whom were added in 2006. At the end of the year, the total number of fixed and mobile telephone subscribers reached 1.2877 million, an increase of 292,900 over the previous year and the telephone popularisation rate reached 46.5 per 100 persons.

The upgrading of the communication networks through fibre optic cables and satellite communication indicates real-time connectivity achieved by the PLa; a quantum jump in communication technology, wherein Command, Control, Communications, Computers, Intelligence, surveillance and reconnaissance (C4Isr) shall be the key. Their upgradation shall enable the conduct of effective operations and sustain increased force levels in the future. The enhanced communication security will continue to tilt the balance in cyber warfare in favour of the PLa.

Interpretation of Infrastructure Build-up in Military Terms although estimates vary, operationalisation of the QTr provides China with the capability to mobilise as many as 12 divisions (approximately 12,000 troops make a division) in a month's time. The infrastructure and logistics build-up shall double up as base support for the PLa to facilitate military operations. Now China could well transfer telecommunications and other command and control facilities, which are needed to deploy missiles from launches at a chosen place. The QTr has, indeed, made tremendous headway by virtue of increasing the transportation capacity, thereby enhancing induction capability and faster build-up of logistics up to future railheads, and providing capability for day and night movement. Unswerving rail links from Lanzhou to kashi and to Lhasa shall aid easy switching of reserves and logistics resources between the Chengdu and Lanzhou Mrs bordering India. Presently, the travel time for troops from Golmud to Lhasa is approximately 72 hours (including night halts and restrictions). The QTr line has reduced this to 16 hours, implying a complete turnaround time of about three days from Golmud to Lhasa. In fact, Chinese troops were being transported on this rail network to Lhasa in December 2007, signifying its use for military purposes. The *Xinhua* news agency cited unnamed sources in the PLa as saying that the railway would become 'a main option' for transporting soldiers. The QTr will also permit easier movement of larger and more capable ballistic missiles into the Tar. Approximately 2.18 percent of the 1,118-km-long railway is made up of tunnels. Once the construction of these tunnels was completed, however, they were kept unused for several months, which led to speculation that some of the tunnels were probably being used as missile bases. The completion of the railway may, therefore, be followed by deployment of such missiles into the Tar, to be able to cover longer range targets in south asia as well as the Indian Ocean region (IOr). It may also facilitate China's second-strike capability by avoiding the reach of Us missiles. Some of the tunnels on the railway line can also be developed as possible secure storage sites for rail mobile ballistic missiles. This, in turn, will minimise the vulnerability of the lines of communication. The QTr will, thus, cause a reduction in military expenditure and an easing of the logistical difficulties faced by the PLA in moving men and materials to/from the frontiers. In addition, the PLa is also concentrating on developing logistics and infrastructure to improve the rapid deployment capability of the integrated forces.

Rapid Reaction Forces

A small, but concentrated high-tech force perfectly suited for flexible use, especially in the case of regional contingencies, is termed as a rapid reaction Force (rrF). Capable of responding to local war scenarios, these rapid reaction units are regarded as the PLA's most capable fighting forces. During the late 1990s, only a small proportion of the PLa logistics system was capable of being restructured to support combat operations under high-technology conditions. Many of these units were attached to designated rapid response units of the ground, air and naval forces, as well as that of the second artillery. The number of rrFs in the PLa, however, has grown steadily since their creation in the mid-1980s. The 15th airborne army is the PLa's primary strategic rapid deployment force, but it has only been used for internal security missions so far. It has been reported that the Chinese have identified and located RRFs with specific emphasis on each particular Mr and the nature of threat associated with it. Accordingly, one Motor Infantry Division in the Chengdu Mr and two additional Infantry Divisions and a Motor Infantry Division in the Lanzhou Mr with special reference to India are reported to serve as rapid reaction units.

The rapid reaction capability of the Chinese armed forces in the Tibet region, particularly their ability to quickly manoeuvre heavy equipment, has been greatly enhanced. This was indicated by the fact that the PLa soldiers on T-90/89 vehicles on the streets of Lhasa were all wearing the "leopard" camouflage uniforms, specifically designed for mountain warfare operations. These uniforms appeared in a video footage of the 149th Division during exercises witnessed in 2008. Calculated on the basis of being able to transport most of the heavy equipment of a whole mechanised division within 48 hours, it is unlikely that all the division's equipment would be moved; the PLa would be able to transport approximately ten light mechanised divisions and some heavy mechanised divisions through the railroad to Tibet from the Lanzhou and Chengdu Mrs within 30 days.

The average load capacity of one Chinese train car is normally 60 tonnes, with about 20 cars in each cargo train. This ideally should imply that each train could transport 1,200 tonnes, and, thus, 11 trains travelling both ways would be enough for each day. In times of war, the actual number of trains running on the railroad could double to roughly 20 trains both ways, each day. If the total weight of the equipment and combat material needed for one rapid reaction division of the Chinese army was around 15,000 tonnes, the Qinghai-Tibet railway could transport a whole rapid reaction division on an average day. In other words, within every one-and-a-half to two days, China could move one rapid reaction division from the Chengdu Mr or one rapid reaction division from the Lanzhou Mr to Tibet. China's air transport capability, including additional airborne troops, rapid reaction troops and armed police, could be directly delivered to Lhasa from the air. Since airdrop operations would take place in the Tibet region, there would be no need for ground-based air defence firepower. The railway would allow the 61st Plateau rapid reaction Motorised Division of no. 21 Group army under the Lanzhou Mr and the 149th rapid reaction Motorised Division of the Chengdu Mr to quickly enter Tibet. A study of the development of the logistics infrastructure in the Tar and along the China-India frontier reveals that there is an increase in the logistics and infrastructural capability of the PLa to induct and sustain a larger quantum of forces up to major townships in the Tar. The crucial restrictive factors for force applications, however, are deployability and logistics sustainability at the places of application. The depth of the operations, undoubtedly, shall continue to be governed by terrain, the vagaries of climate, sustenance capacities of the thrust lines chosen, and the Indian defence preparedness at the chosen area of application. The PLa logistics set-up along the China-India borders currently caters to a limited force level in the border management role. Hence, supplies, ammunition and FOL for almost the entire force level being inducted for an offensive, have to be moved and dumped near likely places of application, prior to the offensive. The key impediments envisaged by the PLa in the Tar include the following:

- Long distance from rail heads to important communication centres (currently being addressed) and periodic disruption due to climatic conditions lead to delay in induction.
- Terrain and weather restrict logistics operations from March to november. Build-up to the rail head, however, is possible throughout the year.
- need for extensive winter stocking; move of logistics resources at the place of application and sustenance of forces during the road closure period necessitate winter stocking for the road closure period.
- reduced airlift capability and long axes of maintenance and disruption due to high altitude conditions.

- adverse effects of high altitude on men and material; need for acclimatisation, especially in the case of air induction.
- application of rrFs along India's borders would also require ground logistics support like other mountain formations, although these can be air-maintained for short directions.
- Logistics induction is vulnerable to the IaF.
- The PLa's modern joint logistics system is still untested in war-like scenarios.

Tibetan Unrest and the PLA

The March 2008 unrest in Tibet undoubtedly raised questions of China's sovereignty over Tibet, with speculation rife over whether the unrest would erode China's bargaining position during border talks, particularly with respect to its claim over Tawang (arunachal Pradesh). The coinciding of the 50th anniversary of the 1959 Tibetan revolt, that resulted in China's military shelling of the Tibetan capital of Lhasa, and consequently crushing the uprising by the Tibetans, which forced the Dalai Lama and some 85,000 followers to flee into exile in India, raised a palpable sense of concern within India. As the Tibetans marked the 50th anniversary of that uprising, which coincided with the Chinese government holding the People's Congress in Beijing, presumably, the last thing they wanted was bad publicity in the world regarding Tibet. The Tibet issue, particularly the factors and conflicts around the Olympics and the torch relay seemed to have moved the whole issue into a very emotional landscape for many Chinese. There is something much larger that is being witnessed; the growth of Chinese nationalism that is a focused springboard to the Tibetan issue.

Following the Tibetan protests, a special security coordination unit, the 110 Command Centre, was established in Lhasa, with the primary objective of suppressing the disturbances and restoring full central government control understandably under the direct control of Zhang Qingli, First secretary of the Tibet Party and a hu Jintao loyalist. Zhang is also the former Xinjiang Deputy Party secretary, with considerable experience in counter-terrorism operations in that region. In addition, significant positions in Lhasa are being held by Zhang Xinfeng, vice Minister of the

Central Public security Ministry and Zhen Yi, Deputy Commander of the People's armed Police headquarters in Beijing. The seriousness with which Beijing treated the unrest was further illustrated by the deployment of a large number of important army units from the Chengdu Mr, including brigades from the 149th Mechanised Infantry Division, which acted as the region's rrF. A United Press International (UPI) report stated that the elite ground force units of the PLa were involved in Lhasa, with the new T-90 armoured personnel carrier and T-92 wheeled armoured vehicles being deployed. The UPI report also brought out that China eventually denied the participation of the army in the crackdown, saying it was carried out by units of the armed police. Such equipment, as mentioned above, however, has never been deployed by China's armed police. Air support was provided by the 2nd army aviation regiment, based at Fenghuangshan, Chengdu, in the sichuan province. It operates a mix of helicopters and short Take-off and Landing (sTOL) transports from a frontline base near Lhasa. Combat air support could be quickly made available from fighter ground attack squadrons based within the Chengdu region. The Xizang Military District forms the Tibet garrison, which has two mountain infantry units: the 52nd Brigade based at Linzhi and the 53rd Brigade at Yaoxian shannxi.

These are supported by the 8th Motorised Infantry Division and an artillery brigade at shawan, Xinjiang. according to srikanth kondapalli, it was widely reported that at the time of the unrest, China had deployed 180,000 troops in the Chengdu Mr and nearly 220,000 troops in the Lanzhou Mr. notably, the Chengdu Mr has operational jurisdiction in sichuan, Tibet, Guizhou and Yunnan regions and the Lanzhou Mr has operational jurisdiction in Gansu, Qinghai and Xinjiang regions.

Although estimates vary about the exact nature and number of PLa's troop deployment in Tar, the fact remains that the quantum of infrastructure activity in the region is well beyond the "genuine needs" of Tibet or the Tibetan people. If read in the backdrop of Chinese reiteration that its concepts of warfare and capability upgradation go well beyond meeting challenges in the form of Taiwan, Tibet and east Turkistan, this for sure, tends to throw caution to the winds.

Responses and Options to China's Build-up in TAR

Given the current backdrop, although the border between China and India is rather calm with no overt mobilisation of troops into Tibet, there is a clear possibility that once the Taiwan issue is resolved by China, the subsequent focus could well shift towards India in the next couple of years, owing to the impending territorial and boundary dispute that continues to loom large. According to the Tibetan Government-in-exile in Dharamsala, the estimated number of troops in Tibet stands at about 500,000 in the form of the People's armed Police, the Chinese Frontier Guards and the Garrison Duty Forces. There have been numerous estimates as far as the quantum of force and build-up logistics in relation to the infrastructure development in Tibet are concerned. Rosita Dellois in her book *Modern Chinese Defense Strategy: Present Developments, Future Strategy,* estimated that China would be able to deploy as many as 30 divisions against India in a potential conflict scenario. Besides, *The Chinese Armed Forces Today* published by the Us Defence Intelligence agency, had revealed that the daily resupply requirement of a standard Chinese division would be about 300 tonnes short for moderate combat and an average of 200 tonnes short for a protracted period of combat. Srikanth kondapalli underscores the Chinese intent vis-à-vis Tibet by stating that nearly 90 percent of the Tar's budget is subsidised by the central government. The Chinese government has spent roughly 40-45 billion yuan in the last 40 years and is spending an added 40 billion yuan under the 11th Five-Year Plan (2006-10). The Chengdu Mr controls the entire Tar, except for western Tibet which is under the Lanzhou MR, with five reserve divisions present for any contingency. Kondapalli further stated that han Chinese influx is amply visible as far as modernity is concerned. In front of the Potala Palace, there used to be kiosks run by Tibetans. As the construction of roads progressed, most of the Tibetan structures were demolished and new malls came up, primarily owned by han businessmen – a very crucial consequence of the growing connectivity between Tibet and the mainland. Thus, the Han Chinese influx is further eroding the Tibetan culture and leading to marginalisation of Tibetans.

According to kondapalli, there are 30 regiments of the PLa stationed at Golmud, which can use the railway line and reach Lhasa, shigatse and other feeder lines. The Chengdu to Lhasa line can bring in five more divisions of the PLA to the border. The airfield, which is being constructed 30 km away from shiquanhe, is a major military installation. Although China is ramping up infrastructure in areas close to the border, it should be mentioned that in the 1990s, as part of the Joint working Group meetings, China had vehemently objected to any construction or air activity in the Ladakh region. The Chengdu Mr houses two Group armies, two tank brigades and one artillery division. No airborne divisions are present in Chengdu or Lanzhou. The 13 and 14 Group armies, present in Chengdu, are called 'monkey troops' in China, similar to the Ladakh scouts in the Indian army, who are trained to rapidly climb mountains and can swiftly adapt to extreme weather conditions. In fact, the 13 Group Army is an RRF – potentially a significant concern for India. The Chengdu MR also commands the Chongqing garrison and a significant number of independent and border forces in Tibet. Both the General headquarters Department and the Chengdu Mr expend great efforts to make sure the forces in Tibet are adequately supplied, primarily by road, but sometimes also by aircraft. Given that the Chengdu Mr caters to southeast asia and the Lanzhou Mr to Central asia and aksai-Chin, kondapalli estimates that there are 400,000 troops in Tibet that face India and other nations.

According to Brahma Chellaney, no country is going to be more affected by the Chinese plans and projects in Tibet than India. The states that the Golmud-Lhasa railway line has significantly augmented China's rapid military deployment capability against India, just when Beijing is becoming increasingly assertive in its claims on Indian territories. This hardline stance, in the midst of intense negotiations to resolve the dispute over the 4,057-km Indo-Tibetan border, opines Chellaney, is no less incongruous than Beijing's disinclination to set up a joint expert-level mechanism on inter-state river waters, as agreed during its President's state visit to new Delhi in november 2006, given that Beijing dragged its feet on setting up an innocuous interaction mechanism. As the tensions on the border escalated in the recent past, with incidents of incessant Chinese intrusions, it reflected a perceptible hardening of China's stance toward India. Chinese troops have repeatedly attempted to gain control of sikkim's evocatively named "Finger area" – a tiny but key strategic location. The fact that China holds the military advantage on the ground and its forces controlling the heights along the frontier, with the Indian troops perched largely on the lower levels, cannot be negated. Furthermore, by building modern railroads, airports and highways in Tibet, China appears to be in a position to rapidly move in large numbers of additional forces to the border with India, so as to potentially strike at India at a time of Beijing's choosing.

Primarily intended to boost the "Go west" campaign under the 10th Five Year Plan, the Golmud-Lhasa railway line alters the military balance, but has been ignored in India. The military implications for China include a reduction in military expenditure and an easing of the logistical difficulties faced by the PLa, in terms of supplies and garrisons along the frontiers. It also allows a feeder line, service bases and airfields. Stobdan claims that China will be able to transfer 12 divisions in a span of 30 days to meet pre-positioned equipment. Tibet's missile launch brigades include the Da Tsaidam 412 Brigade, the Datung-wulan 408 Brigade, the 9th academy (Factory 211) in amdo area, an anti-frigate Missile Centre at Drotsang, a missile launch site at Terlingka, a new launch site in amdo, bases at risur in nagchuka, and bases at the Tago Mountain. In addition, there is also an underground site at Lhasa and kangpo. The implications of such activity for India are significant. The strategic importance of Tibet lies in the fact that China is soon going to control asia's principal source of water. nearly half of the world (47 percent, in terms of population, in 10 countries) depends on Tibetan water for its sustenance. China will use water as a strategic commodity and as a tool for energy and economic diplomacy with neighbours. There is a western route Transfer Project, a south-north water Diversion Project and a west-east Power Transfer Project. Moreover, a barrage near Tsamda gorge near Guge kingdom could disturb the Sutlej flow and enable China to control and regulate the flow of water into India. Similar things could also happen in the Lohit (Zayul Chu), subansiri and

Indus, amongst others essentially, while China launches a new unconventional/non-linear war, the question needs to be asked: is India prepared to respond to such an onslaught?

As a matter of fact, the Pareechu lake controversy in 2004 brought out that the issue of river water sharing was another area of potential discord between the two countries. It is well known that China and India share the waters of the Indus, Brahmaputra and sutlej rivers and are upper and lower riparian states, respectively.

This makes India vulnerable to manipulation of the river water supply by China. In 2004, China had informed India that approximately 35 km from the Himachal Pradesh border, an artificial lake measuring about 230 hectares had been formed on the Pareechu river, a tributary of the sutlej. This incident triggered a debate in India over whether the formation of the lake was a natural phenomenon or a man-made one. If the possibility of the latter was true, it provided China with the capability to devastate the lower reaches of the river in India at will. India requested China to allow Indian experts to examine the topographical details of the lake and study the causes for its origin. China, however, denied visas to a fact-finding team from India to visit the spot of the lake formation, further fuelling speculation. The Pareechu lake incident highlights China's awareness regarding the environmental vulnerability of India.

In a rising asia, while sculpting a global vision, if there is a framework which convincingly captures the overall current scenario, despite the backdrop of strategic uncertainty, it is one of building bridges/synergies and deepening détente. This can be achieved by focusing on common grounds and by accepting that even as both nations are pursuing their respective national interests, the growth of each is based on accommodating the other's needs and emergence.

Of late, the Government of India appears to have taken note of the laxity vis-à-vis the ramping up of logistics infrastructure, especially in the border areas with China in arunachal Pradesh and Ladakh. The Indian armed forces are presently seriously handicapped in the absence of all-weather roads in the states like arunachal Pradesh and the region of eastern Ladakh, and have to depend on logistical support from the air, which is an expensive option.

The Border roads Organisation (BrO) is under directions to complete work by 2013 on at least eight roads termed 'strategic' in arunachal Pradesh, of which four have yet to be completed. The BrO had been directed to complete construction of 608 kms of roads stretching from Ladakh to Diphu La in arunachal, at a cost of rs 992 crore ($203,000,000) by 2010.87 as many as 75 roads with a total length of more than 6,000 km are now under construction at a cost of rs 5,000 crore. Besides this, 7,000 km of roads costing rs 12,000 crore are under various stages of construction in the northeast. The special accelerated road Development Programme for the northeast (sarDP-ne) project was divided into two phases: The first phase involving 1,300 km of roads, primarily in the northeastern states, to be completed by 2010; the second phase involves 5,700 km with a 2013 deadline. Further, the Inter-Ministerial China study Group proposed construction of at least 75 roads all along the border, of which 36 have been earmarked for arunachal Pradesh alone.

While road construction is going on in the border regions, the Indian air Force (IaF) has reportedly begun upgrading its advanced Landing Grounds (aLGs) in Ladakh and arunachal Pradesh. The IaF has built four air bases in Ladakh since 2008, with plans to upgrade such bases in arunachal in a time-bound manner as well. It has been reported that India is also progressively reactivating old aLGs like the Daulat Beg Oldi, Phukche, Chushul and nyoma airstrips in Ladakh. similarly, apart from building new helipads and upgrading air bases, the IAF is also going to soon start basing its Sukhoi-30 MKI fighters in the eastern sector for the first time. In fact, the government had cleared a plan to upgrade nearly 40 airfields all over the country, with most of them in the northeast, in an effort to maintain connectivity and strategic balance with China. Reportedly, these airfields are likely to be completed in the next five to seven years.

Although C raja Mohan contends that China's road-building is unlikely to lead to a military confrontation between the two countries, he believes that the current expansion of Chinese infrastructure in Tibet confronts India with a different set of challenges. For one, it brutally exposes the poor state of transportation networks on the sub-continental side – the southern slopes of the himalayas. raja Mohan sates that the message from China is clear: on the frontiers, infrastructure is power in its broadest sense. In Nepal, for example, China has plans for six additional highways to link up with Nepal, besides the present one that runs through kodari on the sino-nepalese border. Chinese plans are not limited to highways, but include the development of cross-border energy pipelines and optical fibre links in Nepal. The awful state of infrastructure on the border is the result, incredibly enough, of a deliberate policy in new Delhi over the last several decades, not to develop connectivity along the frontiers.

Ds rajan, Director of the Centre for China studies at Chennai, recalls that a few influential strategists in the PRC visualised what they termed a "partial war" with India, to recover "southern Tibet" (the PrC's name for arunachal Pradesh). For the same, China appears to have completed its military preparations to resolve the issue. The 14th army of Chengdu Mr could be stationed in kunming (Yunnan's capital) and 80 percent of China's strategic bomber force is in the Lanzhou Mr. The hardline stance on the arunachal Pradesh issue being adopted at least by a section of Chinese strategists, ostensibly under an indirect government nod, contrasts with Beijing's present official position that China and India are no threat to each other and that the boundary issue can be solved on the basis of "mutual understanding and mutual accommodation" and dialogue on "equal terms."

This forces one to wonder whether China is deliberately blowing hot and cold on the border issue. A probable explanation could be that there are internal differences in China on the arunachal Pradesh issue, between strategic and national security establishments, which give priority to national sovereignty on the one hand, and the diplomatic machinery, which accords primacy to a 'harmonious world' and 'peaceful periphery' concepts to suit China's modernisation requirements, on the other.

India needs to invest heavily in developing infrastructure and transport links along the Sino-Indian border. China holds the benefit of heights, easier acclimatisation and superior airlift capabilities along the border. The initiatives discussed above will only supplement its power projection in the region. As the border talks continue, any potential lacuna in India's preparedness will make the country vulnerable to Chinese pressure. New Delhi should work its way towards negotiating with the Chinese from a position of strength and not one of weakness, and for that, ramping up infrastructure build-up and preparedness is imperative. In fact, poor infrastructure is a key impediment towards an effective deterrence against China. During a field trip to Leh and the interiors of the Ladakh region in July 2009, this author had an opportunity to travel extensively across the mountainous terrain. During the course of numerous discussions that this author had with senior officers, there was a discernible consensus over the potential Chinese build-up that could take place by means of their rrFs. Theoretically, they could build-up within 48 hours; the Indian view, however, is that it would take much longer. Army officers in the region believe that, logistically, the Indian forces are comfortable; able to deploy adequate force levels, i.e., adequate resources are available for logistical support for a high-, medium-, or low-intensity conflict. Nonetheless, it has to be noted that unlike the Line of Control (LoC), the Line of actual Control (LaC) is not physically demarcated on the ground, including on military maps. Thus, when intrusions occur, it ruffles feathers, since it is complicated to determine which country the territory in question belongs to. Moreover, unlike arunachal Pradesh, the situation is quite different in Ladakh (J&k). In the eastern Ladakh (western Tibet) section, China has the capacity to begin the war with two to three divisions in minimal time and that, too, without much preparation. Reportedly, there is one airfield opposite eastern Ladakh; two rrFs are likely to be deployed there, both of which are armoured and mechanised heavily. Officers on the Indian side, however, are of the view that even if they are inside eastern Ladakh in 48 hours, the Chinese forces would require at least six to eight days to deploy and acclimatise. The western highway opposite eastern Ladakh is not all that smooth and convenient, as claimed by the Chinese.

6

Modernisation of China's Geopolitical Influence in South Asia

CONTOURS OF CHINA'S SOUTH ASIA POLICY

Following its takeover of Tibet, China became an integral part of the Southern Asian geopolitical and strategic environment. It shares borders with Pakistan (given its occupation of a portion of Jammu and Kashmir), India, Nepal, Bhutan and Myanmar.

The rise of China, whether in terms of economic growth or military build-up, is bound to have a regional implication. Different countries, however, have their own interpretation and response. As neighbouring states, each is affected, some positively and some negatively, by China's military power, posture, strategic thinking, and evolving role. China thus shapes in a major way the regional balance of power and security environment. Although India and South Asia are not central to China's foreign relations and policy priorities at present, this is a growing area of Beijing's interest. For New Delhi, however, whether positive or negative, "China's military doctrines, forced deployment postures and economic interests are a matter of interest to India."

China's Stance. Interestingly, the Chinese Ministry of Foreign Affairs does not use the term South Asia in its major foreign policy pronouncements and limits it to discussions on Pakistan. It treats all countries around in its periphery (including India) as 'Asian

Neighbours' and claims that it conducts its foreign policy towards them in 'the Asian spirit of coexistence in harmony, good neighbourly friendship, consultations and dialogue, respect for civilization diversity, solidarity and (mutually beneficial) cooperation'. It lays emphasis on consolidating its relationship with its Asian neighbours through frequent high-level contacts, and believes in pushing forward regional cooperation and expanding 'exchanges and cooperation in the fields of TRADE, investment, infrastructure, finance, science and technology, culture and education to unprecedented width and depth'. This, in a way, denotes China's aspirations as an emerging world power with bigger ambitions to make its mark on the world stage as the most pre-eminent power in Asia. Against this backdrop, it is necessary to take a close look at China's relationship with each of the South Asian countries and understand its implications for India.

CHINA AND PAKISTAN

Historical Friendship. Of all of China's relations in Asian neighbours, those with Pakistan outweigh and overlay any other bilateral relationship. The Beijing Islamabad "special relationship" is part of China's grand strategy that moulds South Asian security environment. Despite some improvements in Sino Indian relations Pakistan remains the linchpin of China's South Asia policy. The relationship between the two prospered, especially since the 1960s, against the backdrop of the India–China war of 1962. Pakistan has since looked up to China as a major strategic partner. Pakistan played a major role in the US–China reconciliation in early 1970s. China and Pakistan are united in their antipathy towards India and each uses the other as a strategic ally in southern Asian region against India. Beijing's 'entente cordiale' with Islamabad continues to flourish underpinned by military, economic and infrastructure development and diplomatic cooperation. No one put it better than Chinese President himself during November 2006 Pakistan visit; "We can give up GOLD but we can't give up our relationship with Pakistan. China Pakistan relationship is higher than the Himalayas, deeper than the India Ocean and sweeter than honey". China has engaged itself in critical infrastructure building and business INVESTMENTS in Pakistan. This is amply demonstrated by the construction, and later expansion, of the Karakorum Highway, a deep-sea port at Gwadar, Chashma Nuclear Power Plant, Taxila Heavy Mechanical Complex, Jinnah Sports Stadium, and the Pakistan–China Friendship Centre. Reports in the media indicate that Chinese are increasing their footprints in the Pakistan-occupied Kashmir (PoK) under the pretext of developing infrastructure in the region. Moreover, this 'all weather' relationship is likely to further get strengthened in view of recent strains between Washington and Islamabad and the United States announcing plans for a withdrawal of troops from Afghanistan .

TRADE. China–Pakistan trade hovers around US$ 10 billion and they are taking active measures to raise it to about $15 billion by 2012. According to Pakistan Foreign Ministry, 'over 100 Chinese projects in various fields are underway in Pakistan and thousands of Chinese are working on these projects'.

Defence Cooperation. The two armies have very good relationship. China continues to provide military assistance, both conventional weapon platforms and components for strategic weapons, to Pakistan army. China's transfer of missile and nuclear technology to Pakistan is an uncontested fact. The Indo-US nuclear deal in 2007 has been wrongly interpreted by both as being directed against them and this has brought them even closer together. This is demonstrated by the brazen attempt by the Chinese to grandfather some nuclear deals with Pakistan, as a strategic counter to Indo-US deal. Contrary to some of the Chinese claims, no notable let-up has been observed in China's military cooperation with Pakistan. It continues and finds newer areas like supply of unmanned aircraft to Pakistan. Besides, it has been recorded that whenever India and Pakistan have come close to confrontation in the last 20 years, the Pakistani political and military leadership have paid visits to China and extracted positive political statements from the Chinese leadership about China-Pakistan friendship, seeking to put indirect pressure on India. Besides, it has also been noted that China has, in some cases supplied military assistance to Pakistan in the immediate backdrop of the latter's crises with India. Geostrategic and security considerations continue to be the most important DRIVERS of close Sino-Pakistan relations. This relationship presents India a potential two front war threat.

CHINA-BANGLADESH

Chinese Interest in Bangladesh. China was one of the few countries which did not support the independence of Bangladesh in 1971. However, it did not waste much time and established diplomatic relations with Bangladesh in 1975. The relationship between the two countries is growing, with China substantially increasing its economic and TRADE relations with Bangladesh. For China, Bangladesh is a doorway into India's turbulent north eastern region, including Arunachal Pradesh, to which China lays territorial claims. China prizes Bangladesh for its immense natural gas reserves which rival those of Indonesia. Bangladesh's geographic proximity with Myanmar makes these reserves accessible to China. 'Further as China looks at the possibilities of naval presence in Indian Ocean, the port of Chittagong-where it is developing a container port facility – and the long Bangladesh coastline along Bay of Bengal offer enticing possibilities'.

Blooming Bilateral Relations. China is Bangladesh's largest trading partner and IMPORTS FROM CHINA have increased over a period of time. China has invested in the Bangladeshi market in textiles, energy, and infrastructure sector. The Chinese President had visited Bangladesh in 2010. Agreement on 'Closer Comprehensive Partnership of Cooperation between China and Bangladesh' was signed during Sheikh Hasina's visit to Beijing in March 2010. According to the outgoing Ambassador of China to Bangladesh, 'The bilateral TRADE volume in the first 11 months of 2011 reached $7.5 billion, with an increase of 21.3 percent compared with same period in 2010. Bangladeshi exports to China reached $400 million, an increase of 79.5 percent'. Media reports quoting Chinese foreign ministry reports suggested that China responded positively to the request from Bangladesh side to help it in launching a communication satellite. China and South Korea are the largest foreign INVESTORS in Bangladesh followed by India. China is providing Bangladesh with hydrological data at three points in the upper reach of river Brahmaputra on a daily basis between January to October free of cost. China has also agreed to develop a deep-sea port at Sonadia near Cox's bazaar.

Defence Cooperation. The two countries have extensive defence cooperation, involving regular military-to military exchanges and contacts at high levels. China is largest supplier of small firearms to Bangladesh and also transfers missile to the country. China trains Bangladeshi forces under Defence Cooperation Agreement signed between China and Bangladesh in 2002 and shapes Dhaka's security apparatus. Recently, China has assured to help Dhaka in developing peaceful use of nuclear technology for the implementation of Rooppur Nuclear Power Plant. China has also built six 'friendship bridges' across various rivers in the country. China had agreed to supply frigates to Bangladesh Navy in 2010. Bangladesh is purchasing forty-four military armoured vehicles costing US $ 200 million from China. China and Bangladesh are likely to strengthen their relationship further in the future, especially on economic and security-related issues.

CHINA–NEPAL

Growing Chinese Interest and Influence in Nepal. As a state sharing its border with China's restive province of Tibet, Nepal occupies a special position in Chinese foreign policy. China has three major strategic interests in Nepal: first, containing Tibetan refugees (total number amounts to about 20,000) south of the Himalayas and stopping their anti-China activities; second, neutralizing India's influence in Nepal and setting up a pro-China regime in Kathmandu, for which China has scaled-up its policy of engagement in recent years and adopted even soft diplomatic measures, that is, people-to-people contacts, cultural relations, scholarships to students, economic aid, and spreading of Chinese Buddhism in Nepal; and third, INVESTING in strategically important infrastructure like airports and important highways. The investments in Lumbini and Pokhara airports are a point of reference. China has increased its annual assistance to Nepal from RMB 150 million to RMB 200 million. It also announced an RMB 750 million (US $ 120million or Nepalese Rs [NRs] 9.7 billion) grant to Nepal to be spent on mutually identified projects under a new bilateral Agreement on economic and Technical Cooperation (Link1). China also announced a one-time grant of $ 20 million to be spent on the rehabilitation of former Maoist combatants. China agreed to provide engineering equipment assistance worth RMB 30 million and assistance worth RMB 100 million to the Nepal Army Hospital at Chhauni during recent visit of PLA Chief, General Chen Bingde to Nepal on 23 March 2011.

Policy Shift. Above developments indicate major shift in China's foreign policy towards Nepal since 2008 after the fall of the monarchy. China has increased its political, economic, military, and academic delegations to Nepal, posted one of its better diplomats as Ambassador to Kathmandu, increased people-to-people contacts, opened more customs posts at the borders, increased annual grant assistance, and most importantly, strengthened its engagements at the institutional level leading to greater interaction with Nepalese army, bureaucracy, police, and armed police (mostly deployed along the borders). China, it seems, is positioning itself as an alternative to India in Nepal thereby reducing the salience of Indo-Nepal ties.

CHINA–BHUTAN

While Bhutan and China do not share official diplomatic relations, the two countries are engaged in boundary negotiations since the 1980s. There are pressures from the National Assembly members on the incumbent government to solve the boundary dispute. Economically, China is slowly making inroads into Bhutan. It has made efforts to offer itself as an attractive economic partner to Bhutan, particularly for the development of north and north western areas. China has expressed its intent to INVEST in projects relating to health and education services and it has also been exporting farming and telecommunication equipment to Bhutan. Formalizing diplomatic relations with China will occupy an important place in Bhutan's foreign policy in the coming years. As public pressure builds up to resolve the disputed boundary issue, and as China's penetration into Bhutanese economy grows there may be a major shift in Bhutanese foreign policy, away from its current focus on India.

CHINA–SRI LANKA

Increasing Sino Lankan Bonhomie. China's ties with Sri Lanka have intensified, particularly since 2009. China has now become Sri Lanka's largest donor and third-largest import origin country. According to Sri Lankan President Mahinda Rajapaksa, 'the relations between China and Sri Lanka are at the highest levels of friendship and understanding'. As indicated by very high level visits form Sri Lanka to China the current government is seen to be boosting its relations with China against the backdrop of ongoing international attempts to isolate Sri Lanka over human rights accountability issues. Playing its part China has used its veto power in the United Nations Security Council to block the discussion on steps undertaken by the Sri Lankan Government in its fight against the LTTE.

Trade and Economic Relations. Growing trade and economic relations is another important indicator of the China–Sri Lanka multi dimensional engagement. In 2010, Sri Lanka's export to China was valued at Sri Lankan Rupees (SLR) 8,579 million, which accounted for 0.9 per cent of its total export. On the other hand, Sri Lanka's IMPORT FROM CHINA in 2010 was SLR 140,210 million, 9.2 per cent of its total import value. China became the top-most aid provider to Sri Lanka with a total aid commitment of US $ 759.8 million during January–April 2011. China's INVESTMENTS in Sri Lanka have been directed mainly towards development of infrastructure and specific regions such as Hambantota where it is building a $ 1 billion port that military analysts suspect it plans to use as refuelling and docking station for its navy. Central Bank of Sri Lanka included the official CURRENCY of China, Renminbi or Yuan, in the list of designated currencies permitted for international transactions through banks in Sri Lanka in 2011.

Defence Cooperation. In 2008, Sri Lanka also signed an arms deal with China worth US$ 37.6 million. Recent years have witnessed various high-level visits by a PLA delegation which further enhanced military ties in the field of professional training, exercises, and military assistance to Sri Lanka. The PLA continues to offer training to Sri Lankan military personnel on various training modules. China also gave six F-7 Jet fighters to Sri Lanka free of cost in 2008. China's military aid has substantially contributed to enhancing China's political, diplomatic and strategic influence over Sri Lanka vis-a-vis India, which is a disturbing sign for peace and stability in South Asia in future China-Sri Lanka strategic tie ups are likely to increase further.

CHINA - MYANMAR

China's Strategic Interests in Myanmar. Myanmar lies at the strategic crossroads between South West China, North East India, the Indian Ocean, and South East Asia. Myanmar and China emerged as 'partners in adversity' after they faced criticism and sanctions in the wake of their respective crackdowns against democratic protests in 1988/89. While India opted to politically isolate Myanmar, the PRC took the opportunity to establish a foothold in Myanmar. Myanmar offers a threefold advantage to China: one, port access to China's landlocked and impoverished Yunan Province; two, a transit corridor through Myanmar to mitigate China's Malacca dilemma; and three, military bases in Myanmar that can enhance China's strategic reach in the IOR. Myanmar is also reported to have large gas reserves, a factor that is of immense interest to China.

Chinese Investments in Myanmar. Since 1988, the PRC has made extensive investments in Myanmar. By 2005, this included $100 million in aid, $1 billion in seller's credit, and $2 billion INVESTED in various projects, thus laying a foundation for strong bilateral relations. The main infrastructure project undertaken by China has been improvement of the Irrawaddy corridor linking Kunming to Kyaukpyu, construction of a deep-water port and construction of an OIL pipeline linking Sittwe to Kunming, in addition to the gas pipeline already underway. In 1988, Myanmar undertook an ambitious military modernization program with Chinese assistance; by 1992, military exports from China amounted to $1.4 billion including a squadron of F-7 fighter aircraft, and six Hainan class patrol boats.

Misplaced Perceptions. In 1992, the Kyodo News Agency in Japan reported that a listening post was established in the Coco islands, barely 11 miles from India's Andaman and Nicobar Islands, along with a naval base at Haingyyi Island. In 1997, treaty between Myanmar and China, granted the latter a 30-year permit to fish in Myanmar's waters; further strengthening the apprehensions regarding China's efforts to gain access to Myanmar's military facilities. However, even after years of speculation, analysts have found no concrete evidence of a permanent Chinese military presence in Myanmar. In 2005, India acknowledged that there was no Chinese base at Coco Islands, or anywhere else in Myanmar and in 2008 Myanmar passed a referendum prohibiting foreign troops from being based on its soil.

CHINA–MALDIVES

The growing economic and military power of China along with its dependence on energy sources coming from Gulf and Africa has made Chinese interested in the Maldives. The diplomatic relationship between China and Maldives was established on 14 October 1972. Since then, the country has been trying to build on it with various economic programmes and high-level visits. China's has expressed its desire to maintain friendly exchanges and cooperation at all levels in an effort to expand mutual trust and economic and TRADE cooperation in fields such as fisheries, tourism, and infrastructure building. China also encouraged Chinese companies to further participate in the Maldives' national construction and more Chinese tourists to visit the country.

China–Maldives bilateral relations received a major boost after China opened its embassy in Male on 8 November 2011. China is also trying to increase its leverage with Male by sending larger number of tourists as tourism remains a major contributor to the Maldivian economy.

China is the past has shown interest in creating a naval base for itself in Maldives. It is reported that China may have clinched a deal with Maldives to build a naval facility capable of hosting submarines on the islands of Marao; allowing it to lease the island and develop it for 25 years. It is also interested in developing Ihavandhoo and Maarandhoo Islands, with transhipment ports among other things, as well as grabbing a piece of action in the development of the country's second international airport at Hanimaadhoo. China wants a presence in these islands which will fulfill their desire to get a foothold in the Indian Ocean. China's main aim is to ensure the security of its sea lanes for facilitating its critically needed energy imports. With the changed political environment in Maldives after Mohd Nasheed's resignation, and increasing assertion of the Islamists, there is a fear that India may lose its long-standing advantage in Maldives to China.

IMPLICATIONS FOR INDIA

Replacing India as Reliable Partner. From the given analysis, it is clear that China is upgrading its relationship with all South Asian countries in a determined manner. It is expanding the areas of engagement, creating opportunities for Chinese INVESTMENT where it is profitable, offering aid and assistance, and mostly engaging itself profitably in infrastructure-building projects in most of the countries. It has to be acknowledged also that the Chinese ability to deliver on these fronts has generated popular goodwill in most of the countries. With its increasing economic might and its global presence, it is also being viewed as a reliable partner in the region. While this may not offset the natural affinities that India has with each of the South Asian countries, it is likely to increasingly reduce their dependence on India on many counts. This may inevitably lead to an overall weakening of Indian influence and pose a critical challenge to Indian diplomacy, foreign policy and security. China's interests in the neighbourhood may be benign at the moment, but with increasing penetration into the region through multi-dimensional engagements, it is likely to lead to further assertive posture vis-à-vis India in future.

China – Myanmar. Burmese dependence on China could have a negative impact on the traditional neutrality and independence of Myanmar, strengthen the military regime and create a destabilizing strategic relationship. The Tibetisation of Burma also provides China with an invasion route to India and generates apprehensions regarding a "two and half front war".

China's shadow in the South Asia is lengthening steadily, presenting the security dilemma regarding its rise in front of India policy makers. Unless India takes appropriate diplomatic and strategic measures to arrest its declining influence in South Asia it may face grave security challenges in future.

WEAPONS GROWTH AND THE NATIONAL DEFENCE ECONOMY

It is common knowledge that modern warfare is not only the competition of weapons on the battlefield but is also, at the same time, an all-out competition of the total strength of the opposing side's politics, economics, military, and science and technology. During the development of weaponry, the four aspects of politics, economics, military and science and technology are completely brought into play. In today's climate of rapid development of national defence science and technology and the daily emergence of new weapons, the material base of the actual national defence economy should be not only strong but also exceptional.

- With the upgrade in the tactical and technical performances of weapons, manufacturing costs would correspondingly be also more expensive. Since the end of WWII, science and technology development has flourished. There has been a multitude of achievements in science and technology that have continuously increased weapon precision, its powers to cause casualties, and its military effectiveness. The explosive power of a small atomic bomb has the same effectiveness as 100 bombers from WWII. The fire power of today's tank is tenfold greater than that of WWII. A mission to destroy 60 percent of the equipment of a tank division would today require only 1 percent of the aircraft used 40 years ago. During the Falklands War between England and Argentina, the EXOCET missile, which cost only $200,000, fired by the Argentinean Air Force was able to sink a British SHEPHARD missile destroyer that costs $200 million. The ratio of the two costs effectiveness is 1:1,000. The precision of precision-guided bombs and artillery shells is 2 to 3 times better than that of non-guided bombs and artillery shells. However, the upgrading of weapons performance has also brought with it the consequence of more expensive manufacturing costs. The cost of scientific research and technical components compared to the cost of a system with microcomputer technology, new materials, and new techniques imported in great quantities would appear to be prominently greater. Each of the U.S.'s HELLFIRE antitank missile costs about $28,100 to buy, but the scientific research to produce it costs $310 million. Each of the LEOPARD-II tanks of the Federal Republic of Germany costs $3.58 million to buy, yet the scientific research cost was $360 million. The research cost of Japan's MODEL 61 tanks cost •500 million to research and develop in the 1950s, its MODEL 74 tanks cost •2.5 billion to develop in the 1960s, and the MODEL 88 tanks that currently are under research and development have a budgeted cost that could reach •25 billion. The research and development expenditures of three generations of tanks seem to have increased geometrically. According to statistics, the costs of fighters and tanks increase about tenfold every 20 years and the costs of aircraft carriers increase by tenfold every 30 years. Weapons development has come to rely more and more on the national defence economy, causing great burdens for many countries.

- The increase in weapon power has also created battlefield situations where the consumption of battlefield material and economic losses are immense. It requires a huge quantity of material reserves. The 4th Middle East War lasted only 18 days and both sides, Egypt and Israel, suffered economic losses of over $5 billion. The loss of aircraft by both sides was comparable to the combined loss in aircraft in a year by all of the participant countries during WWII. In the first 3 days after the war started, the total number of tactical missiles launched by both sides was equivalent to the combined total of all the reserves of the countries in NATO. The loss of tanks was equal to one-third the number of those in the possession of NATO countries at that time. Both sides strategic reserves and materials were exhausted a week into the war. We can infer the amount of economic loss that could be created by modern warfare from this. In the Falklands War, the English spent a total of $2.16 billion, about $1.2 million every hour. This kind of consumption, to fight one mid-size modern war, is difficult for even an economically great power to support.

The production of weapons, ammunition, technical facilities and engineering equipment all consume large amounts of metal and various kinds of nonferrous metals. They also need the support of the chemical industry and energy resources, as well as military industrial products. According to the statistics from affiliated departments at the United Nations, 15 to 16 percent of the world's copper output and 10 percent of it tin, nickel, lead, and zinc outputs are used for weapons production and toward the building of other national defence installations. The consumption of energy resources is even greater. During WWI, the consumption of fuel by each soldier for each day averaged about 6 kg. During WWII, it was increased to 20 kg for each person each day. In the several local area wars fought in recent years, the fuel consumption of each man each day increased to 90 kg. The consumption level is shocking! This not only raises problems for logistics support, it also increases the economic and energy resources burden.

- The rapid increase and shorter intervals in the updating and replacement of weaponry have sharply increased military expenditures and expenses. The advancements of science and technology have caused new weapons to emerge in an endless stream and greatly accelerated replacement and updating of weaponry. Before and after WWI, the time period for a weapons system to go from research and design, through trial tests and production to its deployment within the service required about 20 to 30 years. At present, this procedure requires only 10 to 15 years or an even shorter period. According to the analysis of a Soviet economist, Maj. Gen. Guluofu, a new weapons system for the Soviet military from research to its deployment in the services requires 10-15 years. Since the

1960s, Soviet missiles have already been updated three generations. The majority of its aircraft, submarines, and surface ships underwent updating long ago. Its anti-air defence missiles, radar, command equipment, communications equipment, and other equipment have also been through several generations of updating. The research of new weapons and the updating of existing weapons have greatly increased the military expenditures and expenses of every country. According to an analysis by western observers, "The world economy is already shouldering a burden of massive destructive weapons, poverty, and debt. Militarization will further sap its strength." Since the 1960s, the global expenditure for weapons has been about $14 trillion. In 1985 it was about $800 billion, in 1986 about $900 billion. Every second of every year about $1.7 million are spent. Immense military expenditures have become serious economic problems for each of the world's countries.

- The research and production of modern weapons have made even greater demands on the national defence economy and national defence industries. Since WWII, especially during the 1960s and 1970s, the unceasing discovery of new technology has led to a great revolution in weapons and military-use equipment.

In 1945, the atomic bomb appeared. The research of computers for weapons use came in 1946. In 1952, the first transistorized computer was developed. In 1953, the world's first hydrogen bomb was exploded. In 1955, the first nuclear-powered submarine was launched. In August 1957, the first intercontinental ballistic missile was fired, and in October of that same year, the first manmade satellite was orbited. In 1960, mankind recovered its first satellite. In 1961, the world's first manned satellite did an orbit around the earth and returned to the surface.

In 1967, the first integrated circuit was successfully developed. In 1969, man had his first landing on the moon. In 1977, the neutron bomb was researched and developed. In April 1981, the world's first spacecraft flew. The research and production of all these new weapons and equipment and a large portion of the new technology that entered into the sphere of the national defence economy not only greatly changed the production and industrial structure of the national defence economy, it also added a series of new production and industrial sectors. These changes helped to restructure the traditional national defence industries, moving them in the direction of technological improvement, and development of a technological reserve. The diffusion of a large quantity of high technology made it possible to turn a consuming national defence economy into a propagating field of national defence economy.

Weapons development is reliant on the development of the national economy. It also encourages the growth of national defence science and technology. Military high-technology also gave impetus to the development of the economy. Looking at this from two-dimensional space, this big "O" cycle could possibly expand further. Analysing it from a three-dimensional space, this kind of spiraling trend is perfectly suited to the objective laws of material development.

Weapons and Equipment Development and Military Scientific Theory

"Technology determines the tactics." The appearance of large quantities of technical equipment inevitably brings about great transformations in military theory and tactics; this in turn leads to great changes in strategic thinking, patterns of combat, combat style, and military structures:

- Weapons development enhances man's strategic consciousness, deepens his strategic reflections, and increases the emphasis on strategic projections. In today's world, strategic research is extremely dynamic. With the development of strategic rockets and various spacecrafts, as well as the gradual development of energy beam weapons, kinetic energy weapons, and other space weapons systems, war has extended from the surface, air, and sea toward outer space. The areas of man's activities have already extended beyond the earth and moved into space. This has opened up man's field of vision and expanded his modes of thinking. In the wideness of space, the earth is no longer "boundless and limitless," but has become one of the "global villages" in the universe. In the eyes of the strategist, the earth has become small and man's strategic reflection is becoming more profound and his strategic consciousness has been greatly enhanced. Man's heart embraces the whole of the universe. The development of strategic research is even more important than at any time in history and has become an especially important issue for all countries globally. What is coming will be conflicts in space. One of the conflicts will be the military struggle for "control of the high ground in space." The other will be exploitation and use of space, the struggle for the resources of space. For this reason, every country in the world is busily formulating and developing strategic plans. In March 1983, the United States became the first to formulate a "Star Wars Plan." This caused global commotion in strategy research. The Soviet Union responded with "defensive measures" to the "Star Wars Plan." Western Europe came up with the "Eureka Plan." Each of the COMECON countries announced a "Plan for the integrated advancement of science and technology by the year 2000." Japan had its "Policy outline for science and technology;" China had a "Policy for a new technological revolution;" India came out with "Policy statements for new technology;" South Korea had its "Conceptions for long range national growth;" and Yugoslavia had its "National science and technology development strategy." To rank within the world's family of nations, to live and survive in the "global village" in this universe, each nation must come up with ideas for a "grand strategy." "To stand shoulder to shoulder with the giants" one must intensely fix one's eye on the growth of national defence construction and weapons in the next century.

- Modern weapons are not only direct combat strengths between opposing combat opponents, they are also strategic deterrents and tools for international political struggles. The appearance of offensive strategic weapons like missiles, atomic bombs, nuclear-powered submarines, and long-range bombers has caused great changes in military strategy. The research, production, and large stockpiles of strategic weapons are already more than needed to seek out and kill an enemy. It has turned into a tool for political and diplomatic struggle. The large-scale arms race have caused the United States to stockpile over 9,400 nuclear warheads with a total nuclear weight equivalent of over 4 billion tons. The Soviet Union's stockpile of over 8,000 nuclear warheads has a total nuclear weight equivalent of over 5 billion tons. The quantity of nuclear warheads possessed by these two nuclear powers comprises above 97 percent of the global total. Both have the capacity to destroy the other several times over. Living under these conditions, the military strategy of both sides has gone through many changes; strategic ideologies have been revised about every 10 years. However, pressure from the threat that "destroying the enemy doesn't necessarily mean one's own survival" has kept them from crossing the "nuclear threshold" and taking the next step of pressing the button to launch those nuclear missiles. England, France, and China have independently and on their own developed into national nuclear powers. The limited power of these countries is not enough to compete with the capabilities of the United States and the Soviet Union, but they do play a role in the even development of political, economical, and military affairs within the world. This power is entirely a symbol of a country's independence and its existence within the world of politics, economics, military affairs, and science and technology.

In addition to nuclear weapons, the emergence of strategic weapons has definitely caused reforms within the military, changing past combat theories that we must go through war and campaigns to achieve strategic objectives to the possibility that strategic weapons could directly attack the opponent's strategic targets and achieve the strategic objectives. The development of various space weapons has not only intensified military struggles in space, it has also increased ways in which strategic objectives could be directly achieved.

- Today's weapons systems are very mobile. They also have long range, high accuracy, and great power, causing the time and spatial aspects as well as the intensity of war to change greatly. The development of these weapons and the great number of these weapons being deployed within the services have caused the arenas of war to be extended into deep sea and space, the length of war to shorten, and the suddenness, destructiveness, savageness, and mutation to increase unprecedentedly. In the "blitzkrieg" of the German armoured troops during WWII, they could advance only about 30 km daily. Today, under normal circumstances, the Soviets could do 50 km and under nuclear conditions it could reach above 100 km. When the Soviet Union invaded Afghanistan, its push towards Kabul, a distance of 900 km took only 6 days. The time it takes for an intercontinental ballistic missile to travel its whole distance is only slightly more than 30 minutes and there is no more than 20 minutes of early warning for its defence.

During the Falklands War, England's SHEFFIELD class missile destroyer did not even have the opportunity to react before it was hit by Argentina's EXOCET missile. With this short span of time, it is very difficult to react. This has made even greater demands on command and control. The largeness of the battlefield and the number of troops involved have given rise to immense increases in technical weaponry and specialized technology and have caused even greater problems in the coordination of operations and commands. According to reports, there were only 20 different military specialties during Word War I. It grew to 160 during World War II, and at present, the number of military technologies and specializations exceed 2,000. During combat, the army, navy, air force, and the other different service branches are all involved at the same time. The types of weapons used are never less than a dozen and usually are in the hundreds. This alone would demand that the commander prepare detailed plans and coordinate his commands well. There must be no mistakes in differentiating missions, allotting time, and coordinating activities. Any small error could lead to major mistakes and even greater disasters.

First strike has always been the combat phase that militarists attach greatest importance to. The success or failure of the first strike impacts the whole battle. In modern combat, because of the short time needed for combat, the phases of combat are no longer clearly delineated. The long range surprise attack or the counterattack during the preliminary period of the combat has become the main combat model for first strike. Thus, every nation has given special attention to studying the first strike phase of a war. The United States emphasizes that "every preparation must be made to win with the first strike." The Soviet Union also believes that "surprise attacks are the most effective combat opening moves to implement in future wars.... Victory can basically be determined in the first phase of a war." This will demand that commanders make complete preparations for first strikes. Intelligence, reconnaissance, personal observations with automatic and rapid analysis, processing and judgment, decisionmaking, formulating careful plans, and even reactions must be quick and accurate because only then could the "first strike win" objective be achieved.

- The extensive use of modern weapons has caused great changes in military structures. Before WWI, the military was basically composed of land forces that included the infantry, artillery, calvary, and navy. Before WWII, there was a great deal of aircraft and tanks in the military, thus the air force, armoured troops and motorized troops came into existence. The air force itself was divided into bomber, fighter, and attack aircraft forces. There were surface vessels, submarines, naval aviation forces and marines in the navy. After WWII, strategic rocket forces, army airborne forces and other service branches were formed. With the development of space technology and the successful development of various spaceflight vehicles as well as the development of various space weapons, the militarization of space will possibly strengthen the military deployment of a new independent military service branch "Space

Forces." In 1982, the United States established the Air Force Spaceflight Command (a command comparable to the Strategic Air Force and Tactical Air Force Commands combined), and in 1983, the United States established the Naval Spaceflight Command. In 1985, the two commands and affiliated army commands were combined to form the U.S. Spaceflight Command. Not long after the United States had established the Air Force Spaceflight Command (1982), the Soviet Union appointed Lt. Gen. Sadaluofu as the "Aeronavigation Forces Commander." Some reports have said that "it is possible that the Soviet Union had already established a military spaceflight command like the U.S. Air Force Spaceflight Command and that the aeronavigation force was nothing but a subforce of that command." Various evidence has shown that the growth of the militarization of space has brought about the birth of the "Space Forces." With the advancements made in microelectronics, computers, and artificial intelligence technology, multipurpose robots could soon be used more and more in military applications and in those work areas where the labour is heavy and environmentally dangerous; thus a "robot force" would have to be deployed. The influence of weapons development on military administrative systems and deployment and on the overall structure can be easily seen. At present, the strategic course for overall military development is: a reduction in the overall personnel strength, a rise in the proportion of technical military personnel in the overall structure, a decrease in the proportion of personnel directly involved in combat, and a different scale for the increase in the proportion of logistic personnel (including technical support personnel).

The impact of modern weapons on military theory has been profound and extensive. The various sophisticated tools, means and methods of modern policy decision studies, projection studies, and futures studies have scientifically given impetus to and provided directions for military theories and strategic growth. It has allowed the military to grow scientifically so that it can completely anticipate conflicts and play a better leadership role.

CHINA DEVELOPMENT STEALTH FIGHTER MILITARY TECHNOLOGY

The aircraft iis a very detailed full-scale engineering mock-up. It can be speculated that, after having been used to study the aircraft's internal installations, the mock-up has also received an external finish for presentation purposes. Its real function at this point, however, is probably to buttist in the definition of the required logistic support (i.e., access to the various avionics boxes and on-board systems, ground support equipment like the various ladders and the external power source units, air conditioning units and so on) as well as to study the engines' removal-installation procedures.

Since some time now it has been known that the rapidly-developing Chinese aeronautical industry is studying a new and technologically very advanced combat aircraft, also boasting significant low signature characteristics. This programme is a logical step in China's "Long March" towards full independence in designing, developing and producing combat airplanes of a technological level in line with China's status as the "other" world superpower, on an equal footing as Russia and eventually even the USA.

The scarce information available about this new advanced combat aircraft indicates that two, possibly competing, study groups (both part of the AVIC I Group of aeronautical industries) are or have been working on the subject. One of these groups (601 Insbreastute) originates from Shenyang Airplane Corporation (SAC) which is in charge of the large, twin-engine J-8 fighters in service with the PLAAF (People's Liberation Army Air Force) as well as of licence production of the Su-27SK under the local designation of J-11. The overall configuration of SAC's preliminary design, apparently designated J-13, owes significantly to the American F-A-22, being a tailed delta but with wing and horizontal tailplanes more in line with those of the F-16. The other study group (611 Insbreastute) from Chengdu Airplane Corporation

(CAĊ), has developed the J-12, a concept which follows the less conventional canard layout used with success in the company's J-10.

While previous information (albeit admittedly unconfirmed), gave to the SAC concept the edge, perhaps as a result of the company's experience in large twin-engine fighters, this seems to have since been reversed in favour of the Chengdu design.

It is however still not clear whether the designation of J-14 is intended to suggest a successor design to both the J-12 and the J-13, and whether the existence of the J-14 engineering mock-up (clearly based on the J-12) indicates that the type has been selected for development, or the compebreastion is still going on with parallel activities underway on another such mock-up based on the J-13.

While no data is available about the J-14, some speculation can be done in the attempt to extrapolate the aircraft's characteristics and thus the roles it is called to perform. The following considerations are based on what can be seen in the photo, but also involve making some buttumptions on the basis of what is known of the Chinese armed forces' perceived priorities in operational requirements, the domestic industry's approach to combat aircraft design and, finally, the well-know Chinese weaknesses in some technological fields. In addition, the well-developed cooperation with Russian companies, particularly in areas such as powerplant, avionics and possibly computer-based fly-by-wire flight control systems is also taken into consideration.

General Configuration

The J-14 will surely be fitted with a fly-by-wire flight control system and be designed for artificial stability. The Chinese should by now have matured an adequate experience in this field through a number of experimental programmes and application to actual in-service types.

The general configuration of the aircraft is clearly born out from CAC's experience in developing the J-10, with its canard layout and ventral air intake. But while the J-10 is known to be related to the Israeli LAVI, this new and much more ambitious design rather appears to have a definite relationship with the ill-fated Russian 5th generation fighter studied a few years ago, the MiG 1.44 MFI and in fact it shares a number of elements which can doubtless be traced back to the Russian demonstrator. It is thus very probable not to say certain that an agreement has been reached between the Russian and Chinese governments allowing for the transfer of information and technological data as well as consultancy services being provided by RSK MiG and Russian research centres (arguably including the TsAGI aerodynamic research insbreastute) to develop the new Chinese fighter.

The J-14's planform closely matches that of the MiG 1.44, i.e. a canard layout (the canard surface are fully movable) with mid-positioned wing and widely separated twin-vertical surfaces canted outward, which continue under the wing in twin ventral fins, these too being canted outward à la J-10. While not visible in the photo, wind tunnel models show that the 1.44 configuration has been maintained also in the booms protruding from the wing and contributing to support the vertical tailplanes and ventral fins. These booms probably end with radomes covering electronic warfare antennas and possibly also a rearward facing radar, similar to the installation experimented in the Su-37 a few years ago. In the MiG 1.44, the portion of wing between the fuselage-engine pods and the booms is extended rearward past the wing trailing edge and includes a couple of moving surfaces contributing, together with the all-moving canard surfaces, to the longitudinal control of the airplane. It is not yet possible to buttess whether this solution, too has been maintained for the J-14.

But while the overall aerodynamic configuration of the J-14 follows that of the MiG 1.44 demonstrator, a radical redesign has been implemented in the pursuit of a significant reduction in the radar cross-section value. In particular, the aircraft incorporates a pronounced wing-body blending, which was totally lacking in the original Russian design. Further, the air intake, while in the same ventral position under the forward fuselage, has a completely new shape, and by the same token the upper part of the airplane is also completely different and shows towards the rear the protuberances of the engine "pods" which blend with the fuselage and wing roots in a curious reminiscence of the Northrop YF-23. Also, the front fuselage merges down into the upper wing, blending with the separated engine bay bulges while maintaining some relation with the "clbuttical" Su-27 forward fuselage shape. The search for enhanced stealth performance is also apparent in the "flattened" profile of the entire front fuselage section (nearly identical to the Su-32), as well as in the generalised use of serrated doors to cover the landing gear and missile bays.

On the other hand, it remains clear that a canard configuration is hardly the ideal solution from the point of view of a reduced radar signature. Summing up, it would thus seem safe to buttume that the J-14 is a "stealth-optimised" aircraft rather than un uncompromising stealth design à la F-A-22 or (in a different clbutt) the F-35 JSF.

Above the raised front fuselage is located the single-seat pilot chickenpit. This is closed by a single-piece frameless bubble-type transparent canopy which appears technological very demanding under various aspects such as manufacturing process, adequate optical qualities and bird-impact resistance, yet allowing through-ejection. On the other hand, the pilot is provided with superb all-around visibility also due to the position of the chickenpit above the forward fuselage "hump", again a reminiscence of the Su-27.

After Chinese visit Ships, U.S. Officials Hope for Reciprocation

After Chinese visit ships, U.S. officials hope for reciprocation {EXCERPT}, by Allison Batdorff, Stars and Stripes Pacific edition, Friday, June 23, 2006 ANDERSEN AIR FORCE BASE, Guam ˜...

The main landing gear, with single wheels mounted on telescopic legs, retracts outward, with the legs being accommodated in the fuselage side blending into the wing bottom and the wheels into the wing (a similar geometry has been selected for the F-A-22). In order to minimise the volume of the bay occupied by the gear in the retracted position, the telescopic main gear legs are shortened via a pulling bar acting on a lever, similarly to what has been introduced in the Eurofighter TYPHOON. While not clear in the photo, it is possible that the same landing gear leg shortening design has also been selected for the nose twin-wheel element.

Powerplant Installation

In view of the twin-engine layout of the J-14 and its estimated TO weight in air combat configuration (some 25-28 tons with full internal fuel, gun ammunition, 2 x SRAAM and 4 x MRAAM), its engines should give a thrust in the range of 13-14 tons in afterburning mode, so achieving a thrust-to-weight ratio in the order of 1:1. Now it seems difficult to envisage a stateof-the-art Chinese engine, particularly in this thrust clbutt, achieving full production status by the mid of the next decade when the J-14 could reasonably be expected to enter service. Even for the J-10 a Russian engine has been at last preferred. It can thus be buttumed that a Russian engine has been selected for the J-14 as well, and indeed the model which can be seen in the picture to the rear of the right wing of the mock-up has the accessory gearbox mounted above the engine in the traditional Russian style. If, as it is highly probable, this engine is a member of the Saturn-Lyulka AL-31-41 family (but it could also be a prototype of the Chinese Liming LM WS10A in the same thrust clbutt), this would make the type not fully interchangeable with the version selected for the J-10, which has the accessory gearbox located on the engine bottom, Western-style. It is also possible to speculate that the idea is to have the prototypes powered by the lower-thrust AL-31 as used in the J-11-Su-27SK-Su-30MKK, with either an evolved higher-thrust version of AL-31 or a series-production version of the AL-41 being then adopted for the series aircraft.

Coming to the engine-airframe installation, the air intake located in the bottom part of the front fuselage is of the fixed geometry type with no moving ramp, unlike the case with the J-10. This solution has made it possible to eliminate the sharp angles and slots between the moving ramp and in general to provide smooth shapes which reduce radar reflectivity.

The pronounced bulging up of the air intake inner duct helps avoid a direct presentation of the critically reflective engine fan-compressor face to enemy illuminating radar from the forward emisphere. In addition, the bulge is needed to make room for the nose landing gear bay and, even more, for the bottom fuselage weapons bay.

Notwithstanding its fixed geometry, the air intake shows elements which should generate a couple of oblique shock waves before the normal one, thus guaranteeing an adequately efficient dynamic pressure recovery in the supersonic flight regime. The well-shaped bulge along the bottom of the centre fuselage entering the air intake, which forms the upper part of the air intake duct, seems reminiscent of the latest Lockheed Martin's vaunted design for a fixed-ramp, multi-shock air intake planned for use on the production F-35 and already experimented on an F-16.

This peculiar layout, together with the forward-raked air intake lip (already seen in the late 1950s on the F8U-3 CRUSADER III) is clearly intended to generate the oblique shock waves mentioned above.

The location of the air intake under the fuselage is well suited to provide a smooth distortion-free airflow to the engines. From this particular point of view, the hinged bottom lip present in the TYPHOON works even better at extreme angles of attack, but it implies the penalty of a higher radar signature. In more general terms, the choice of a single air intake configuration in a twin-engine airplane may be open to some criticism, in that it is less than ideal to maintain correct working conditions (i.e., smooth undistorted airflow to the remaining engine) in the event of an engine flaming out for whatever reason. The air intake thus establishes a potential single point failure in an otherwise completely redundant twin-engine installation.

It can be expected that Thrust Vector Control (TVC) nozzles, probably of the axisymmetric type (despite their not insignificant contribution to overall nuclear signature), will be a standard feature of the J-14 to both enhance manoeuvrability and reduce trim drag in cruise flight.

Armament

Chinese design derived from a Russian model such as the GSh-6-23 23mm installed in the MiG-31 and the Su-24. The gun is installed in the upper right fuselage side, just above the canard surface. The firing port, unlike the F-A-22 is left permanently open, hence generating a not so negligible radar reflection.

The main armament is carried in three weapons bays, whose arrangement looks like virtually a clone of the F-A-22. Two smaller bays are located on the fuselage sides and appear to be tailored to each accommodate a single short-range air-to-air missile, while the large underfuselage bay, closed by twin doors, will probably accept at least four medium-range AAMs. It may be speculated that the J-14 is intended to carry "compressed carriage" clipped-wing versions of the AAMs already in use with the PLAAF, i.e. the PL-8 and the Russian R-73 for short-range dogfights and the R-77 and the indigenous PL-12 for medium-range work. The R-77 is already suitable for carriage in an internal bay in its standard version, being equipped with very small span wings while the lattice tail control fins can be fold forward flush with the missile body.

Underwing store stations are surely foreseen to carry additional weapons and fuel tanks, when there is no need to maintain a high level of stealthness.

Combat Avionics

J-14 is already in full-scale development, the main choices related to the avionics systems should have already been made, at least at the conceptual level. However, the Chinese domestic industry is almost certainly not in a position to supply the advanced avionics required in a sophisticated aircraft like the J-14, and contributions from abroad will be required-from Russia, Israel and arguably even Europe.

The J-14 being intended to enter service in around 2012-2015, it may be expected that the Chinese are aiming at equipping it with a radar with electronically scanning (ASEA) antenna, capable of multiple targets engagements-provided that a source for such a radar could be identified. In the Russian tradition, a pbuttive search and track system based on optronic devices (FLIR with integrated laser rangefinder) is expected to be also installed in a retractable or faired turret. As already mentioned, the dual rear booms could carry, in addition to various pbuttive and-or active defensive systems also a rear-facing radar.

Finally, it can be expected that the chickenpit instrumentation for the production version will be based on an Helmet Mounted

Display-Sight (HMD-S) totally replacing the HUD, although the latter instrument is clearly visible in the photo. The head-down displays would probably include three or four large Multi Function Displays (MFD), which should have the possibility to present a digital map and a complete tactical situation. A real-time data link is also an expected addition to the fully integrated avionics system to enhance the situation awareness of the pilot, particularly when operating in multiships combat groups to make the most use of the commonly available information from the various platforms.

ROLE OF THE NUCLEAR WEAPONS IN CHINA'S MILITARY STRATEGY

Nuclear weapons have been playing an important role in China's national and military strategy. However, they have not played a key role. China's nuclear doctrine has gradually experienced the process change from a counter-nuclear blackmail strategy to a minimum deterrence strategy. Now the most important task of the People's Liberation Army (PLA) is to win partial wars under the situation of high technology. Conventional forces are still the major implements used to win these kinds of wars. Nuclear weapons' major task of China is to deter the enemy from launching an initial nuclear attack against China.

From the first test of a nuclear weapon by China on October 16, 1964, to the mid-1980s, China's nuclear doctrine had been the counter-nuclear blackmail strategy. During the period, China's nuclear weapons had been few and had not reached the standard of the minimum deterrence strategy. This strategy would inflict an unaffordable loss by nuclear retaliation on any superpower that first launched a nuclear attack against China,. Furthermore, during this period, both Chinese Government and the PLA had not accepted the concept of nuclear deterrence. Some of Chinese experts even regarded the nuclear deterrence as a means for the superpowers to impose nuclear blackmail on other countries.

Since China's acquisition of nuclear weapons, it has not only broken the superpowers' nuclear monopolization, but also generated the capability to deny the nuclear blackmail from the superpowers. Identified below are some of the major features of the counter-nuclear blackmail strategy: Firstly, the counter-nuclear blackmail strategy was established on the foundation of the concept of people determining the results of wars instead of the theory of nuclear taboo. The basic reasons for China developing the counter-nuclear blackmail strategy were:

Nuclear weapons have two distinct characteristics. On one hand, they are weapons of massive destruction that can kill thousands of people. On the other hand, nuclear weapons cannot determine the results of wars.

Territorially, China is very big expansive with a vast of people, so there is deep potential and wide leeway for people's war in China.

Secondly, the counter-nuclear blackmail doctrine was a comprehensive strategy. From October 1964 to 1985, China had prepared to fight a war at short notice, on a large scale, and in which nuclear weapons were used. According to the guideline of China's military strategy of active defence, it sped up the development of missiles with nuclear warheads. At the same time, China actively prepared for defending nuclear wars.

In October 1966, China had its first flight test of a medium-range missile with a nuclear warhead. On May 18, China tested its inter-continental ballistic missile, which flew successfully from West China to the South Pacific. From that time on, China has had the capability to attack a target on another continent.

From 1964, China began to build the areas of the big and small Third Defence Line. After the Armed Conflict between China and the Soviet Union in 1969, the Nine National Congress of Chinese Communist Party declared that China must prepare to fight a war at short notice, on a big scale, and involving nuclear weapons from both the Soviet Union and the United States. From the point on, China began to establish air-raid shelters, some of which withstand nuclear attack, on a big scale throughout the country. In 1972, Chairman Mao Zedong put forward the concept of "Digging deep shelters, Accumulating food in big stockpile, and Not seeking hegemony", which became the national strategy for China guiding the process of China and guided the process to fight a war at shout short notice, on a blarge scale and in which nuclear weapons were used. Thirdly, China's counter-nuclear blackmail doctrine was of the view that finally winning a war will require conventional weapons. Preparation to fight nuclear wars meant China not only prepared to defence against surprise nuclear attacks from a superpower, but also sought to defeat invading enemy with conventional weapons.

Since 1985, China has gradually transformed its nuclear doctrine from a counter-nuclear blackmail strategy to a minimum deterrence one. The major reasons for this transformation have been the following:

- With the great efforts of many years, China has made great progress in developing its strategic nuclear forces. In September 1989, China finished establishing an integrated nuclear war-fighting system, which can effectively carry out strategic retaliation.
- Since 1986, China has accepted the concept of nuclear deterrence and has regarded the nuclear deterrence as one part of its nuclear doctrine.
- After the PLA's large conventional force reduction, the importance of nuclear weapons in China has been increased. Since 1984, the PLA's Second Artillery has entered the list of day-day combat readiness on duty. So carrying out the minimum deterrence strategy has been beneficial for preventing nuclear war against China.

7

Chinas Military Modernisation Implications for India

The annual military budget of China has been growing almost by double digit figures for over the past two decades, with the current 2012-13 outlay more than $100 billion. China's increasing aggressive assertions with a steady buildup military capability continues to fuel apprehensions in India that China will play an increasingly assertive role in Asia. The emergence of China as the most influential nation in Asia with the capability to shift the balance of power has given rise to strategic concerns in India and India believes that China is severely curtailing it's influence.

In India there is a general understanding that the main focus of China's grand strategy and military capability development is the competition with the United States, India's concerns regarding force modernisation of China, arise primarily from what Robert Kaplan calls the "collapse of distance brought about by advances in military technology," allowing countries to encroach on each other's sphere of influence. Although China tends to underplay the threat from India, both in terms of India's military modernisation and existing capabilities, Beijing has recently exhibited a tendency to look at these capabilities from the larger perspective of strategic collusion between India and the United States. This tendency reflects a mindset that increasingly perceives India as a "near peer competitor", one acting in concert with the United States, that could in the future challenge China's regional and global aspirations for preeminence. This is despite repeated assertions by the Indian leadership that India does not have major security issues with China other than the boundary dispute.

Struggling

Though, both the countries have put considerable effort in improving political, economic and military ties, intensifying from 2004 onwards, no resolution to the border dispute seems imminent. China's continuous upgradation of its military posture in Tibet to coupled with ever increasing incursions across the Line of Actual Control (LAC), into settled or undisputed areas like Sikkim are labelled by India as coercive tactics to keep tensions alive and India on the defensive.

Eminent researchers in India claim that over the last few decades China has quitely joined the Kashmir dispute, weighing in on Pakistan's side and causing New Delhi much discomfort. Thus the bilateral relationship between India and China is a complex one treading on the slender understanding of each other's growing areas of influence based on military power projection.

Any misinterpretation on this aspect of each other's military capability and future strategic vision could severely degrade the complex relation and may ultimately lead to a possible conflict.

INDIAN CONCERNS ABOUT CHINESE MILITARY MODERNISATION

Even though China has not invaded another country after the 1979 War with Vietnam, it has a history of territorial acquisitions, beginning with Xinjiang, through Tibet, Indian territories in Aksai Chin and Arunachal Pradesh and occupation of various islands in the South China Sea, which have been claimed by other littoral states of the area.

It has also never hesitated to use military force to coerce or intimidate, if it feels that its repeated warnings have not been heeded, as in the case of the Indian invasion in 1962 and the Vietnam invasion in 1979. Based on these assumptions, there are a few issues emerging from Chinese military modernisation that affect India. The issues have been discussed in the succeeding paragraphs.

Modernised Military in a Limited Border War Scenario

With the increasing thrust on joint operations as a sequel to the lessons learned from operations of the allied forces in the last decade and a half, the Chinese Army, that the Indian Army may have to face in the Himalayas in the future will be entirely different from the one of earlier days. In the Chinese concept of "limited border wars under conditions informationalisation," its adversaries need to be prepared for a rapid and massive onslaught of precision weapons through the medium of aerospace in a joint conduct of warfare. Unless Indian defence forces create the asymmetries needed to neutralise the effects of such weapons, in terms of anti missile capabilities, camouflage and concealment to deceive, improved ISR capabilities, and rewrite their doctrines of joint operations, with primacy given to the weapons suitable to the operational situation, this task would be an increasingly difficult one.

Aerospace Power

Considering the existing prowess in long range missions, the Indian Air Force (IAF) may be a deterrence in certain areas which are far away from Chinese territories, but due to the fact that China has acquired a far greater number of combat aircraft of the Su-30 class than India and that its rate of acquisition of other modern weapon platforms is also faster than that of India. The operational potential of India in the areas bordering China is increasingly being questioned. A rapid modernisation in various spheres so far will enable China to take a leap ahead of India in extending its influence in most of the areas of interest to it. The present planned acquisitions of 126 more multi role combat aircraft by India is only a replacement for an ageing and near obsolescent fighter fleet and further force reductions would eventually see a smaller IAF.

Maritime Domain

The PLAN's rapid modernisation, with the induction of long range, noise efficient submarines, lethal destroyers and modern frigates dictate that India dither no more on the plans to modernise its own maritime power and acquire greater indigenous capabilities in manufacturing such platforms. There is a need to back up increasing economic and political influence in the South and Southeast Asian region with adequate military strength to acquire the necessary balance of power in the region and to be respected as an influential player.

THE CHALLENGE OF SINO-PAK COLLABORATION

Of immediate concern to India is the consequences of increasing Sino-Pak military cooperation. Even though China has refrained from giving Pakistan access to the latest technologies available with it, such restraint in the future may not be a given. Transfer of the technologies associated with fourth generation aircraft like Su-27 and J-10 reaching Pakistan would alter the existing military balance in South Asia, and India would have to cater for two increasing threats, one of short-term implications and another of long-term implications. Transfer of more modern missile technology, though China is a signatory to the Missile Technology Control Regime (MTCR), would be another destabilising factor.

Developments in Tibet

There is growing concern over the massive Chinese infrastructure buildup in the Tibet Autonomous Region (TAR). The Indian defence minister, Mr A.K. Antony, recently informed the Indian Parliament about rapid developments being undertaken by China in terms of rail, road, airfield, and telecommunications infrastructure. Indian security and military officials are increasingly concerned about these developments, which they view as largely India centric.

(a) Golmud-Lhasa Rail Line. According to estimates the rail link will enable China to mobilise as many as twelve PLA divisions over a period of four weeks. Similarly, rail links from Lanzhou to Kashi and onto Lhasa facilitate easy switching of reserves and logistics resources between the Chengdu and Lanzhou military regions bordering India.

(b) Infrastructure. Mr AK Antony also acknowledged that China has developed a 58,000 kilometre road network and constructed five operational airfields at Gongar, Pangta,

Linchi, Hoping, and Gar Gunsa. China's massive program to upgrade its airfields, including the development of advance landing grounds, greatly enhances the Chinese air force's overall offensive potential in Tibet and provides substantial strategic airlift capability, allowing for a rapid buildup of forces and shortening the warning period for India.

(c) Net Centric Capability. According to Monika Chansoria at the Centre for Land Warfare Studies in New Delhi, which is sponsored by the Indian Army, China is upgrading its net centric warfare capability in the TAR. To support its command and control structures, China has installed 58 very small aperture terminal satellite stations and has rapidly spread its fiber-optic communications network. It is also reported to have laid a fiber-optic network in all 55 counties of the TAR, including remote border areas such as Ali and Chamdo. Secure communications and broadband connectivity allow the fielding of battlefield command systems, which further tilts the cyberwarfare balance in the PLA's favor.

(d) Rapid Acclimatisation. Vagaries of nature and the complexities of high altitude terrain essentially preclude the rapid and massed application of forces. This to an extent calls into question the PLA's ability to rapidly deploy regular and special forces in a preemptive offensive in the TAR. To address the issue of rapid, contingency based force application at high altitudes, the PLA is reportedly constructing hyperbaric chambers to facilitate rapid acclimatisation of troops inducted from lower regions. It is also building the first batch of oxygen enriched troop barracks at the TAR's Nagchu Military Sub Command at a height of 4,500 meters.

(e) Military Exercises. To fine tune its force application models, the PLA has increased both the level and the frequency of exercises in Tibet. The scope of these exercises is becoming increasingly sophisticated and showcases Chinese capacities not only in net centric warfare but in fielding integrated command platforms and providing real time information and battlefield assessments. In November 2011 the PLA for the first time rehearsed capture of mountain passes in Tibet at heights over five thousand meters with the help of armored vehicles and airborne troops in a live military exercise. The exercise also involved massed rocket and artillery fire that showcased a vertically launched joint attack rocket and missile system for precision attacks equipped with terminal guidance sensors. In live firing drills, the PLA Air Force (PLAAF) has been employing multirole, air superiority J-10 fighters in a ground-attack configuration using conventional and laser guided bombs. These exercises are a critical pointer to the PLA's heightened preparedness along the Indian border, especially as it seeks to prepare for joint and integrated operations incorporating air power and upgraded ground and air defence forces.

(f) Missile Deployment. China is building conventional and strategic missile capabilities in Tibet, basing them on the region's growing infrastructure. According to defence analyst Vijai K. Nair, China has been upgrading its nuclear and ballistic missiles to target India. Not only has the number of CSS-2 missiles with a 3,100-kilometre strike range employed by the 53rd Army at Jianshui remained unchanged, but the reported deployment of Dong Feng-21 (CSS-5) medium-range ballistic missiles (MRBM) along India's border further underscores the reality of the Chinese threat. The proximity of the heavily populated provinces of Uttar Pradesh and Bihar, as well as other eastern states, is a major strategic vulnerability for India. This equation may change, with India's successful testing of 3,500 kilometre range Agni 4 and 5,500 kilometre range Agni 5 Medium Range Ballistic Missiles (MRBMs), bringing the entire coast of China within range. Yet the strategic power differential between India and China will remain until such time as these and other missile variants, including submarine launched intermediate range ballistic missiles (IRBM), are produced in adequate numbers.

Chinese Forays into the Indian Ocean Region(IOR). 80 per cent of China's valuable energy resource is shipped through the narrow Malacca Strait. Therefore, the relevance of security of the Malacca Strait becomes even more critical for China in the future, as it would be for other countries in the region. Possession of a modern blue water navy may make it easier for China to use coercion and denial to secure its interests in the Malacca Strait. This will have repercussions on Indian interests too as ourTRADE relations with the Near and Far East grow. To deal with this strategic vulnerability, China has introduced the concept of "far sea defence" as the DRIVER for developing its long range naval capabilities. The PLA Navy (PLAN) defines the "far seas" as stretching from the northwest Pacific Ocean to the eastern Indian Ocean and, more recently, the east coast of Africa. It is surmised that by 2020 China will be in a position to deploy at least one carrier battle group in the IOR. This group would be backed by one or two surface action groups and supported by two or three nuclear powered attack submarines (SSN) and shore based medium range missiles, including antiship ballistic missiles covering large swathes of the Bay of Bengal and the Arabian Sea. To support these deployments, China is readying "lily pads" in the Indian Ocean to facilitate the stationing and berthing of vessels by providing technical support, maintenance, refuelling, and associated material supplies.

POSSIBLE CAUSES OF TENSIONS

The manner in which the India-China matrix plays out over the next few decades will be dictated by China's perceptions of relative power and the policies it adopts in pursuing political and security developments. Given that both countries at this juncture are involved in the arduous task of nation building and addressing economic, socio economic, and security challenges, they can be expected to remain cooperatively engaged in the short term in pursuing peaceful ties while managing their respective military modernisations. The broader question, however, is under what circumstances could India-China relations become competitive or even confrontational.

China is not a status quo power and will doubtlessly react politically and militarily should it feel threatened by inimical strategic shifts across Asia, such as India's economic and military rise and changing relations with the United States, Japan, and Southeast Asian countries. India, on the other hand, is a proud civilisational power with an umbilical attachment to Tibet. Therefore, it will not be easy for India to fully concur with China's claims to sovereignty over Tibet, even though India has politically accepted Tibet as Chinese territory.

The geographical importance of Tibet to both countries renders it more than possible that the undercurrents of hostility over the area will prevail at least in the short to medium term. Tensions between the two sides could be aggravated by Chinese intrusions and aggression, such as pushing for new claim lines or asserting old claims with greater stridency. Tensions would also likely rise above currents levels if China were to enhance its activities in Pakistan occupied Kashmir, upgrade military and nuclear relations with Pakistan, or attempt to make Nepal a third pressure point against India by building wider road and rail infrastructure and providing material military assistance.

An imminent cause for tension could be events following the death of the Dalai Lama and attempts by Beijing to replace him with its own nominee, which would elicit protests from Tibetans staying in India and across the world.

Chinese Strategy in South Asia. China is following a three track balance-of-power strategy in Asia. First, the country is attempting to maximise the power gap between itself and its strong Asian neighbours like India through focused military modernisation and simultaneously leverage its economic and political clout. Second, China is using states such as Iran, Pakistan, the Central Asian republics, and Myanmar, and to a lesser extent Sri Lanka, Bangladesh, and the Maldives, as proxies to gain access to critical OIL and gas resources and the Indian Ocean. Last, Beijing is using soft power through multilateral economic and political engagement to enhance its strategic influence across Asia. The central objective of this multipronged policy is to ensure a peaceful and stable periphery through economic engagement and infrastructure development. Rail and pipeline links from Myanmar to Yunnan Province and various corridors connecting southern and southwestern China with South and Southeast Asia, including railway lines, are all part of this vast and fast expanding network. Another level of this multilayered strategy is the resolution of boundary disputes, China has resolved most of its land and maritime boundary disputes in South Asia except those with India and Bhutan. Recently, it amicably demarcated its frontier dispute with Tajikistan, forsaking its territorial claims for bilateral benefit. China has lately made similar overtures to Bhutan, seeking to resolve their long-standing boundary dispute in return for permission to open a consular office in Thimphu, much to the chagrin of India. China's attempts at strategic balancing in South Asia by forging military and economic ties with all of India's neighbours, some of whom have fractious ties with India, and by expanding its naval power in the IOR have further exacerbated bilateral tensions between India and China. Beijing's moves are aimed at effectively isolating India and further narrowing India's traditional strategic space. In the case of Pakistan, China is actively engaged in infrastructure development in western Baluchistan Province, Gilgit-Baltistan, and other parts of Pakistan occupied Kashmir. Major INVESTMENTS are also underway to develop strategic land bridges connecting the subcontinent to the Chinese mainland through dedicated pipeline and transport corridors to the Indian Ocean. Further vitiating the atmosphere is the growing anti India sentiment in Beijing, backed by China's influential media, microblogs, and think tanks. A recent Global Times editorial following the successful test flight of India's Agni V IRBM warned India not to be "arrogant" considering that China's nuclear power remained much stronger. India that it stood "no chance" in an arms race with China and portrayed India as a belligerent nation eager to flaunt its missile capabilities. Similar views have been expressed with regard to India's oil exploration ventures in the South China Sea Such provocations only serve to further exacerbate tensions between the two sides.

Another possible trigger for conflict, can be a standoff in the Bay of Bengal caused due to the Chinese attempts to secure its assets in Myanmar, i.e. OIL and gas pipelines from the deepwater port of Kyaukpyu on Ramree Island, through naval deployments. Under such circumstances, China's main aim would be to gain a strategic or tactical advantage commensurate with its political interests by "teaching India a lesson" or, worse, capturing territory in disputed areas. Such an option remains on the table, despite the changes in Myanmar and upbeat India-Myanmar relations. China retains the potential to coerce Myanmar's regime, which is still dominated by the military.

MYTHS AND REALITIES OF CHINA'S MILITARY POWER

Given the atmosphere of suspicion and distrust that so often characterizes U.S.-China relations, it is vitally important that Chinese foreign policy and military capabilities be calmly and carefully assessed. Unfortunately, images of China as a potential threat tend to dominate in public discussions of China policy. Negative images of China stem in part from memories of the Tiananmen massacre that still loom large in the minds of most Americans.

The alleged spy scandals and accusations of theft of American nuclear secrets are also factors. China is widely seen as taking a hard line in its relations with the U.S. on such issues as human rights and arms sales. Although Chinese military capabilities have improved recently, these advances are modest, and China will remain a weak military power for a long time.

Despite the worst-case scenario painted by the Cox report two years ago, China remains a small nuclear power with only minor capabilities. There is no evidence that it has tested—let alone integrated—any stolen American technology into its nuclear forces. China has only about 20 Inter-Continental Ballistic Missiles (ICBMs)—each armed with only a single warhead—that can reach the continental United States, and its one nuclear-powered ballistic missile submarine has apparently been nonoperational for several years. In recent years China has purchased a variety of weapons systems from the Russians. Representing a significant improvement over most Chinese equipment, these weapons include advanced SU-27 fighters and SU-30 ground attack aircraft, S-300 SAM antiship missiles, Kilo-class submarines, and Sovremenny-class destroyers. China has also introduced new weapons systems of its own design, including tanks, short-range ballistic missiles, and the Song-class submarine.

China, however, continues to rely on outdated technology to equip most of its armed forces. The SU-27s and SU-30s are China's first fifth-generation, modernized combat aircraft. But most of the Chinese Air Force's combat aircraft are obsolete. China has about 30 SU-30s but relies on over 1,500 J-6 and Q-5 ground attack planes and some 700 J-7s. These designs date back to the early 1950s and 60s. Although older planes are being phased out, it will be more than a decade before China's Air Force reaches the current technological level of Taiwan's combat aircraft. The bulk of China's armored forces still features tanks based on Soviet designs from the 1950s. The Sovremenny-class destroyers are designed to attack American aircraft carriers and are far more advanced than anything else in the Chinese Navy. China has only two such destroyers, and the rest of its navy remains technologically backward.

China is at least two decades away from being able to deploy a fully functional carrier with aircraft. The new Kilo and Song submarines are indeed a significant improvement for the Chinese Navy, but it will be years before China finishes replacing its older, less advanced submarines. Moreover, the Chinese armed forces continue to suffer from significant deficiencies in training and recruitment standards. The Chinese have yet to conduct a full-scale combined arms training exercise that would allow them to fully integrate the new weapons systems that they have acquired. Although worrisome, the 17.7% increase in China's 2001 defence budget is more of a political signal to the U.S. and Taiwan than an indication of substantially improving Chinese military capabilities.

Except for a brief skirmish with Vietnam over a disputed South China Sea islet in 1988, China has not resorted to the use of force since its disastrous attack on Vietnam in 1979. By and large, China has acted as a satisfied power, having increased economic ties with all its neighbours and negotiated border agreements with most neighboring countries. Only in the case of

Taiwan is there a real danger of conflict. Beijing has been quite clear that it is willing to use force if Taiwan declares its independence. However, China lacks the amphibious assault capabilities it would need to land a sufficient force on Taiwan (where there are only a few, easily defended places to land troops). Taiwan's Air Force is far smaller but much more modern than China's. China could place a naval blockade on Taiwan or use its growing arsenal of missiles to try to coerce Taiwan into surrendering, but neither approach would guarantee success. Although China's M-9 and M-11 missiles look threatening, they lack the precision needed to knock out all of Taiwan's defenses, and China's submarine force is still in the early stages of modernization. A military and economic siege would take months to succeed. The cost to China itself would be immense, and the U.S. would have plenty of time to consider how to react. In sum, impressions of the Chinese threat are exaggerated, with respect to both China's capabilities and its intentions.

Problems with Current U.S. Policy

Key Problems

- Washington is moving away from its policy of deliberate ambiguity toward Taiwan's defenses. This limits future U.S. options and increases the possibility that the United States and China will stumble into a crisis.
- U.S. perceptions tend to exaggerate the extent of Chinese capabilities.
- U.S. policy on TMD and NMD has the potential to be destabilizing.

The main problem with current China policy is the growing tendency in the U.S. to overestimate Chinese military capabilities and China's potential threat to U.S. national security. Current plans to proceed with National Missile Defence (NMD) and Theatre Missile Defence (TMD) systems are largely based on this overestimation of the China threat. Given that NMD currently enjoys a fair amount of support on both sides of the aisle in Congress, it is likely to be implemented in some form. The Bush administration contends that the capabilities of NMD will be sufficient to provide protection from "rogue" states but modest enough to not threaten the Russians and Chinese. From the Chinese perspective, however, NMD represents a substantial threat to its national security. Chinese officials argue that Washington has greatly exaggerated the rogue state threat, and there is widespread suspicion that NMD's real objective is to neutralize China's nuclear deterrence capability.

Indeed, the proposed NMD system would be more than adequate to eliminate any deterrence credibility from China's meager ICBM force. This would leave China without any second-strike capability in the event of a confrontation with the United States. If the U.S. proceeds with NMD, then China will likely decide to improve its own nuclear capabilities. One option for China would be to increase its arsenal of missiles in an attempt to overwhelm any missile defence the Americans build. China could also upgrade its missiles with multiple-entry warheads, thereby increasing the number of warheads aimed at the United States. It might even do both. However, any plan by China to increase the size or capability of its nuclear forces would likely also increase sentiment among U.S. policymakers that China is indeed a potential threat to America's security. Thus, the deployment of NMD could easily trigger a series of events that would trap the U.S. and China in a classic security dilemma of mutual misperceptions.

Extending a missile shield to Japan and Taiwan may also be destabilizing. Washington regards TMD as necessary in northeast Asia to defend Japan (and U.S. forces stationed there) against a North Korean missile threat. A TMD system could also help Taiwan resist a potential attack from China. (See Missile Defence and China by Wade Huntley and Robert Brown, FPIF, January 2001.) Beijing, which sees TMD as a threat to its territorial integrity, argues that such a system would encourage Taiwanese independence and otherwise foster the political separation of Taiwan from mainland China. China's most obvious response would be to increase the number of its battlefield missiles, so it could overwhelm any Taiwanese missile defence system. Less obvious to many American observers is that China is also concerned about TMD in Japan. Within China's military, TMD is seen as a potential first step in the remilitarization of Japan. Far from creating greater stability in the region, TMD systems in East Asia may set off an arms race.

Arms sales to Taiwan also remain problematic. The Taiwan Relations Act (TRA) commits the U.S. to offer arms for Taiwan's self-defence. Over the past decade the U.S. has sold Taiwan 126 F-16s as well as Patriot antimissile systems, eight Knox-class frigates, seven Perry-class frigates, M-60A3 tanks, and electronic equipment. Combined with arms purchases from France, these sales have substantially improved Taiwan's defence capabilities. The Taiwanese government is currently seeking further arms purchases from the U.S., including four Aegis-class destroyers, designed to provide air defence for Taiwan's Navy. Other items reportedly on the list include submarine hunting aircraft, missiles, AIM-120 air-to-air missiles, ship-to-ship missiles, antiaircraft missiles, and submarines.

The Aegis-class destroyers have come to assume enormous symbolic value as a litmus test of the degree of U.S. political support for Taiwan. From both the Chinese and Taiwanese perspectives, any sale of Aegis destroyers would signal that the United States is moving closer to a de facto military alliance with Taiwan, rendering Washington a potential enemy in Beijing's eyes. Ironically, for all the controversy over the proposed sale, the Aegis is not necessarily the best military choice for Taiwan. These ships will do little to counter China's newer submarines, which represent Taiwan's primary threat. Taiwan would be better off buying antisubmarine weapons, which are also less politically offensive to Beijing.

Worst-case scenarios and ideological considerations are pushing the U.S. in the direction of providing Taiwan with more than is necessary for its defence. This creates a negative reaction in China and reinforces Beijing's perception of the U.S. as a potential enemy. China, in turn, is taking a more hard-line stance toward the U.S.—thereby confirming Washington's suspicions of Beijing.

Washington is also moving away from its traditional policy of deliberate ambiguity toward a more clear-cut commitment to

Taiwan's defence in advance of any actual crisis. This limits future U.S. options and increases the possibility that the United States and China will stumble into a crisis that neither country wants or desires. This is especially worrisome in light of renewed congressional pressure to end or sharply curtail military exchanges between the U.S. and China. These exchanges have come under criticism, because they are perceived by some as rewarding China, despite its bad human rights record, and because the exchanges have not produced as many positive results as had been hoped. However, mutual misperceptions about military capabilities and intent are most likely to occur in the absence of communication. The April 2001 spy plane controversy, for example, was aggravated by a lack of trust on both sides. If the Bush administration decides to end the exchange program, there is a risk of fostering even greater mistrust between the two powers and increasing the chance of more dangerous incidents in the future.

MODERNIZING CHINA'S MILITARY: PROGRESS, PROBLEMS AND PROSPECTS

In early February 1991, China's High Command was stunned to realize just how far behind modern militaries the People's Liberation Army had fallen. The opening days of the Gulf War convinced PLA analysts that they were witnessing a revolution in military affairs (RMA). American stealth bombers penetrated Iraqi airspace undetected to strike their targets in Baghdad and elsewhere with impunity, while the allied naval armada sat comfortably offshore in the Persian Gulf, well outside the range of Iraqi defenses, launching wave after wave of air strikes and cruise missile attacks. The surgical bombing substantially degraded Iraqi air defenses, while electromagnetic warfare attacks blinded command and control networks. Allied information warfare experts spread viruses into Iraqi computers, scrambling software programs and causing confusion.

With its intelligence eyes and ears incapacitated and its air defenses knocked out, Iraq had no effective defenses against carrier-based air strikes or the saturation bombing of the elite Republican Guards by B-52 and B-1 bombers (which flew round-the-clock missions). Once the allied ground invasion began, Iraqi tanks (ironically, many of them of Chinese origin) became easy fodder for the far more advanced allied tanks, which could target them with laser rangefinders and used night vision equipment to illuminate the desert battlefield. In the infantry offensive that followed, allied units (which were linked to each other by means of global positioning systems, or GPS) quickly decimated Iraqi ground forces. Finally, when Saddam Hussein was forced to play his trump card—Scud missiles potentially armed with biological and chemical weapons—American antimissile defenses were able to intercept many of them in flight after calculating trajectory and targeting coordinates and relaying them to Patriot missile battery commanders via satellite within minutes of the Scud launches.

The Gulf War, with its awesome display of firepower, stealth, electronics, computers, and satellites, revealed that warfare had made a quantum leap into a new era. It was a profound shock to the PLA, but it was not the first time that the Chinese brass had been forced to acknowledge their military shortcomings. Twelve years earlier, during China's punitive attack on Vietnam, the PLA found it difficult to carry out a modest cross-border incursion to subdue a few small cities and suffered enormous casualties against smaller, albeit experienced, opposition. The Chinese army had proven incapable of carrying out a coordinated ground assault from three directions. Command and communications were disjointed, and Chinese forces fell victim to their own "friendly fire." Nor did the PLA bring any air power to bear on their adversaries. As a result, battle-hardened Vietnamese troops were the ones who "taught lessons" to the PLA.

The weaponry that the allied forces threw at Iraq, which was generations ahead of what China had encountered on the Vietnam border in 1979, forced China's generals to the harsh realizations that a new, high-technology era of warfare had dawned and that the Chinese military was unprepared to deal with it. The shock of the Gulf War was all the more traumatic because, since the Vietnam fiasco, China's military had begun a fairly comprehensive modernization and reform program. Deng Xiaoping, who chaired the Central Military Commission, Marshall Ye Jianying, and

General Yang Shangkun all harshly criticized the PLA's bloated size, disorganization, political factionalism, lax discipline, and combat ineffectiveness. Deng, Ye, Yang, and others accordingly set in motion a series of initiatives intended to truly "modernize" the military (although military modernization came distinctly last in the "Four Modernizations"). Throughout the 1980s, the PLA was restructured to prepare, first, for "people's war under modern conditions," and then for "limited war." The changes reconfigured ground forces, consolidated military regions, began combined arms and joint service exercises, undertook a new recruitment drive along with the demobilization of redundant and incompetent personnel, and pursued new weapons procurement programs. The PLA had been implementing reforms for more than a decade when the Gulf War starkly demonstrated that it was still operating in terms of a bygone era of warfare.

The Catalysts for Reform

The Gulf War stimulated deep introspection and analysis in the PLA about the nature of contemporary warfare and the reforms necessary to ready the Chinese armed forces to wage it. In the wake of the Gulf War, PLA strategy was revised to focus on "limited wars under high-technology conditions." Evidence of new defense policy and doctrinal initiatives, structural changes, altered training regimen, new weapons procurement programs, and other changes became noticeable during 1995-96. These reforms had some continuity with previous programs and reforms undertaken in the late 1980s and early 1990s, but others were entirely new and could be traced to the lessons learned from the Gulf War.

Then, in March 1996, another event jarred the PLA, provoking further reflection, rethinking, and readjustment. The PLA's strategic rocket forces, the Second Artillery, began to practice coercive "missile diplomacy" in the Taiwan Strait—firing M-9 missiles within miles of the entrances to Kaohsiung and Chi'lung harbors—and the United States dispatched two aircraft carrier battle groups, centered on the USS *Independence* and *Nimitz,* to the vicinity. With their deployment, the powerful American task forces displayed the greatest show of strength directed at China since the Sino-

American rapprochement of 1971. From positions in the waters east and north of Taiwan, the small armada flew combat exercises and monitored the PLA's own live-fire "exercises" in the Strait. Washington, Beijing, and Taipei all drew different lessons from the U.S. deployment, but for the PLA it meant only one thing: to expect American military involvement should the PLA use force against Taiwan. PLA leaders had long wondered whether they would have to confront the vaunted U.S. military in a Taiwan crisis—now they could assume so.

The 1996 "Taiwan Crisis" added new urgency to China's military modernization and reform program, focusing some of the lessons of the Gulf War. But it also diverted broader efforts to create a more comprehensive force structure and a balanced military modernization program. Since then many elements of PLA planning, training, and procurement have become contingency-driven, dominated by the specter of a military conflict with the United States over Taiwan. Exercises, force deployments, and weapons procurement (particularly from Russia) are preparing the PLA for such a conflict. Hard allocation choices channeled resources into services, programs, and weapons thought necessary to fight not only Taiwan's military but the United States as well.

Resources that might have contributed to a broad-based and systematic military modernization have instead gone into the purchase of expensive Sovremmeny-class destroyers from Russia, built principally to counter Aegis-equipped destroyers and cruisers (which escort aircraft carriers) and the on-board defenses of American carriers, as well into the procurement of Su-27 and Su-30 fighters, Kilo-class submarines, and other equipment intended to plug critical gaps in PLA capabilities against Taiwanese and U.S. forces. China pursued the acquisition of Israel's Phalcon airborne early-warning and control systems—a sale aborted by the Israeli government in July 2000 under considerable pressure from Washington—as a key to controlling the skies in the Taiwan theater. (Chinese pilots currently only have ground control links and no aerial multiple-tracking capability). PLA marines and ground forces practice beach assaults and amphibious landings in mock invasions of Taiwan or the offshore islands and increasingly train with air and naval units in joint-force exercises. Knowing that Taiwan currently has no effective defenses against short-range ballistic missiles, the PLA is embarked on a major and rapid buildup of these weapons opposite the island (approximately 300 by 2000 and increasing by about 50 per year). Also, the steady program to modernize and deploy more nuclear-capable intercontinental ballistic missiles is in large part driven by the need to have a bona fide second-strike minimum deterrent against the United States.

Just as the PLA was adapting to the new military challenges posed by the Taiwan situation, the third rude shock of the 1990s struck: the Kosovo crisis and NATO's war against Serbia in 1999. This time the jarring effect on the PLA was both political and military.

On the political level, Beijing perceived NATO's actions as illustrating a new propensity on the part of the United States (which China's media always dubbed "U.S.-led NATO") to intervene in regional conflicts, under the pretext of "humanitarian intervention," for the purpose of extending and consolidating American global "hegemony" and domination. During and after the war, the Chinese media (including the military media) unleashed a barrage of invective against the United States unequaled since the Cultural Revolution and the Vietnam War. NATO and American actions forced Chinese analysts to question the core assumptions about international relations and the global strategic landscape that had guided their worldview since the late Deng Xiaoping's 1985 pronouncement, that the threat of war was on the decline, that the global system of power relations was inexorably moving toward multipolarity, and that all countries sought "peace and development." Instead of sinking into relative, if not absolute, decline, as Chinese analysts had predicted just a few years earlier, the unrivaled strength and unipolar power of the United States now seemed to be growing significantly. Furthermore, contrary to the touted thesis of "peace and development," regional conflicts, and the American propensity to intervene in them, were seen as increasing. Moreover, American military deployment around the world remained at high, even expanded, levels. Although Chinese strategic theology predicted, and the Chinese government had officially called for, the abrogation of alliances and withdrawal of forces from foreign soil, Washington had in fact strengthened and broadened its network of global alliances in the aftermath of the Cold War.

Thus the U.S. role in the Balkan war had a profoundly disturbing and dissonant effect on Chinese military and strategic thinkers as well as on national leaders. When the NATO intervention was considered in the context of the 1991 Gulf War and 1996 Taiwan crisis, China perceived itself to be facing a United States bent on global dominance and the permanent separation of Taiwan from China. The possibility of U.S. intervention in China's ethnic troubles in Xinjiang and Tibet as a result of the "Clinton Doctrine" of humanitarian intervention added to Beijing's sense of urgency.

On a military level, too, the Yugoslav campaign jolted PLA analysts, who paid close attention to how NATO prosecuted the war. They set up two 24-hour centers to monitor the military dimensions of the conflict—one in the General Staff Department's intelligence "Watch Center" and the other at the Academy of Military Sciences. They witnessed tactics, technology, and weaponry similar to those used in the Gulf War eight years earlier, but they also observed a number of new features. Information and electronic warfare appeared to play a more important role in disabling enemy command infrastructure and defenses. Cruise missiles had improved accuracy. NATO suppressed Serbian air defenses in the early stages of the conflict and gained complete command of the skies; aerial bombardment was significantly more intense (in operational tempo, if not in tonnage of ordnance). With the use of in-flight refueling, bombing raids using the newly deployed B-2 strategic bomber were initiated half a world away instead of within theater. One such bombing raid tragically and mistakenly targeted the Chinese Embassy in Belgrade. The bombs themselves were equipped with new satellite and laser guidance systems. Perhaps most important, PLA analysts watched a war prosecuted from great distances—where the Serbs could not see, hear, or reach their attackers. With all of the high-tech weaponry deployed, not a single allied soldier was lost to hostile fire.

The 2001-2 U.S. military campaign against the Taliban regime and al-Qaeda terrorists in Afghanistan was also carefully studied by PLA analysts, although the lessons derived remain unclear at this time. As in the case of the war against the Serbs in Bosnia, PLA analysts were alarmed on both the political and military levels.

Politically, they were quite uncomfortable with the prospect of U.S. and allied military forces deployed in Pakistan and particularly in Central Asian countries on China's northwestern periphery. The prospect of a long-term American military presence in the Central Asian republics is particularly unsettling to Chinese national security planners, as it represents (in their somewhat paranoid view) a major new step in what is perceived as an American strategy of encircling China. From this perspective, only the direct northern frontier, where China borders Russia, is free from a U.S. military presence.

At the outset of the Afghanistan conflict in October 2001, PLA officers at the PLA National Defense University in Beijing warned, mistakenly, that like the British in the nineteenth century and the Soviet Union, the United States would become bogged down in an Afghan quagmire. They warned that this was a different kind of enemy, which could not be subdued by aerial bombing, and doubted whether America was prepared to insert ground troops and risk casualties (arguing that the United States continued to suffer from a "Somalia syndrome"). If the United States did deploy ground troops, PLA analysts warned, they would be consumed in a quagmire of guerrilla war, which they were not prepared to fight, and U.S. helicopters and aircraft would be shot down by Stinger missiles in possession of the Taliban and al-Qaeda. Similar prognoses had been offered by PLA analysts at the outset of the Gulf War and the Bosnian bombing. They were proven wrong each time, reflecting fundamental misunderstandings of U.S. military strategy and tactics.

Militarily, in Afghanistan, PLA analysts witnessed displays of high-technology warfare similar to those seen in the Gulf War and the Serbian conflict, as well as some new techniques and ordnance. Long-range strategic bombing with extremely sophisticated precision-guided munitions (PGMs) played a key role. During ninety days of bombing, the United States dropped a total of nearly 13,000 bombs on Afghanistan, of which 9,000 were PGMs. The accuracy and lethality of these weapons proved far more advanced than had been witnessed in Iraq or Bosnia. In addition to sustained precision bombing, and early suppression of Afghan defenses, PLA analysts also noted the key role played by real-time allied intelligence. In addition to the kinds of sensors and satellites previously seen, two new elements appeared in Afghanistan that did much to provide instantaneous intelligence: special operations forces on the ground and aerial unmanned drones. Other new factors noted by PLA analysts included AH-64 attack helicopters and A-130 airborne gunships. These and other new capabilities attracted the attention of PLA analysts. As was the case with the Iraq, Taiwan, and Bosnian conflicts, the Afghan war will be intensively studied for some time in the PLA, with alternations in doctrine, tactics, and training subsequently becoming apparent over time.

The lessons the PLA drew from these conflicts are discussed at much greater length in chapters 3 and 7; suffice it to note here that it increased the Chinese leaders' sense of the urgent need for military modernization, and, particularly, of a looming threat from the United States. Funds for the military continued to rise, on average by 15 percent, in fiscal years 1999-2002. Certainly, popular sentiment against the United States peaked following the Chinese embassy bombing, and there were public calls in China for a reordering of modernization priorities with increased emphasis on the military.

Throughout the 1990s, the PLA was reading and hearing about the "revolution in military affairs" (*xin junshi geming*) that was evolving in the United States. As if the Chinese military was not humbled enough by the impressive display of firepower and electronic wizardry on display in the 1991, 1996, and 1999 and 2001-2 conflicts, PLA strategists were led to believe that the U.S. military was entering one of those periods of technological advance that come along every few generations, when there is a quantum leap in a family of technologies and operational concepts that push warfare into completely new realms. Such technological advances stimulate concomitant changes in the way forces are structured and deployed, how logistics are managed, and how force is used. Not only was the PLA High Command thus obliged to witness a series of powerful demonstrations of modern military prowess, but it also had to reflect on the prospect that, while it was trying to upgrade its equipment from the 1960s to the 1970s, and its doctrine from the 1980s to the 1990s, the already impressive American military of the late twentieth century was on the verge of a significant leap forward into the twenty-first century.

THE NATURE OF INDO-CHINA CONFLICT IF IT OCCURS

There are four possible theatres for conflict namely Ladakh, the central theatre in Uttar Pradesh, Sikkim, and along the McMahon Line in the northeast. The latter was agreed to by the British colonial administration and Tibet in 1914 as the boundary between China and India but later rejected outright by the Communist Chinese government. An all out conflict, although possible, appears highly improbable because it could spiral into a nuclear war and would upset the prevailing harmonious development model adopted by both sides. Hence, it is more likely that military conflict between the two states would be marked by a calibrated use of force and careful management of escalation.

Degeneration of India-China friction into a conflict would be an incremental process that would pass through various stages of escalation. Indian analysts have also considered a scenario in which China resorts to hostilities under the garb of training exercises, an old and tried method. The use of force and the nature of escalation would be driven largely by relative conventional and strategic balance, the perception of a "quick victory," and the political and military payoffs. A large perceived asymmetry in the military balance could embolden China to act unilaterally in the hope of forcing India to accede to Beijing's terms on the boundary issue or sending India a broader strategic message about Chinese regional military preeminence. Nonetheless, the threat of nuclear war and the likelihood of disruptions to the global order are perceived as restraining factors on China.

Coercive Muscle Flexing or Intimidation. In one scenario, China could use force posturing or a calibrated display of force to induce Indian compliance through coercive muscle flexing, without resorting to the application of major force. Chinese intimidation could take one or more of the following forms:

(a) Targeted cyber attacks against India's command and control facilities and commercial entities.

(b) Partial PLA mobilisation to change the balance in the disputed areas, backed by the. PLAAF and missile deployment.

(c) Aggressive patrolling (both on land and at sea) and encroachments in selected areas as a show of strength.

(d) Increased support to the numerous insurgencies in India's northeast and to Pakistan in J&K, backed by overt military operations.

(e) Support to Indian. Maoist insurgents through proxies to foment unrest in the border regions.

(f) Increased. PLAN presence in the IOR, Bay of Bengal, and Arabian Sea as part of an intimidation strategy.

(g) The degrading of India's satellite-based communications systems, including a show of force by testing an improved version of its anti-satellite weaponry on a Indian satellite.

(h) Attacks on preselected, politically sensitive economic and military targets to coerce. India's political leadership and convey the price of any reactive escalation.

Intermediate level Conflict: A Limited War of High Intensity.. China could launch a limited war confined to a specific area that is limited in duration and amenable to a negotiated termination. Alternatively, the PLA could take over selected places such as Tawang to drive a partial victor's bargain. Resorting to either of these two actions has the potential of escalating a limited conflict into a broader one encompassing both the northeastern region and Ladakh. For China, this could be a stand alone tactic driven by larger political and strategic considerations or an extension of coercive muscle flexing. However, a high-intensity limited war under "informationised" conditions remains China's basic military doctrine and its decision to escalate will be a calculated one. China could also initiate hostilities in the belief that it could successfully fight a short punitive campaign. The PLA could attempt to rapidly and clandestinely change the force balance in the border areas to catch India off guard. Such an option would largely be driven by India's sketchy ISR (intelligence, surveillance, and reconnaissance) cover over Tibet and its force mobilisation and firepower disadvantages along the LAC. This could take the form of a punitive strike campaign to teach India a lesson.

The Chinese military modernisation, capacity building, infrastructure development in Tibet, and increased assertions in the Indian Ocean pose a serious challenges to India's security. China's attempts to increase it's area of influence in South Asia and actions to influence peripheral states only add to the Indian concerns. There is nonetheless a growing realisation that India needs to develop credible hard power as a dissuasive strategy against China. Thus, the dilemma that India faces is in giving a shape to it's political response to external balancing.

CHINA: MILITARY MODERNISATION AND STRATEGY

Military modernisation cannot be seen in isolation from economic modernisation, and both go hand-in-hand. This aspect needs to seep in the decision-making process. The emerging international environment today forms a strategic triangle of which the two obvious participants are the US and China; empirically speaking, India should be the third power forming this triangle. What we need to look into is where China is heading especially in light of the fact that as a nation, China has been far ahead of India since the past decades. It was in 1996 that the Chinese government passed a law that reunification was the sacred duty of the PLA. We need to question whether that duty ends with Taiwan, or does it go any further? Arunachal Pradesh is well-entrenched in the Chinese thinking and strategy and India should not be complacent about that. In this regard, India also needs to increasingly focus upon logistics infrastructure in the border areas. This has been visible in the official Defence White Papers which have spelt out the strategy of active border wars. In today's date, the Indian Air Force will prevail over the PLA Air Force given that even though PLAAF stands way ahead, however, in terms of professional capability of its personnel, the IAF holds the edge.

A facet that stands opposed to vociferous Chinese claims of a 'peaceful rise' is the robust military modernisation that the PLA has undertaken since the past decades. The entire debate centering on China's 'peaceful rise' is meant for public consumption. Beijing has chosen to undertake swift and robust modernisation of the PLA by planning to make up for its poor hardware capabilities while at the same time enhancing abilities to wage asymmetric warfare in the space, cyber-space and information warfare domains. The post-1991 Gulf War period witnessed the Chinese leadership take note of the rapidly changing nature of modern warfare. As a response, the leadership of the PLA set upon a path of reform aimed at building a more professional force in a corporate and institutional sense, and a more capable force in the operational sense. The Chinese White Paper on national defence issued in 2004, stated that the objective of the PLA was to win local wars under the conditions of informationisation. The 2010 Annual Pentagon Report on the *Military and Security Developments Involving the People's Republic of China* underlines this Chinese emphasis on the concept of informationisation which would enable integrated joint operations that require integration of the entire PLA with common information systems.

The primary obstacles acknowledged by the Chinese military leadership in realisation of integrated joint operations at the moment include:

- Inadequate training
- Shortage of qualified staff of PLA personnel
- Equipment
- Tactics of the other services.

In an effort to rectify this existential paucity, the PLA reportedly is undergoing robust training for integrated joint operations on future battlefields. In line with the strategic requirements of high mobility operations and three-dimensional assault, the PLA has been moving from regional defence to trans-regional mobility. The units are becoming small, modular and multi-functional in organisation through appropriate downsizing and structural reform. While accelerating the development of aviation, light mechanised and information counter-measure forces, it is giving priority to the development of tactical missiles, surface-to-air missiles and special operations forces, so as to increase its capabilities for land-air integrated operations, long-distance manoeuvres, rapid assault and special operations.

The PLA has chosen to justify pre-emptive military action at the operational and tactical level under the guise of a 'defensive posture' at the strategic level. The Chinese doctrinal concept of "active defence" *(jiji fangyu)* thus, could be interpreted as a tactic of employing the weak against the strong. Although stated to be defensive in purpose, the doctrine seeks to take the initiative and stay on the offensive from a conflict's earliest stages in order to bring hostilities to a swift and more importantly, a favorable conclusion. The concept is in concurrence with the doctrine that puts a premium on surprise, pre-emption, indirect/asymmetrical confrontation and concentrated strikes on the most critical platforms and capabilities of the adversary, particularly its C4I2SR systems, and on high-value psychological targets. The effort is to overwhelm and undermine the adversary's will to resist during the early stages of conflict.

Thus, the focus on anti-access, area-denial strategies, procuring platforms with the capability and intention to deter, prevent or complicate the intervention of the US (and/or others) in a Taiwan-like scenario. From an Indian stand point, the scenario is applicable to a Tibet-like situation. China's force structure for long-distance air and naval operations is consistent with a limited regional force projection capability. The production of conventional missiles and upgrading the quality and survivability of China's nuclear arsenal from silo-based to road-mobile and from liquid-fuelled to solid-fuelled, accentuates PLA's aim to render its strategic nuclear forces as more survivable and hence provide a far more credible deterrent.

Realising the shortcomings in inter-service cooperation and actual experience in joint exercises and combat operations, the Chinese leadership appears to be stressing more upon asymmetric strategies to leverage China's advantages while exploiting the perceived vulnerabilities of potential opponents, for e.g., the counter-space and cyber warfare programmes. As computer technology increasingly integrates itself into modern military organisations, including the PLA, military planners shall assign it the twin role of being both a target and a weapon. Cyber forces are most likely to be integrated into an overall battle strategy as part of a combined arms campaign.

China's negotiating strategy is to resolve the dispute when the Chinese are in a much stronger position in terms of comprehensive national strength so that they could bargain from a position of strength—an instance is Beijing's strengthening of its military capabilities and infrastructure development in Tibet. PLA's larger aim is that of radically boosting rapid military deployment in the border areas with India. Would enhance China's military capability and enable Chinese coercive diplomacy especially with regards to the border dispute with India.

The PLA realised that modernising its military had become inevitable in wake of Gulf War I—which eventually became the catalyst for its military modernisation campaign. China's thrust areas of modernisation have been the strategic forces, navy and air force with heavy defence budget allocations with every passing year. China's intent as it formulates its strategy is one in which it envisions a multi-polar world and a uni-polar Asia. India needs to take serious note of its lagging logistics mechanism and infrastructure in the border areas which have been neglected. Significantly, the armed forces have to be made a part of the policy formulation, especially while formulation of India's China policy.

The PLA is greatly driven by strategy. There needs to be a wider understanding that Chinese military strategy is not a defensive one but an offensive one. It is a strategy that is tailored in a sense to go well beyond the enemy lines of communications. The concept of 'informationisation' that the PLA is greatly emphasizing upon can be related to RMA-based warfare. However, the levels of information warfare platforms in the Chengdu and Lanzhou MR are very low. The campaign strategy of the PLA can be attributed to the lessons learnt from Gulf War I. As the higher ranks of the PLA advocate the military strategy of active defence, there is an understanding that is emerging that the PLA is less likely to enter a conflict unless and until it is absolutely confident of victory. Although, a lot of speculation has been raised regarding the rising Chinese defence budget, it is still too low in order to achieve full-spectrum dominance like the US military. China is focusing a lot on the levels of training including both tactical and technical training, with multiple platforms for training. Another area of focus are the modernisation levels vis-à-vis equipment which will further reflect upon their usage in future battlefield environments as China readies to confront Taiwan, Vietnam, Japan, South China Sea region or South Asia. From an Indian stand point, it is important to note as to how this equipment would be used in terms of future warfare. Another important facet is how China is coping up with all these technological advances despite the US embargoes.

8

'New Front' of China on Indo-Nepal Border

The Chinese clamour over Arunachal Pradesh has raised many eyebrows in India. Even as the meeting between Prime Minister Manmohan Singh and Chinese Premier Wen Jiabao in Thailand on Saturday was being looked at as an effort to cool down the tension between the neighbouring countries, the Dragon nation has opened another anti-India front. This time in Nepal. Silently but speedily China is spreading its wings in the erstwhile Hindu kingdom, mainly to unleash anti-India propaganda. Besides acquiring some major construction projects in Nepal, the Chinese are also making their presence felt by opening language centres in Nepali cities on the Indo-Nepal border. These centres are teaching Chinese language. But, what raises suspicions on Chinese intentions is the fact that these centres are open only for Nepali citizens.

The surge in Chinese activities in the neighbour country is a matter of concern for India which is already fighting terrorism being pushed into the country from Pakistan. It's a known fact that China often uses Nepal as a buffer state against India. After the Indo-China war of 1962, the Dragon country has made constant efforts to increase its influence in Nepal. Though it did not succeed much till Nepal was under the rule of monarchy, the fall of monarchy and growing Maoist grip over Nepal has given a fillip to Chinese plans.

A clear indicator of this is the construction of Sikta barrage in Agaiya village of Banke district (Nepal). Its construction was delayed for almost three decades owing to Indian protest. But, once Maoists held sway over the Nepali government, the construction was given a go-ahead in 2006. Moreover, the contract for the project was given to Chinese firm — Sinehydro. In fact, a team of 40 Chinese engineers is engaged in the construction of the Sikta barrage in Agaiya district of Nepal. The district touches the Indian district of Shravasti. The distance from Indian border to the barrage is barely 14 kilometres. The possibility of Chinese infiltration in important zones of war on Indian border areas due to the presence of Chinese engineers cannot be ruled out.

Also, after the completion of the barrage the flow of river Rapti towards India will be diverted towards Nepal which will create acute water shortage in Indian area. Efforts have also been started to divert the flow of rivers flowing towards Indian area from Parchu lake located in Chinese area adjoining the state which may lead to floods in the borders districts of India during monsoon. Not only this, if the and Sikta barrage ever breaks down due to technical reasons it will severely impact the security arrangements made on the India border. China, thus, seems to be working on these two projects under well-planned policy to tease India. Similarly, China has established the office of 'Maitri Sangh' in Nepal adjoining Indian border territory. Meanwhile, a 10-member team comprising five Chinese and five Tibetan national recently visited Nepalganj headquarters of Banke district (Nepal). The team toured the Indo-Nepal border and secretly clicked photographs of the Rupaidiha main gate located on Indo-Nepal border. The Indian intelligence agencies, however, learnt about this when the team had already left for Kathmandu. Assistant army Nayak Devendra of Shashtra Seema Bal (SSB), when contacted, told TOI that he will report the incident to his senior officers.

Nepal's Prime Minister Mr. Madhav Kumar Nepal and Chairman of the Nepalese Congress (NC) Party Girija Prasad Koirala have assured China that Nepali soil will not be allowed to be used against China under any circumstances. Talking with the Chinese delegation led by politburo member of the Chinese Communist Party, Mr. Zhang Gaoli, separately, September 1, 2009, the two veteran politicians of Nepal, according to the high placed sources, did try to convince China towards Nepal's firm stand on 'One China Policy'. However, Beijing is not that fool to believe such parroted/repetitive assurance of Nepali politician, say Kathmandu based analyst.

"The lame duck government has not even asked official clarifications from those lawmakers from the Madhesh parties who had assured the Tibetan community in exile in India that they will raise the issue of 'Free Tibet' in Nepal's Constituent Assembly (CA) during their last meet with Dalai Lama in Dharmasala of Himanchal Pradesh, India", laments a Kathmandu based analyst who preferred anonymity. 'The recent meet of the Nepal law makers has raised suspicion in the minds of the Beijing authorities as regards the Nepalese structured stance that she remains firm on "One China Policy' of Nepal. And Beijing understands the Nepali intentions well. According to PM's political advisor Mr. Raghujee Panta, PM's upcoming visit to China, Constitution drafting process and ongoing peace process were also discussed during the meet.

CHINA'S MISSILE EXPORTS AND ASSISTANCE TO THE MIDDLE EAST

China's missile trade with various countries in the Middle East has been a subject of substantial concern in Western nonproliferation circles. China has reportedly transferred missiles, missile technology, materials, and production assistance to a number of Middle Eastern countries, including Iraq, Turkey, Libya, Egypt, Saudi Arabia, and the United Arab Emirates. In some cases, Chinese trade activities have been masked using cover names for businesses. The Shandong Arts and Crafts Co. reportedly sold Iraq test equipment for inertial guidance systems. In another case where trade activities were obfuscated, a North Korean company based in China allegedly sold Egypt specialty steel used in the making of missiles. However, the most serious sources of concern in this region, from a nonproliferation standpoint, are Chinese missile trade and cooperation with Iran and Syria.

Allegations of Chinese M-9 ballistic missile transfers to Syria in the early 1990s contributed to the US decision to impose Missile

Technology Control Regime (MTCR)-related sanctions on China in 1991. China's transfers of anti-ship cruise missiles and ballistic missiles to Iran, along with related components, technology, and materials, has been a source of continuing friction. Of particular concern, from a nonproliferation perspective, are Chinese transfers of production technology and expertise that contribute to indigenous missile programs. Transfers of production technologies could contribute to Iran's production of medium and long-range missiles which are banned by the MTCR.

China has generally denied an extensive missile technology trade with the Middle East, although it has on several occasions conceded that certain transfers, previously denied, had taken place. As early as 1989, China denied that it sold missiles to the Middle East despite US information to the contrary. For example, on 12 December 1989, a Chinese Foreign Ministry spokesman stated, "Except for Saudi Arabia, where a small number of mid-range missiles were sold, China has never sold, nor is planning to sell, missiles to any Middle East country." Throughout the 1990s, China insisted that its missile sales to the Middle East are modest and responsible. Since 1991, China has pledged to abide by MTCR guidelines and parameters in all its missile technology exports, although that commitment has been called into question on several occasions. As of 1999, the central issue of concern regarding missile exports to the Middle East are Chinese sales of missile technologies to Iran which could be used for non-MTCR compliant systems.

MISSILE TECHNOLOGY CONTROL REGIME (MTCR)

The Missile Technology Control Regime (MTCR) is a set of guidelines regulating the export of missiles, unmanned air vehicles (UAVs), and related technology for those systems capable of carrying a 500 kilogram payload at least 300 kilometres, as well as systems intended for the delivery of weapons of mass destruction (WMD). The MTCR was formed in 1987 by the G-7 partners, and is an informal voluntary arrangement, not a treaty or an international agreement. The MTCR consists of common export policy applied to a common list of controlled items. Each member implements its commitments in the context of its own national export laws. In addition to the MTCR's members, a number of countries unilaterally observe — or "adhere to"— the Guidelines.

The MTCR considers "missiles" to include: ballistic missiles, space launch vehicles (SLVs) and sounding rockets. UAVs include: cruise missiles, drones, and remotely piloted vehicles (RPVs). The MTCR Guidelines specifically state that the Regime is "not designed to impede national space programs or international cooperation in such programs as long as such programs could not contribute to delivery systems for weapons of mass destruction." The MTCR was originally concerned only with nuclear capable delivery systems. In January 1993, the Partners extended the guidelines to cover delivery systems capable of delivering all WMD (nuclear, chemical, and biological).

The MTCR's annex of controlled equipment and technology is divided into "Category I" and "Category II" items. It includes equipment and technology, both military and dual-use, that are relevant to missile development, production, and operation. According to the Guidelines, export of Category I items is subject to a presumption of export denial. Category I includes complete rocket systems, unmanned air-vehicle systems such as cruise missiles, target and reconnaissance drones, specially-designed production facilities for these systems; and certain complete subsystems. Category II covers a wide range of parts, components and subsystems such as propellants, structural materials, test equipment and facilities, and flight instruments. These items may be exported at the discretion of the MTCR Partner government, on a case by case basis, for acceptable end-uses. They may also be exported under government-to-government assurances, which provide that they not be used on a missile system capable of delivering a 500 kilogram payload to a range of at least 300 kilometres.

November 2000 Pledge

On 21 November 2000, the Chinese Foreign Ministry issued its most stringent and specific policy statement on missile nonproliferation to date. The Chinese government promised, for the first time, to issue export control laws covering missile technologies. In the past, Chinese officials have stated that its controls on missile exports were governed by internal documents and not public laws. The Chinese pledged that the new laws would include such regulations as license application and review, end-user certifications, and a "catch-all" clause. The Chinese statement did not, however, specifically reference the MTCR or its control list and the statement did not mention when China would issue the new export control law. Some experts argued that the latter elements represented a loop-hole in the accord. The Chinese government also denied that it engaged in illegitimate trade with either Iran or Pakistan. The *China Daily* reports Chinese Foreign Ministry spokesman, Sun Yuxi refuting US allegations that China supplied Iran and Pakistan with missiles. Sun denounced the allegations as "rumors with ulterior motives." Sun said the PRC had exercised strict control on the export of missile technologies.

On the same day, the State Department announced that it was waiving sanctions on Chinese entities for the past sales of missile technologies to entities in Iran and Pakistan. These exports, which date back to 1992, violated the 1990 Missile Control Act which calls for sanctions on entities engaged in export of MTCR-controlled items. The sanctions were for the export of both MTCR category I and category II items. The US also pledged to resume discussions with China as soon as possible on extending the 1995 US-China Agreement on International Trade in Commercial Launch Services. Under this accord, US companies can export satellites to China for launch on Chinese rocket boosters.

Old Problems Arise

The November 2000 deal did not hold for very long. On 1 September 2001 the US government imposed economic sanctions on a Chinese company for shipping missile technology to Pakistan in violation of a bilateral agreement in November 2000 and US law. The US government said that the China Metallurgical Equipment Corporation in late 2000 and early 2001 shipped missile technology to Pakistan that would assist its Shaheen 1 and Shaheen 2 programs. The sanctions, under the 1990 Missile Control Act, ban US companies from doing business with the Chinese entity for two years. The Bush administration has also invoked a ban on new licenses for U.S. companies to put their satellites on Chinese rockets or transfer satellite technology. These transfers were subsequently confirmed in September CIA report on global proliferation developments.

The Chinese government vociferously denied a Chinese company had shipped proscribed missile technology to Pakistan. The Foreign Ministry spokesman said: Over a period of time, the US has repeatedly alleged that MECC was engaged in missile proliferation activities according to its so-called "intelligence information". In-depth investigations by the Chinese side indicate that MECC has never engaged in any activities as alleged by the United States and the US allegation is groundless. However, the US side is bent on making the erroneous decision based on its wrong intelligence information, in disregard of the constructive position and the investigation results of the Chinese side. Such a US move is totally groundless and irresponsible, which the Chinese side can never accept.

The Foreign Ministry called for the US to immediately lift the sanctions. China threatened repercussions of the sanctions were not lifted. "China strongly urges the US side to immediately withdraw its wrong decision, so as to avoid any damage to Sino-US cooperation in non-proliferation. Otherwise, the US side should bear all the responsibilities for the consequences arising therefrom."

2002 Regulations

In the aftermath of the September 11th terrorist attacks, US-China relations showed signs of improvement. Beijing extended its support to the US-led campaign against global terrorism. However, the Bush administration continued to stress that the issue of nonproliferation and export control was essential to further improvements in bilateral relations. In an effort to resolve bilateral tension, in August 2002 Beijing announced new export control regulations and an expanded control list, fulfilling its November 2000 pledge to issue export control laws covering missile technologies. The announcement coincided with a visit by Deputy Secretary of State Richard Armitage to Beijing, and was seen as an aspect of preparations for President Jiang Zemin's upcoming visit to the US in October 2002. The new regulations included both the MTCR's "presumption of denial" approach, end-user certifications, and a "catch-all" clause. The new regulations appeared to mark a realization in China's leadership of the dangers of the proliferation of WMD and their delivery systems to its own security, as well as an attempt to remove this issue as a barrier to bilateral cooperation. The 2002 regulations and control list are comprehensive and closely follow the MTCR. The discrepancies with the MTCR were explained by senior Chinese diplomat Liu Jieyi as: "If you compare the List with MTCR, you will find that the categorization is a bit different for the sake of easy administration.

There are items not contained in MTCR in the List. So in this respect, this List covers a wider area than MTCR. Of course there is also a very limited number of MTCR items that are not in the list because they are not really that relevant, either because we don't have them, or they have never come into the picture, or because our experts do not know exactly what they are. Some discrepancies, however, may still allow for license-free export of some technologies that would be useful for countries to establish indigenous missile programs.

The US response to the regulations was cautious, with many in the Bush administration taking a "wait-and-see" approach before making a final judgment as to whether Beijing had fully committed itself to comprehensive implementation of these regulations. In an example of this cautious attitude, State Department spokesman Richard Boucher stated that: "It is an important part to have the regulations in place, it is an equally important part to see that they are enforced." On 9 May 2003, the U.S. expressed its dissatisfaction with China's implementation of its new export control regulations and control list by imposing sanctions on North China Industries Corporation (Norinco) for allegedly supplying missile technology to Iran. The sanctions barred all exports to the US by Norinco and its subsidiaries, and forbade any contracts between the company and US government agencies. The measure was expected to have more of an impact than previous sanctions; in 2002, Norinco exported an estimated $100 million worth of products to the US.

CHINA MILITARY POWER IS STILL HIDDEN

President Hu Jintao called for even stronger armed forces as China flexed its muscles in a National Day parade, but experts said the PLA's marching skills might exceed actual fighting ability. Illustrating the importance China attaches to its growing military strength, the People's Liberation Army kicked off a dazzling celebration in Beijing of the nation's 60th birthday by showing off a range of home-grown weaponry.

China has boasted that the nuclear-capable missiles, fighter jets, aerial drones and other advanced arms on display mark a "quantum leap" made possible thanks to a long-running campaign to upgrade the once-backward PLA. Hu hailed this push in a speech to a packed Tiananmen Square, ahead of the massive military parade. "The PLA... must carry forward their glorious tradition, build up military strength and perform their duties earnestly," he said.

Official media gushed after the parade about the "cutting-edge" arms that have caused concern overseas about Beijing's military intentions, but analysts noted China had far to go before it could truly project military power abroad. "We can make absolutely no conclusions about the actual tactical abilities of the troops or the capabilities of the equipment from what we have seen," Dennis J. Blasko, a former US military attache to China, told AFP. "The fact that nothing broke down en route and all marchers completed the parade is admirable, but does not speak to tactical capabilities," he said.

Blasko noted one apparent advancement — the intercontinental ballistic missiles which state-run Xinhua news agency described as a military "trump card" were now on mobile launchers. "The key is its mobility, thus improving its survivability and insuring a true second-strike capability," he said. But aside from hardware such as the Jian-10 fighter jet, much of what was seen on Thursday represented upgrades or variations on weapons seen in the 50th anniversary parade in 1999, he said.

However, the array of home-grown systems showed China was making clear progress in moving away from its long-term reliance on Russian arms purchases, experts said. And the mix of ground, naval and air force components showed the PLA — which encompasses all those branches — was growing more diverse.

"The era of a 'heavy' PLA is over. A lighter, more diversified and capable military able to complete various missions was on display," a Western diplomat well-versed in military issues, who spoke on condition of anonymity, told AFP.

Chinese Defence Minister Liang Guanglie boasted last month that much of his nation's weaponry now rivals that included in Western arsenals, but analysts said China has much to do before it comes close to challenging American power. "Despite rapid strides in military modernisation, China still has a lot of catching up to do," said Minxin Pei, a China scholar at the Washington-based Carnegie Endowment for International Peace. "Most of its neighbours, including Japan, India, South Korea, and Taiwan, have more advanced and better-trained air forces and navies than it does," he said in a research note.

China also is believed to possess too few of some systems, such as major missiles, for them to be significant in strategic terms in the near term. "This was a demonstration of what China knows how to do but this is just a show — the entire military is not equipped with what we saw this morning," said the Western diplomat.

INSECURE BORDER MANAGEMENT OF NEPAL

Nepal is situated between two emerging Asian giants, China and India. The frontier of Nepal is surrounded on its south, east and west by India and on the north by China. China has expanded its economic market almost all over the world against the background of its emerging political scenario. And India is attaining economic prosperity in South Asia by enhancing its global political image. Historically, Nepal was elongated 1,415 km east to west from Tista to Kangra with an area of 267,575 sq. km. But it was shrunk to Mechi and Mahakali, after the Treaty of Sugauli on 4 March 1816 and subsequent Boundary Treaties of 11 December 1816 and 1 November 1860 with British East India Company. As a result, present Nepal's territory has been limited to an area of 147,181 sq. km having 885 km east-west length.

Nepal has a regulated border management system with China, whereas there is an open border between Nepal and India. This paper analyses how Nepal's open border with India is faced with external threats due to cross border terrorism. It further analyses the implications of open border system in order to maintain law and order, peace and security not only in both the nations but also in other countries of South Asia. Besides, it describes what border management strategies are available between the two countries and how they are working in practice. It also emphasizes that the existing border management system needs some change to prevent cross border terrorism.

Historical outlook

Nepal-China border management : There is a regulated/controlled border system between Nepal and China from historic time. It has a demilitarized zone of 20 km on either side of the borderline. However, there is a frequent infiltration of Tibetan refugees in a disguised manner to move to Dharmashala of India where the Dalai Lama resides. It is notable that compulsory ID Card system has been recently introduced for the inhabitants of Nepal-Tibet (China) frontier from 1 January 2006 to cross the border point. But earlier, authentic ID was not required for the inhabitants of 30 km of both the frontiers.

Nepal-India border management : If we look back at the history of border management of Nepal with India, it was a closed border system in ancient period. There was restriction on entry into Nepal, especially for third country nationals. In course of time, controlled border system was informally initiated after the Treaty of Sugauli of 1816 with the East India Company. Eventually, western people would require special permission from the Prime Minister.

The open border system started unknowingly after the Boundary Treaty of 1860. However, passport or travel document was necessary to cross the border till 1957. The border between Nepal and India became more open after India's independence in 1947. It was wide open after the establishment of democracy in Nepal in 1950. The border became further wide open after the construction of Tribhuvan Highway in 1957 linking Katmandu, capital city of Nepal, to an Indian frontier town, Raxaul.

As a result, anyone could cross the international border and shuttle back and forth, many times a day, without any interrogation. As a consequence, Passport/permit system gradually and unknowingly disappeared after the connection of roadway. On the other hand, there was a kind of closed border system during economic blockade by India from 23 March 1989 to 30 June 1990 as India unilaterally closed its entire 22 border crossing points and 15 transit points for Nepal. Meanwhile, India has also adopted a kind of discretionary system from time to time. It unilaterally implemented the temporarily closed border system in some of the sensitive border crossing points.

For example, the Falelung border point of Taplejung district of Nepal is a case in point. This point was closed for the Nepalese nationals to go to India during 2004. But before this, India was allowing Nepalese nationals to enter India from this point, after depositing ID or Citizenship Certificate.

As another example, India has laid down unilaterally that the Nepalese nationals, who enter India from third country, must produce visa. Tanka Lal Shrestha (Nepalese working in German Embassy, Kathmandu), while travelling by Indian Airline flight on 26 January 2005 from Lahore to New Delhi was obstructed by Immigration Officer asking him to produce visa. Earlier, ID card was sufficient for the Nepalese nationals.

In due course of time, open border system changed into regulated system for the air-route passengers travelling from Nepal to India and vice versa. ID Card system was introduced for air passengers of both the countries from 1 October 2000. It was done after Indian Airline Aircraft with flight number IC-814 which took off for New Delhi from Katmandu had been hijacked on 24 December 1999. The plane ultimately landed at Kandahar, Afganistan.

Very recently, open border was transformed into regulated system in one of the land-routes at Nepalganj-Rupaidiya border crossing point from 1 November 2005. Both the governments have introduced regulated border management system to this point, as ID Card system has been made compulsory. This is, more or less, a short account of the historical background of Nepal-India border management system. All these points show that Indo-Nepal border management is complex, as history tells.

REASONS FOR KEEPING THE BORDER OPEN

The main reason to make Indo-Nepal border gradually and unknowingly open was to facilitate easy access to recruit the young and raw Nepali boys in the British Gorkha Army Regiment without any border restriction. British Army Officers did appreciate the bravery of young and sturdy Gorkha fighters during Anglo-Gorkha War, 1814-16. Second, it would be easier to sell the finished British and Indian goods and merchandise in the market of Nepal and even Tibet via Nepal with open border. At the same time, open border facilitated the import by India of Nepalese cheap raw materials for its manufacturing industries.

The third reason was to make easy and frequent visits of the Indian politicians and bureaucrats as advisors and consultants to the Nepalese Ministers and Secretaries after the democratic movement of Nepal in 1950. In the same way, wide open border also made it easy for Indian Overseers to come to Nepal as Engineers and semi-educated persons as teachers in remote-area schools of Nepal. Fourth and the most important factor for the border to remain open is social relationship at people to people level of both the nations.

There is no Treaty to make the Border Open

There is no such treaty/agreement or memorandum to keep the border open between two countries. Even Nepal-India Peace and Friendship Treaty of 31 July 1950 does not have the provision for open border system. Article-VII of the treaty says: "The government of India and Nepal agree to grant, on reciprocal basis, to the nationals of one country in the territories of the other the same privileges in the matter of residence, ownership of property, participation in trade and commerce, movement and privileges of a similar nature."

But there is no mention of the open border between two countries. It only suggests that the border management system must be reciprocated by both the countries. What it means is that if open or regulated system is enacted by one country, the same system should be implemented by the other on the basis of reciprocity. If we examine some regulations, there is no mention of open border system. Passport Regulations-1952 says: "In case of the Nepalese residing for long or permanently settled down in any foreign country want to visit Katmandu, they will require to have the permit issued from the concerned District/City Magistrate or Passport issued by the Embassies or Consulates of Nepal in the respective country or from the Alainchikothi (as Consulate Office of Nepal) in Patna, India."

In the same way, the Sample of Rahadani/Permit-April 1862 says: "Nepalese to go out of Katmandu Valley and Nepal to Nepal via India should require to obtain Rahadani/Permit from Rahadani Goswara (Office) or Gadhi/Gaunda." There was also arrangement to provide permanent passport paying Nepali Rupees Five for one year to the general people, who come and go through Gadhi and by aero-plane from 14 April 1952.

On the other hand, if we make a study on the existing Immigration Act-1992, even the Indian nationals should produce visa to enter Nepal. Article-3 (1) of the Act says: "No foreigners are entitled to enter into the Kingdom of Nepal and reside in Nepal without having passport and visa." In this connection, the question arises: who are the foreigners?

Immigration Regulations-1992 (Second Amendment-2002), Article 2(B) defines: "Foreigner means any person, not being the citizen of Nepal at present, as it must be understood." In the regulations, no special provision has been made for Indian nationals.

It indicates that the regulated border system should also be followed for the Indian nationals. If there was some memorandum or agreement to maintain open border system between two countries, the Immigration Act and Regulations would not have been issued in this manner.

Next, Article-7 of Nepal-India Joint Press Statement-23 March 2000 reads: "The two Prime Ministers agreed on the need to prevent the misuse of the open border by terrorists, criminals and other undesirable elements and directed that co-operation in this regard be enhanced. Discussions on the management of the border would continue in the Joint Working Group on Border Management between the two Home Secretaries." This scribe had published an article in a daily newspaper on the regulation of border. In response to this article, Sanjaya Verma, Counselor of Indian Embassy, Katmandu wrote in the Letter to the Editor column of the same daily supporting this scribe that "Open border between two countries is not mentioned in any of the articles of 1950 Nepal-India Treaty. Open border is an emblem of most intimate friendship that has existed between both countries from ancient time to this date."9 So all these facts reveal that there is no black and white document on the prevalence of open border system between Nepal and India.

How the Border is made Open

There may be a query as to how the open border system prevailed between two countries. The answer may be, it prevailed only on the basis of mutual understanding, good neighbourly relations, religious sentiment, the same topography, social similarities, and family relationship. The next factor may be political. There was a very close contact among high-ranking political leaders of both nations. While Nepalese leaders had participated actively in the independence movement of India, Indian leaders also contributed to establish democracy in Nepal. And the open border made the movement of political leaders and bureaucrats of India and Nepal easy to shuttle back and forth without any interrogation or check in the border. The third factor is the social one. Socially, Nepalese boys are the sons-in-law of Indian nationals and Indian girls are the daughters-in-law of the Nepalese, mostly those who reside in the frontier. As a consequence, Indian and Nepalese parents are Samdhi (parents of daughter-in-law) to each other. So the border was made open socially for frequent visits to the kith and kin on either side of the frontier. The administration did not obstruct them in practice.

NEPAL AND THE SINO-INDIAN RIVALRY

The inevitable passing of the Fourteenth Dalai Lama, the radicalization of the Tibetan diaspora and the fervor of the international campaign to free Tibet are bound to keep the Himalayan dispute on the world's front pages. India, which has sheltered the Dalai Lama and tens of thousands of his followers, today increasingly sees Tibet as a bargaining chip with China in its overall bilateral relationship. Home to some 20,000 Tibetan refugees and wedged precariously between the assertive Asian giants, Nepal is likely to become an even more important theatre.

From Nepal's perspective, at least, the issue of Tibet goes beyond the freedom of a land, the liberation of a culture and a celebration of a way of life. The region always has been a conduit for major external protagonists to pursue wider objectives. The British Empire considered Tibet a critical part of the imperial chessboard, a legacy that lives on in today's geo-strategic milieu where China sees the region as a front rivals are intent on using to contain its rise. The Tibet issue has a peculiar psychological subtext in Nepal. Some of the same people, who profess the greatest admiration for the Dalai Lama and his cause, also hope that Tibet remains under Chinese control. Many Nepalese recognize that an independent Tibet would leave their country without a border with China. They believe such a situation would allow India, which has long invoked its own version of the Monroe Doctrine in the land-locked nation, to tighten its grip.

Although Tibet has been central to the Sino-Nepalese relationship, Nepal's formal contacts with China did not originate through the region. It began with China's quest for Buddhist texts, artifacts and codes from the wider Gangetic heartland. In the mid-seventh century, a powerful Tibetan king extracted consorts from Chinese and Nepalese royal households on the principle of peace through kinship. The two wives helped bring Buddhism to Tibet and opened a direct Himalayan route between Nepal and China, bypassing the more arduous one across Central Asia. As religion and trade began traversing the same Himalayan passes, peace and goodwill began losing ground. As the British sun rose higher over India, Nepal fought two wars with Tibet, precipitating a Chinese invasion. The Nepalese gained peace by entering into a tributary relationship with the Middle Kingdom, a duty they would discharge with utmost diligence. The Nepalese became the last foreigners to pay tribute to the Qing, as the arrangement helped maintain their independence as most of modern South Asia fell under the sway of the British Empire.

Nepal, which fought a third war with Tibet in 1855-56, refused to aid the Tibetans against a British invasion in 1904, but helped secure the withdrawal of the invaders. The diplomatic triumph was short-lived as the tottering Qing formally claimed suzerainty over Nepal.

Seeking to preserve its interests in Tibet - and project its independence - Nepal mediated between Beijing and Lhasa in 1912, after which Tibet enjoyed a period of de facto independence. For all their antipathy for the Qing and for each other, Chinese nationalists and communists pressed their country's claims on Nepal: Sun Yat-sen and Mao Zedong both included Nepal among territories China had lost to imperialism.

The Chinese invasion of Tibet in 1950 impelled the leaders of independent India to restore the monarchy at the top of a multiparty democracy in Nepal to forestall a communist advance southward. On the eve of Nepal's first democratic elections in 1959, Tibetans rose up in a failed revolt against Beijing, prompting the Dalai Lama's flight into exile in India. Nepal's first elected prime minister, B.P. Koirala, sought unsuccessfully to consolidate democracy by asserting Nepalese independence from India and China. When King Mahendra dissolved parliament, jailed Koirala and most of the elected leadership, and abolished multiparty democracy, much more than royal ambition was at play.

Nepal had become a center of Cold War intrigue where the United States and India - the world's two largest democracies - were working to undermine each other as were the communist giants China and the Soviet Union. By the end of the 1960s, Sino-American rapprochement put the two nations on the same side in Nepal for the duration of the Cold War. As the 1980s drew to a close, a new round of unrest in Tibet merged with student protests in Beijing, culminating in the bloody crackdown in Tiananmen Square. The fall of the Berlin Wall inspired the Nepalese to bring down the palace-led partyless Panchayat system, with Beijing a mere bystander. With the kingdom's democracy turning rancorous,

Nepalese disciples of Mao launched a bloody insurgency, a convulsion exacerbated by the assassinations of King Birendra and almost the entire royal family in a June 2001 palace massacre.

India, like the United States and Britain, opposed King Gyanendra's February 2005 coup, widely perceived to have enjoyed Chinese backing. Beijing, which accused the Nepalese Maoists of soiling the Great Helmsman's memory, armed the palace against the rebels. Yet a year later, as the royal regime faced massive popular protests, Beijing distanced itself from the monarchy and befriended the Nepalese Maoists. Chinese policy toward Nepal has been marked by much ambiguity, which both Beijing and Kathmandu have benefited from. One school of thought sees limited Chinese interest in Nepal, where phases of Beijing's assertiveness are the exception. In keeping with its foreign policy of unsentimental pragmatism, this school contends, China could easily concede Nepal as part of India's sphere of influence.

Chinese assertiveness, however, is likely to grow as its interests in Nepal go beyond the issue of Tibet to encompass its wider South Asian strategy. Nepal is only country that maintains diplomatic representation in Lhasa and Beijing reminds Kathmandu with ever greater regularity the responsibility that flows with the privilege. Enticing Nepal with promises of greater commercial benefits as part of its massive investments in Tibet, Beijing is intent on committing Nepal to firm political, security, economic and cultural agreements.

Should tradition become a more dominant part of Chinese regional diplomacy - as also seems likely - Nepal's status as a former tributary to the Middle Kingdom is likely to drive Beijing's policy. This is bound to raise anxiety levels in India, whose own relations with China sit uneasily atop planks of cooperation, competition and confrontation that are vulnerable to extra-regional pressures.

WEAKENING SINO-INDIAN RELATIONS

It was a very perturbed Sardar Patel who wrote to J L Nehru on November 7, 1950, pointing out that by our silence at the UN, we had accepted Chinese suzerainty over Tibet. In a forceful letter, Patel, not a man to mince words, warned that "The Chinese

Government has tried to delude us by profession of peaceful intentions" but in fact "it is not a friend speaking in that language, but a potential enemy". He then detailed ten steps that needed to be considered to strengthen our internal border security and defenses especially in the North-East. The tragedy is that this letter was apparently never discussed.

Till 1950, India had borders with Tibet not with China and by accepting China's suzerainty we became direct neighbours. Also this concession in effect gave China a border with Bhutan, Nepal, India and Pak-occupied Kashmir. It was in April 1954, India and China (People's Republic of China) signed an eight-year agreement on Tibet that set forth the basis of their relationship in the form of Five Principles of Peaceful Coexistence, or Panch Shila. On this political move, Nehru observes, "in the absence of either the wherewithal or a policy for defence of the Himalayan region, India's best guarantee of security was to establish a psychological buffer zone in place of lost physical buffer to Tibet."

Though India's diplomacy with China in 1950's was Hindi Chini bhai- bhai, but Nehru did not trust the Chine at all. By annexing Tibet, China now had the potential to be a player in South Asia. China and India are two of the world's oldest civilization and have coexisted in peace for millennia. Cultural and economic relations between China and India date back to ancient times. The Silk Road not only served as a major trade route between India and China, but is also credited for facilitating the spread the Buddhism from India to East. The revolt in Tibet in March 1959 leading to the Dalai Lama's flight to India added to China's paranoia. The Chinese thought it necessary to warn India through its ambassador Pan Tzu-Li in a letter to Prime Minister Nehru in May 1959, saying that China would make common cause with Pakistan. This would force India to face diplomatic and military pressure on two fronts. Therein lay the beginning of an all weather affair that is deeper than the ocean and higher than the mountains.

Relations between contemporary China and India have been characterized by border disputes, resulting in three major military conflicts-the Sino-Indian war of 1962, the Cholas incident in 1967, and the 1987 Sino-Indian skirmish. But 1962 and 1965, were landmark years when India was involved in conflicts with both her neighbours. This provided an opportunity for Pakistan to get closer to China and the two have remained locked in warm unusually unquestioned embrace. For China, becoming Pakistan's largest arm supplier to match Indian acquisitions-conventional, delivery system and nuclear weaponry was a convenient hedge against India, and Pakistan thus strengthened by American indulgence and Chinese connivance felt emboldened to hone its assistance to freedom fighters (militant) as a low cost, highly effective foreign policy option.

However, since late 1980s, both countries have successfully attempted to reignite diplomatic and economic ties. In 2008, China emerged as the largest trading partner of India and the two countries have also attempted to extend their strategic and military relations.

Despite growing economic and strategic ties, several issues continue to strain Sino-Indian relations. Though bilateral trade has continuously grown, India faces massive trade imbalance heavily in favour of China. The two countries have failed to resolve their long-standing border dispute and Indian media outlets repeatedly report Chinese military incursions into Indian Territory. In order to become a regional power, China aspires to destabilize India, and for this purpose it maintains good relations with all anti-India elements, whether it is insurgency in North-Eastern India, or Pakistan. To make Pakistan capable to equalize India in power, China gave its nuclear and missile technology. Pakistan is one of the largest users of Chinese military equipment. This has doubled India's harbour of suspicions about China's strong strategic relations with its arch-rival Pakistan while China has expressed concern about India's military and economic activities in disputed South China Sea. Consequently both nations have steadily built-up infrastructure along border areas.

Pak-India hostility has been well exploited by China as a bridge for accessing West Asia not just as a counter to the US. It seeks geostrategic space and the rich mineral deposits of oil and gas, copper, gold, zinc, lead, iron-ore and aluminum in these countries including Afghanistan and Central Asia. There are reports of Saudi-

Pakistan-China tie up on nuclear issues as well. Chinese ambitions extend beyond using Pakistan as a low cost secondary deterrent to counter India. Ayesha, a Pakistani analyst observes, China is an 'empire by stealth' which is "growing steadily without necessarily taking on the socio-political or economic liabilities of its client states." China will invest only in the extractive industries of Pakistan not in the country's development.

China is surrounding India from all the sides, By building a railway station for Pakistan at zero line, would mean that PLA is at stone's throw It is building a naval base in Gwarda on the Makran coast that has great significance and importance for China only if has unimpeded access through Gilgat and Baltistan, from where it can keep an eye on all Indian, European and American vessels passing through Persian Gulf, the recent development where Pakistan is leasing Gilgat and Baltistan to China for fifty years has been a cause of great concern to India authorities. Building of a base in Maldives, developing a civil port in Sri Lanka, building a naval base in Myanmar etc, is adding more fuel to the fire. Whatever is happening with India, India seems to be very much affected by continuous bullying by China, but can India do something to control it? If India won't act, China will take India soft and will either include it in its own influence and try to maintain its monopoly in the region or it will crush India. The need of the hour is that India has to do something, it should have a strong economy first, strong international relations second, and good military third. Then only India can keep its stand otherwise messing with China will be like inviting punishment for India. Had India heeded Sardar Patil's advice in 1950 it would not perhaps been in this state of feeling surrounded by China from all sides?

NEPAL'S FORECAST AND CHALLENGES AMIDST GREAT RIVALRY

These instances of interference and rivalry bring both opportunities and challenges to Nepal. The biggest challenge so far is to balance the relationship between both India and China. Since for Nepal, both neighbours are equally important. India has been historically and culturally the most important neighbor for

Nepal whereas recent posture of China as an emerging economic superpower is equally important for Nepal to boast its economic performance and investments. Thus, for Nepal, maintaining equidistant relationship between these two big neighbours is one of the most challenging foreign policy imperatives and interestingly there are signs of optimism and potential benefits as well.

There is consensus on both sides in India and China that stability of Nepal is in their best interest. Tibet is of vital importance to China, which is why Beijing wants peace and stability in Nepal whereas, due to the historical, socio-economic and cultural relationship between Nepal and India, political stability and economic development is major concern for India as Nepal and India shares open and porous borders. Thus de-stable Nepal is direct security imperative to India.

India has recently redefined its strategy towards Nepal. The current Indian Ambassador to Nepal Shri Jayant Prasad opined on a recent program that "India and Nepal are equal and sovereign states, and in keeping with the spirit of non-intervention in each other's domestic affairs, India does not have preferred electoral outcomes, preferred ruling arrangements or favourites among political parties".

Chinese Prime Minister Wen Jiabao, paid a visit to Nepal in January this year. During his short official visit to Nepal, interestingly encouraged the continuation of Nepal's traditional and cordial relations with India. At the luncheon that Prime Minister Baburam Bhattarai had hosted in Premier Wen's honor at Singha Durbar quoted the Chinese leader as saying that Beijing wishes to see the "continuation of Nepal's warm and friendly ties with India", pointing that relations between China and India are also deepening. Later Indian Prime Minister Manmohan Singh in his meeting with Nepal's Deputy Prime Minister Bijaya Kumar Gachhadar in New Delhi later that month indicated that it is comfortable with Nepal's close relationship with its northern neighbor China, India has said it is positive about recent developments in the Sino-Nepali relationship.

Prime Minister of Nepal Dr. Babu Ram Bhattarai on his first address to parliament as Prime Minister on August 28, 2011, "We should abandon a 'Buffer State Policy' between two giant neighbours China and India" and added "Instead, Nepal should act as a 'friendship bridge' between the two countries". Since Nepal is strategically placed between the two largest growing economies and China has become India's largest foreign trade partner with US$ 60 billion dollars worth of transactions. The bilateral trade is expected to reach US$100 billion. Transportation cost, on average, amount to 10% of the total trade. In other words, in a trade of 100 billion, transportation cost will be to the tune of US$ 10 billion. If Nepal can tap only 10% of the transportation moving from Nepal, the country can generate about US$ 1 billion worth of business annually, a substantial amount for a country like Nepal. As not all goods can be economically moved from one country to another by air or sea route alone, surface route can provide an attractive alternative for movements of goods. However, Nepal needs to develop its infrastructure (road and railways) to handle this traffic in trade. Nepal can seek the assistance from both countries in this respect. Also, development of such an infrastructure will help boost Nepal's bilateral trade with each of these neighbours.

Final Remarks

Given the perceived competitive and in some cases even adversarial potential of Sino-Indian relations, China expects to find itself pitted against India's national interests, possibly even in concert with the US. For India on the other hand, it is critically important to balance China's rising power. By not doing so, India's own increasing role as a regional power would be reduced. This would also have serious ramifications for India's interests in South Asia but also other parts of world like Southeast Asia where there is increasing rivalry and competition between Delhi and Beijing. Reinforcing India's contradictory engagement with the region is the fact that while India has got a seat at the table, it has yet to shape the rules of the regional architecture of which it is a member. Underlying New Delhi's inability to be a proactive shaper of regional security is the fact that it lacks a strategic vision of its regional role. On the other hand, the very diverse set of challenges confronting India in South Asia make it very difficult to adopt overall consistent, universal strategies.

This leads to our observation that Nepal should clearly prioritize its national interests and adopt a policy in managing its relationships with India and China, that best preserves and promotes her national interests.

As the country has recently undergone political transformation, such national interests could be: security, internal stability, economic development, and establishing a sound democratic mechanism. In order to preserve its long term security, it is necessary for Nepal to understand the sensitivity of India and China in terms of their security related issues and adopt policies wisely, following a middle path, that respects the interests of both neighbours without endangering its own sovereign and independent position.

Given the historic role of India in the political transformation of Nepal, India being the largest democratic system, may potentially serve as an example for Nepal to establish democratic mechanisms. Furthermore, given the historic ties of Nepal's major political parties and the military with India, the diplomatic and non-diplomatic involvement of India in establishing conditions in order to institutionalize democratic values, and to bring political stability, has been observed as an asset to mature the democratic practices and political institutions of Nepal whether the example mentioned in this paper of New Delhi's intervention into the military reshuffle can be viewed in this manner remains an open question.

In contrast, China has always expressed that Nepal is capable of solving its own internal problems, and has largely kept itself out of the Nepalese political affairs. The findings of this paper also show a clear preference for stability and order on the Chinese side and cordial working relations with all political parties in Nepal. Implicitly Chinese ODA and its 'One-China' policy with regard to the Tibetan question may be regarded as pressure and a clear attempt to influence the polity in Kathmandu. Another vital national interest of Nepal has been the economic development, which ultimately helps to promote stability.

Nepal has benefitted from the economic assistance of both India and China, and considering the economic rise of both countries such assistance could provide substantial benefits in the future. It would be highly beneficial for India too, if she conducts her external affairs, positively and matures the "standard of diplomatic dealing," towards her smaller neighbours. This could contribute to extracting goodwill and considerable willing respect by pulling surrounding neighbours towards India, which would substantially, facilitates to establish its desire as a regional power and assist in lessening China's influence, "perceived and potential.

SINO-INDIAN RIVALRY PLAYS OUT IN NEPAL

While mocking the severe dependency of Nepal, particularly the politicians, to India and the Indian establishment, it is often joked that if it rains in Delhi, they open umbrella in Kathmandu. While people keep debating whether particular government in Kathmandu is pro- or anti-Indian, the relationship between the two very dissimilar neighbours in South Asia remains highly complex and quite often veers towards trouble.

Nepal's geographical proximity to India apart, the 'dependency' factor has become historic as the latest uninterrupted period of such relationship exists for almost two centuries by now. It was in the fateful Sugauli Treaty of 1815 that Nepal was forced to cede almost one third of its territory in the east, west and the south to the British India thereby also ensuring that the British would not encroach further north.

Ever since, regardless of the nature of regime in Kathmandu and the ups and downs in the formal political relations, the social and economic realities of the Indo-Nepal relationship have remained largely unchanged, with the low-productivity subsistence economy of Nepal being dependent on the industrializing Indian economy.

After the Indian independence, the Indo-Nepal Treaty of Peace and Friendship of 1950 was signed, which galvanized the relationship between Nepal and independent India. Even though the calls for amending or even scrapping the 1950 treaty are ccommon and occasionally become very loud in Nepal, the persistent economic dependence on India as a result of chronically under-performing economy and lack of clarity about alternative of that treaty has ensured that the treaty endures even though it can be scrapped unilaterally with a year's time.

Interestingly, the time of the latter treaty between Nepal and India almost coincided with the invasion of Tibet by the newly born People's Republic of China led by Mao Zedong. In the context of new found determination of the Chinese to reassert themselves after the triumph of communist revolution, it became necessary for India to maintain and even strengthen the existing relationship with Nepal. Even now many analysts in India regret the act of their then government which condoned the Chinese act of transgression eventually loosing the important buffer zone between the two Asian giants to China.

With eventual peaceful takeover of Sikkim in 1975, however, and the whole-spectrum dominance that India enjoys in another buffer country Bhutan, some of the scores of loosing Tibet to China were settled, many others argue. By any means, the only effective and strategically important buffer zone between the two rising Asian powers is now Nepal with its whole length separating the northern provinces of India from the Tibet Autonomous Region of China. With increasing economic and military clout of both the powers, the stakes for both in maintaining influence in Nepal have risen significantly.

The increasing importance attached by both the countries to the relationship with Nepal is shown by the fact that both of the new envoys sent to Nepal by India and China recently are senior most till date. Even as successive governments in Kathmandu keep reassuring the Chinese side about Nepal's firm commitment to 'One China Policy' and the Chinese keep praising that commitment, the real and overwhelming concern of the Chinese is somewhat different.

There is no denying the facts that there is steady traffic of Tibetans fleeing to India through Nepal and that there is a significant Tibetan refugee population inside Nepal. Given China's determination to project Tibet as a part of Chinese economic miracle and not the socio-culturally exploited periphery, this flow of refugees through Nepal has become very sensitive issue between Nepal and China while dragging other countries into spotlight occasionally. The other important issue for the Chinese has been, particularly in the recent past, to ensure that the government in

Kathmandu should not be so pro-Indian as to threaten the Chinese interests in Nepal.

On the other hand, the core interests of India in Nepal go even further. Even though Nepal, small and landlocked as it is, has historically been dependent on India economically, the cost of having a regime in Kathmandu overtly hostile to India serves worst the Indian interests in Nepal. Unlike Bhutan where India has become hugely successful in harvesting the hydropower in addition to establishing itself as a trusted big brother in all strategic matters, similar attempts in Nepal have brought patchy success at best. The lingering border disputes and the perception in Nepal that India is exploiting Nepal for its weakness and systemically encroaching the Nepali land has all along generated a strong anti-India sentiment in Nepal. It is to take advantage of this sentiment that the politicians in Nepal have time and again resorted to anti-India rhetoric even though there is little prospect of meaningfully confronting India in any front.

On the other side, the Indian elites are not at all enthused by the fact that the leftists and apparently pro-China parties have been constantly gaining ground in kathmandu pushing the traditionally India-friendly parties like Nepali Congress to the corner. And they repeatedly show this displeasure through anti-Nepal rhtoric in India where many draw a parallel between the rise of Maoist insurgency and eventual ascent to power of the Maoist party in Nepal and steadily growing Naxalite insurgency in many Indian states. Above all this, around 800 km long open border between the two countries means that any strife or instability in Nepal obviously tends to spill over to the northern part of India. Moreover, given the eternal hostility between India and Pakistan the issue of Pakistan-based terror-groups using the Nepali land and open border to attack Indian targets has been a constant source of attention and apprehension for India. It is in best interest of India to have a compliant or at least cooperative regime in Kathmandu.

In wider geopolitical context also, the overarching concerns of both the neighbours intersect in Nepal. With increasing warmth in the Indo-US relations and the worsening stand-off with the East Asian countries in the South China Sea, the matters are only worsening for China with the latest news of Indo-Vietnam deal to jointly explore for oil in the waters that China says are 'contested'. Further collaboration between or among other Asian countries that share the apprehension about China's rise can create further trouble. In this context, it only makes sense for China to strengthen relationship with Nepal which despite its tiny size, forms an important buffer with India. All this said, the act of balancing the interests of the south and the north has been a very delicate task for the government in Kathmandu. When the acts of deporting back the Tibetan refugees on China's pressure anger the western benefactors like US, the matters get further complicated.

While the two Asian powers are involved in active exchange of gestures and even threats with each other in 'hot' issues like the Sino-Indian border dispute or the Indian deal with Vietnam, a silent but crucial diplomatic game goes on Kathmandu. With Chinese ambassador to Nepal Houlan recently blasting the "international forces" for instigating the Tibetan movement to contain China's rise, it takes little for these issues to come in the front. With increasing mercury of the diplomatic tensions between the two giant neighbours because of a host of issues ranging from border disputes to increasing Indo-US and Sino-Pakistan proximity to increasingly hot dispute in the South China Sea, striking a balance could be increasingly hard for Nepal.

And so long as Nepal remains mired in dismal economic performance and politics starting and ending at demagoguery, thereby perpetuating its endless dependence on India, little will be Nepal's ability to choose what policy vis-à-vis each of the neighbor best suits its interest. As of now Nepal is focused at just at not offending or annoying any of the neighbours, oblivious to the greater geostrategic rivalries and games.

CHINA'S GROWING POWER IN NEPAL: IMPLICATIONS ON TIBETAN REFUGEES

There are more than 20,000 Tibetans residing in Nepal, living with no defined legal status as the Nepalese law does not recognise the rights of refugees under the principal treaties that govern their status under international law. Provided they have a Nepalese "refugee identity certificate" (RC), Tibetans who arrived before 1989 can remain in Nepal with certain limited rights. Most live in an uneasy state of subsistence, principally in a small number of isolated settlements in the Kathmandu valley and Pokhara. Tibetans residing in Nepal are essentially stateless. They are neither citizens nor refugees under the law, and they possess neither the legal status nor the rights with which to improve their welfare. Moreover, legally resident Tibetans cannot travel to certain "restricted" regions of Nepal, typically those near the border with China. Nepal has not acceded to the 1951 Refugee Convention, or its 1967 Protocol, and has no domestic asylum law. In the absence of formal refugee legislation, the Government of Nepal has embraced different approaches for different refugee populations. Given the nearby scenario, the state of Tibetan refugees' condition in Nepal continues to be grim, more or less, due to the Chinese mounting pressure in the region. According to the latest United States State Department Human Rights Report for 2009, Tibetans repatriated from Nepal reportedly suffered torture, including electric shocks, exposure to cold and severe beatings and were forced to perform heavy physical labour...Tibetan refugees in Nepal also witnessed curtailment of freedom of expression as police imposed restrictions on demonstrations and sometimes detained demonstrators.

As China continues to rise as one of the Asian giants and a superpower in the making, its dealings with the Tibetan movement has scaled the borders and one can observe the alteration in international political dynamics on this issue. Regarding Sino-Nepal relations, on the inter-national front there has been mounting concern over the growing economic relationship between Kathmandu and Beijing, and the escalating ignorance of human rights and fundamental freedoms of Tibetan refugees in Nepal.

In the beginning of March itself, when the Tibetan exiles marked the 51st anniversary of Tibet's invasion by China, the Nepal Government deployed more than 500 policemen in Kathmandu. Also, the Chinese authorities snapped most links, including the Friendship Bridge, between the former Buddhist kingdom and its neighbour Nepal.

It also insisted to control Nepal's nearly 1800 km open border with India, to tab the Tibetans' movement from this side. Moreover, the detainment of Thinley Gyatso by the Nepal Police also hit the news headlines. Gyatso is considered as the unofficial messenger of the Dalai Lama. In addition to this, recent months have witnessed the Nepal Police conducting raids in areas around the Tibetan religious shrine of Boudhanath, a major pilgrimage destination for Tibetan Buddhists. Besides, at least about 25 Tibetan refugees, imprisoned in Nepal for protesting against the Chinese occupation of their homeland, began a hunger strike, demanding their release. However, the Nepal authorities have made it clear that the 'protests against friendly nations such as China will not be tolerated'.

China's power on Nepal is not a new issue, especially when it comes to the Tibetan question. Historically, the Nepalese royals used to have a close and cordial relationship with China. As per the historical records, in the eighteenth century China and Nepal signed the Sino-Nepalese Treaty, to put a halt to Kathmandu's adventurism in Tibet.

The accord was in itself marked by Chinese political domination in the region. During twentieth century, after a lot of crests and troughs in the relationship, both the countries concluded a treaty based on the "five principles of friendly relations". In contemporary times, both the countries are working together to gain economic prosperity, and to contain India's emerging status in Asia. The very foundation of Nepal's policy towards China is to counter India's influence in the region. Moreover, Nepal supports the 'One-China policy', which considers both Tibet and Taiwan as inseparable parts of China and forbids its territory to be used for anti-China propaganda. With the collapse of the Nepali monarchy under King Gyanendra in 2006 and the ascendance of the Unified Communist Party of Nepal (Maoist) and the Unified Communist Party of Nepal (Marxist-Leninist), Nepal has been constantly working on to cultivate deeper economic ties with China. One glaring example of Sino-Nepal relations and its influence on Tibetan refugees was witnessed during the Beijing Olympics in 2008, when the Nepal Government came down heavily on the Tibetan refugees' protest against China.

Exhibiting a alike trend of Beijing's escalating influence in Kathmandu, the International Campaign for Tibet Report 2009 brought to light the growing influence of China over the Nepali Government, judicial system, civil society and media. It further revealed how the Tibetans are experiencing a rise in harassment and extortion, more restrictions on their movements and greater difficulty in securing education and jobs than ever before.

As the situation continues to remain the same, the United Kingdom's 12th Annual Report on Human Rights has voiced its serious concern about the Tibetan refugees' freedom of expression in Nepal. According to media reports, there is an increasing despair among the community in Kathmandu, particularly among the most vulnerable, that is, those without papers. The Nepali Government had made a decision that all Tibetan shops, restaurants and businesses be officially registered. To do that, one needs 50,000 Nepali rupees ($ 500) and proper residence status in Nepal.

The issue of Tibetan refugees has forever made headlines in the international community who look forward for the resolution of the issue.

International entities like the United Nations (UN), United States (US), European Union (EU) and international donors are playing a vital role in providing relief to the Tibetan refugees. For over three decades and six presidential administrations, the US has remained steadfast in its "One-China" policy.

Reiterating the one-China principle and recognising that Tibet is part of the China, the US Government under the leadership of President Barack Obama in 2009 supported the early resumption of talks between Beijing and representatives of the exiled Tibetan spiritual leader, the Dalai Lama. Moreover in 2009, US Secretary of State Hillary Clinton vowed not to let human rights concerns hinder cooperation with China.

However, in 2010 the US State Department singled out China alongside Iran, Cuba, North Korea and Myanmar as among the worst rights abusers in 2009, which led to a series of terse exchanges between the US and China. In February 2010, the Obama Administration invited the non-governmental organisations to submit their proposals to run a one-year-long project supporting the Tibetan refugees in India, Nepal, and to a lesser extent, Bhutan. Proposals targeted solely or predominantly to the Tibetan refugee population in Nepal come to about $ 250,000. The programmes for Tibetan refugees focus mainly on protection, including prevention and response, to gender-based violence, health and nutrition, livelihoods and education, water and sanitation sectors in Nepal.

Over the years, the European Parliament has followed proceedings in Tibet closely. In 2009, the European Parliament has also urged China to negotiate and resume talks with the Dalai Lama's representatives with a view to bringing about a "positive, meaningful change in Tibet", not ruling out autonomy for the region, a solution that Members of the European Parliament (MEPs) believe need not compromise China's territorial integrity. In its key demand, the Parliament urges the Chinese Government to consider the Memorandum for Genuine Autonomy for the Tibetan People of November 2008 as a basis for substantive discussion leading towards positive, meaningful change in Tibet, consistent with the principles outlined in the Constitution and laws of the People's Republic of China.

The resolution called on the European Union (EU) Council Presidency to adopt a declaration on the same lines. Again in March 2010, the MEPs held a debate on the current situation of Tibet and voiced their concerns about the human rights situation. During the debate EU Commissioner and Vice-President of the European Commission Maros Sefcovic said: The EU position does not leave any room for misunderstanding.

Therefore, let me stress: the EU respects the sovereignty and territorial integrity of China, including Tibet. We respect the 'one China' policy... However, we have always supported peaceful reconciliation through dialogue between the Chinese authorities and the representatives of the Dalai Lama. This dialogue has to be constructive and substantive, addressing all core issues such as the preservation of Tibet's unique culture, religion and traditions and the need to achieve a system of meaningful autonomy for Tibet within the Chinese Constitution.

China has played an important, if at times hidden, role in the Nepali Government's crackdown on Tibetan demonstrations. The unusual number of statements from Nepali leaders reiterating the ban on "anti-China" activities suggests increasing pressure from

Beijing. China has long claimed that the bedrock of its foreign policy is "non-interference" in the internal affairs of other countries. Yet it has directly involved itself in Nepali affairs. China's ambassador has publicly exerted China's influence on the Nepali Government through strong and frequent statements, calling for the arrest of protesters and urging the government to take strong action. With the Chinese influence creating deep impression on the Nepal's politics, the Tibetans refugees in Nepal face another challenge for their survival.

9

Modernisation Plans of the Indian Army

Despite the army leadership's best efforts, the ongoing Revolution in Military Affairs (RMA) had, till recently, almost completely bypassed the Indian Army. For well over a decade the army's efforts to modernise had been thwarted due to political neglect and lack of adequate budgetary support. The funds made available for modernisation are extremely limited and a large portion of these funds is surrendered year after year. For Financial Year 2006-07, a sum of Rs 3,000 crore was surrendered as unspent. The fact that 155 mm ammunition for the Bofors howitzer had to be imported from South Africa during the Kargil conflict in 1999 tells its own tale of persistent shortages. Had the conflict not been confined to the 150 km frontage of the Kargil sector, T-72 and 130 mm medium gun ammunition too would have run short and it would have been politically embarrassing for the government as well as the army. In the plains the army would have had to fight with obsolete Vijayant tanks and several other vintage equipment that were unsuitable for combat. However, sustained efforts by Army HQ have now borne fruit and the army's modernisation drive is once again well underway.

In the prevailing era of strategic uncertainty, while terrorism has become the primary threat, the external and internal threats and challenges faced by India are such that a large army is still required to be maintained. Also, a high degree of preparation and operational readiness is still necessary as conventional war, though improbable, cannot be categorically ruled out. At the same time, heavy capital investments in modern defence equipment are undoubtedly a drain on a developing economy that is ill-equipped to handle the burgeoning defence expenditure. Several eminent analysts have recommended that qualitative upgradation should be accompanied by quantitative downsizing of personnel strength of the army. However, given its responsibilities for border management and the manpower-intensive low intensity conflict that the army is involved in, this is easier said than done.

Future conventional conflict on the Indian sub-continent will in all probability result from the ongoing low-intensity limited war on the Line of Control (LoC) with Pakistan or the unresolved territorial and boundary dispute with China and will be predominantly a land conflict. The Indian Army seriously lacks a potent firepower punch, especially in the mountain sector. Precision-guided munitions (PGMs) have still to enter service in numbers large enough to make a real difference. The reconnaissance, surveillance and target acquisition (RSTA) assets necessary for the optimum exploitation of even the existing firepower assets are grossly inadequate. Automated command and control and decision support systems have been on the drawing boards for several decades but are yet to mature.

In a future conventional war that will be fought under the nuclear shadow, manoeuvre will be extremely limited. This restriction will lead to much greater emphasis being placed on firepower to achieve the laid down military aim. Hence, it is imperative that artillery modernisation is undertaken with alacrity so as to generate firepower asymmetries on the future battlefield. After a long spell of keeping the powder dry, action on modernisation of the Indian artillery is livening up once again. Since January 2008, the Ministry of Defence (MoD) has issued three global tenders for 155mm guns and howitzers for the mountains, the plains and self-propelled guns for the deserts. Summer and winter trials are expected to be held over the next one year and, red tape permitting, contracts may be awarded as early as in the first half of 2010.

Artillery firepower had paved the way for victory during the Kargil conflict. Despite the lessons learnt in Kargil, modernisation of the artillery had continued to lag behind. The last major acquisition of towed gun-howitzers was that of about 400 pieces of 39-calibre 155mm FH-77B howitzers form Bofors of Sweden in the mid-1980s. This gun had proved its mettle in the Kargil conflict. Just when a contract for 120 tracked and 180 wheeled self-propelled (SP) 155mm guns was about to be concluded after years of protracted trials, South African arms manufacturer Denel, a leading contender for the contract, was alleged to have been involved in a corruption scam in an earlier deal for anti-material rifles (AMRs). The other two howitzers in contention, from Soltam of Israel and BAE (Bofors) of Sweden did not meet the laid down criteria according to the COAS and Army HQ recommended fresh trials, setting the programme back at least three to four years. Another key issue was that the howitzers that had been offered were technology demonstration models and not guns that were in actual service with the home country armies.

The probability of the next conventional war breaking out in the mountains is far higher than that of a war in the plains. With this in view, the artillery recently conceptualised a requirement for a light-weight towed howitzer of 155mm calibre for employment in the mountains. Neither the present Bofors howitzer nor its replacement will be capable of operations in the mountains. A light-weight 45-calibre 155mm howitzer weighing less than 5,000 kg, with a light but adequately powered prime mover, is ideal for the mountains. The gun-train should be capable of negotiating sharp road bends without the need to unhook the gun from the prime mover. The two British 45-calibre 155mm howitzers that competed for the US contract for a similar howitzer some years ago – the UFH (Ultra-lightweight Field Howitzer) and the LTH (Light-weight Towed Howitzer) – could be considered for licensed production with transfer of technology.

In January 2008, the MoD floated a Request for Proposal (RfP) for 140 pieces of ultra-light 39 calibre 155mm towed howitzers for use by the Indian Army's mountain formations and, presumably, by its rapid reaction divisions – as and when these are raised as it will be easy to transport by air. 140 howitzers will be adequate to equip seven medium artillery regiments and will cost approximately Rs 3,000 crore. The RfP has been reportedly issued to UK's BAE Systems (which now owns Bofors), for the M777 howitzer claimed to be the lightest in the world at under 4,220 kg, and to Singapore Technologies for the Pegasus SLWH.

India has floated a global tender for the purchase of 400 155mm towed artillery guns for the Army, to be followed by indigenous manufacture of another 1,100 howitzers, in a project worth a whopping Rs 8,000 crore. The RFP was issued to eight prospective bidders including BAE, General Dynamics, Nexter (France), Rhinemetall (Germany) and Samsung (South Korea). An RfP has also been issued for 180 wheeled self-propelled guns for around Rs 4,700 crore for employment by mechanised forces in the plains and semi-desert sectors.

Since the Bofors 155mm Howitzer was introduced into service, the indigenously designed and manufactured 105 mm Indian Field Gun (IFG) and its (not so) light version, the Light Field Gun (LFG), have joined the 75/24 Indian Mountain Gun, the 100mm Russian field gun and the 122mm Russian howitzer on the obsolescence list. Approximately 180 pieces of 130mm M46 Russian medium guns have been successfully "up-gunned" to 155mm calibre with ordnance supplied by Soltam of Israel. The new barrel length of 45 calibres has enhanced the range of the gun to about 40 km with extended range ammunition.

A contract for the acquisition of two regiments of the 12-tube, 300mm Smerch multi-barrel rocket launcher (MBRL) system with 90 km range was reported to have been signed with Russia's Rosoboronexport in early-2006. This will be a major boost for the long-range firepower capabilities of the army. If this weapon system had been available during the Kargil conflict, Pakistan's brigade HQ and forward airfield at Skardu and other targets deep inside POK could have been hit with impunity. Extended range (ER) rockets are being introduced for the 122 mm Grad MBRL that has been in service for over three decades. The ER rockets will enhance the weapon system's range from 22 to about 40 km. A Rs 5,000 crore contract has also been signed for the serial production of the Pinaka MBRL weapon system, another DRDO project plagued by time delays and completed with help from Larsen and Toubro and the Tatas.

The modernisation plan of tube artillery alone is likely to cost Rs 13,000 crore. The major acquisitions will be of initial lots of 400 towed howitzers of 155mm calibre, with a barrel length of 52 calibres, costing about Rs 4,000 crore, 140 ultra-light weight 155mm towed howitzers, with a barrel length of 45 calibres, costing Rs 3,000 crore and 180 SP 155mm howitzers costing Rs 5,000 crore. The "Shakti" project for a command and control systems for the artillery, called Artillery Combat Command and Control System (ACCCS), has reached the stage of maturity and is now being fielded up to the regimental level.

The BrahMos supersonic cruise missile (Mach 2.8 to 3.0), with a precision strike capability, very high kill energy and range of 290 km, was inducted into the army in July 2007. It is a versatile missile that can be launched from TATRA mobile launchers and silos on land, aircraft and ships and, perhaps in future, also from submarines. Fifty BrahMos missiles are expected to be produced every year. Efforts are underway to further increase its strike range. BrahMos Aerospace has orders worth Rs 3,500 crore from the army and the navy, which has opted for the anti-ship as well as the land attack cruise missile (LACM) versions. These terrain hugging missiles are virtually immune to counter measures due to their high speed and very low radar cross section and are far superior to sub-sonic cruise missiles like Pakistan's Babur. Chile, Kuwait, Malaysia and South Africa have shown interest in acquiring this missile.

The Indian army is extensively engaged in ongoing internal security (IS) and counter-insurgency operations (CI) and simultaneously needs to prepare itself for a future border conflict that may spill over to a larger conventional war in the plains. In keeping with these twin requirements, Army HQ have apparently decided to upgrade the IS and CI capabilities of infantry battalions as well as enhance their Infantry firepower-mobility-EW (electronic warfare) punch for a possible war in the plains against Pakistan or in the mountains against China. The Army Chief's modernisation vision is to "adapt to high-end technology, improve night-fighting capability... (and) information technology, information warfare and network centric warfare."

Despite its large-scale employment on border management and extensive commitments in Internal Security and Counter Insurgency operations, infantry modernisation had been languishing for several decades when the Ministry of Defence (MoD) finally cleared a visionary plan to modernise the army's infantry battalions by according "in principle" approval in the form of Modification 4B to the war establishment (WE) of a standard infantry battalion in 1998. However, no funds were specially sanctioned for this purpose till the BJP-led NDA government approved the expenditure of Rs 3,500 crore in September 2003. Thereafter, approval had to be sought on file for each new weapon system or piece of equipment on a "case-by-case" basis as has become the norm. It is by now well-known how each such case chronicles the saga of an uphill struggle to get approval first from the MoD, then MoD (Finance) and, finally, the Ministry of Finance (MoF). All this is only possible after the DRDO has first certified that the weapon system or equipment in question cannot be developed and manufactured indigenously and such a certificate is hard to come by.

While 250 Kornet-E anti-tank guided missiles (ATGMs) with thermal imaging sights have substantially increased the anti-tank capability of infantry battalions, most efforts to modernise the equipment held by infantry and Rashtriya Rifles (RR) units are aimed at enhancing their capability for surveillance and target acquisition at night and boosting their firepower for precise retaliation against infiltrating columns and terrorists holed up in built-up areas. About 200 hand-held BFSRs with practical ranges up to seven to eight km where clear line of sight is available, 2,000 hand-held thermal imaging devices (HHTIs) with ranges up to 2,000 metres for observation at night and stand-alone infra-red, seismic and acoustic sensors with varying capabilities have enabled infantrymen to dominate the Line of Control so completely that infiltration has come down to almost a trickle.

The newly acquired weapons, which complement these surveillance and observation devices, include: 1,500x84 mm rocket launchers, including some disposable ones; 1,000 AMRs (anti-material rifles); 8,000 UBGLs (under-barrel grenade launchers); 4,000 new generation carbines; 300 bullet proof vehicles; and, several hundred accurate sniper rifles. However, the numbers acquired and the ammunition stocks are still inadequate and need to be made up more rapidly. While the INSAS 5.56 mm assault rifles have now been in service for almost 10 years and proved to be effective, the light machine gun (LNG) version is still facing teething problems and the carbine version for close quarter battle has not found favour with the army. New 5.56 mm assault rifles of bull-pup design with an integrated laser range finder and grenade launcher are under development. Efforts are also being made to provide infantry platoons and sections with integrated GPS-based navigation system, secure light-weight walkie-talkie radio sets and better protective gear with a helmet that incorporates a built-in head-up display.

The mechanised infantry is now equipped with the BMP-2 ICV Sarath of which over 1,000 have been built since 1987. A new variant is the 81 mm Carrier Mortar Tracked Vehicle (CMTV) that is based on the chassis of the Sarath ICV and has been indigenously developed to enhance the integral firepower available to mechanised infantry battalions. Other variants include a command post, an ambulance, armoured dozer and engineer and reconnaissance vehicles. Mechanised reconnaissance and support battalions need better surveillance radars, fire-and-forget ATGMs and effective night fighting capability. However, their capabilities can be upgraded on a lower priority compared with infantry battalions that are engaged in border management and IS/CI operations.

The army's infantry battalions also need their own mini or micro UAVs like Elbit's Skylark or Rafael's Skylite, among others, to partly reduce the extent of patrolling necessary in internal security environment and to improve their surveillance capability in conventional conflict. These UAVs should have a range of about 10 to 15 km, should be light-weight (less than 10 kg), hand-launched, carry a single payload, e.g. a daylight video camera or infra-red camera for night operations, and should be inexpensive enough to be dispensable. A mini ground control station should be authorized at battalion HQ for planning and control. Ideally, these should be indigenously designed and developed and locally manufactured.

A new DRDO project, that is reported to be ongoing, aims to equip future soldiers with lightweight force multipliers. Soldiers of the future will have miniaturised communication and GPS systems, small power packs, weapon platforms and smart vests with fibre-optic sensors. The soldiers will also have better and lighter combat fatigues, boots, belts, ammunition pouches, rucksacks and rations in the form of meals-ready-to-eat. Though somewhat akin to the US Army's Land Warrior programme, the Indian Army programme for modernisation of infantry battalions will result in only incremental changes. However, these would be significant enough to make a difference on the battlefields of the Indian sub-continent. The infantryman's average combat load is approximately 27 kg, including the 3.06 kg 5.56 mm INSAS assault rifle and its "on weapon" ammunition. If this can be reduced by even a few kg, it will enable the soldier to improve his agility in battle and counter-insurgency operations. Ultimately an infantryman has to be prepared to engage in hand-to-hand combat and agility can make a difference between life and death.

For over 350 infantry battalions, plus about 150 Rashtriya Rifles, Assam Rifles and Territorial Army battalions, these major changes will be extremely costly to implement and will spill over at least 10 to 12 years – that is, if the funds can be found. What is certain is that there is no alternative to making the financial commitment that is necessary to enhance the operational capabilities of the army's infantry battalions. Without modernising this cutting edge of its sword, the army will soon begin to resemble the armies of India's lesser neighbours.

The indigenously designed Arjun main battle tank (MBT) has been in the pipeline for over two decades. Though the tank has many good features, it has consistently failed to meet the army's GSQR for an MBT and orders have been placed for only 124 tanks to be manufactured. The lack of progress on the Arjun MBT had slowed down the pace of armour modernisation. India then signed a deal with Russia to acquire 310 T-90S tanks in the year 2000. Subsequently, India began to assemble these tanks at Avadi. It has recently been reported that in addition to these, India has decided to acquire another 347 T-90S tanks and assemble them within the country.

The first Indian assembled T-90S (Bhishma) rolled off the production line on January 8, 2004. While T-90S Russian tanks have provided new teeth to India's strike formations in the plains and corrected the imbalance that had resulted from Pakistan's acquisition of T-80 UD from Ukraine and the Al Khalid tanks jointly designed with China, a large number of T-72 (Ajeya) tanks are still awaiting modernisation. The lack of a suitable fire control system and night fighting capability are major handicaps. As soon as the obsolescent Vijayanta tanks are phased out of service, it will be time to also discard the old T-55s as well as they can no longer be either upgraded or modernised. Armour modernisation is now proceeding apace and can be classified as a success story.

The air defence (AD) of mechanised forces is another area that is crying for attention. The Kvadrat missile system that has been the backbone of AD for strike formations since the early 1970s are now ageing and need urgent replacement. With the DRDO's indigenous Akash medium-range and Trishul short-range missile projects not making major headway, it is time to start looking at import substitutes. In fact, the assets of Army Air Defence corps of the army are grossly inadequate to provide effective protection against enemy aircraft during war. This young corps requires substantial capital infusion to really come into its own.

Another DRDO project that is way behind schedule is the Nag anti-tank missile system. The antiquated Jonga-mounted SS-11 B1 anti-tank guided missile (ATGM) system has been replaced in missile battalions by MILAN shoulder-fired ATGMs. However, a vehicle-mounted missile system like the Nag is definitely necessary for reconnaissance and attrition tasks. The experimental Plan AREN tactical communications system for strike formations needs early replacement. The ability to carry broadband data needs to be enhanced in particular. Even the more recent static communications network called ASCON lacks ISDN capability for the real-time transmission of maps and streaming video.

While some Stentor long-range BFSRs have been in service for over a decade, medium-range radars are still to be acquired. At least about 30 to 40 weapon locating radars (WLRs) are required for effective counter-bombardment, especially in the plains, and only a few have been procured so far. Israeli Searcher-I unmanned aerial vehicles (UAVs) have been introduced into service but these are few in number and it will be a long time before these will really make a difference by providing a real-time surveillance capability so that ground forces can initiate action even as a fresh input is received. Only a small number of Searcher – II UAVs, with an upper ceiling that makes them suitable for the mountains, have been acquired.

An automated command and control and decision support system for use by the General Staff is still a far cry and so are supporting systems like the battlefield surveillance system and air space management system. The urgent requirement of real-time satellite reconnaissance systems has still not been accepted despite the nuclear overhang under which the armed forces now operate. Even though the cameras on India's remote sensing and cartographic satellites now have sharply enhanced resolutions, less than one metre, military-grade photographs of still better resolution are needed to be purchased from the open market. These sources may dry up quickly during war.

A "system of systems" approach must be followed so that scarce RSTA and communications resources can be synergistically configured and optimally exploited. The war in Iraq fought in March-April 2003 was based on the concept of "network-centric warfare" in which surveillance sensors, targeting systems and "shooters" are fused together in a seamless "system of systems" that reduced response time between the acquisition of a target and its destruction to 15 to 20 minutes. While such a system may take over a decade to establish, a beginning must be made right away.

PGMs are increasingly gaining currency as weapons of choice in conflict on land, both to accurately destroy critical hard targets quickly as well as to avoid or at least minimise collateral damage. During the Gulf War I in 1991, despite all the CNN-generated hype of smart bombs flying unerringly through ventilators, PGMs formed less than 10 percent of the total high explosive dropped over Iraq and were rather inaccurate. The "collateral" destruction of an air raid shelter harbouring women and children has been too well documented to bear recounting. The coalition forces did not destroy a single Iraqi Scud missile launcher. In Kosovo, PGMs accounted for about 30 per cent of the ordnance dropped and accuracies had improved considerably by 1999. In the post-September 11, 2001 retribution inflicted on the Taliban militia and its al Qaeda supporters in Afghanistan, the share of PGMs had risen to nearly 60 percent. In Gulf War II in Iraq, the ratio of PGMs went up to nearly 70 per cent. The Indian artillery does not have any PGMs worth the name. Only limited quantities of the Russian Krasnopol PGM have been imported for the Bofors 155 mm howitzer. Among others, the Bofors Bonus PGM is a suitable candidate, subject to successful trials in the deserts and the mountains.

Finally, the approach to army modernisation must be more focused; the priorities must be clearly established and then adhered to. The government must give a firm commitment in terms of funds and the Ministry of Defence must streamline its procedures and processes for speedy procurement of high priority weapons and equipment. It is time to institute a rolling, non-lapsable defence modernisation fund of Rs. 25,000 crores as a viable method of ensuring that defence procurement is not subjected to the vagaries of annual budgets. The present situation is disturbing and, if allowed to go on indefinitely, will seriously compromise the army's preparedness to fight the next border war that inimical neighbours like Pakistan can be expected to thrust on India.

INDIAN ARMY

National security, is that ambience, in which a nation is able to protect and promote its national values, pursue its national interests and aspirations, in spite of, or, in the absence of, external or internal threats, real or perceived. Threats to national security may impact on any aspect of a nation's life, ranging from its territorial integrity and internal cohesion to its economy, political structures and institutions, diplomacy, national leadership, national character, morale and so on. The armed forces of a nation have a vital role to play in meeting these threats.

India's National Interests

India's national interests, simply stated, are as follows :-

- National sovereignty.

- Unity and integrity of the country.
- Democratic and secular polity.
- Economic development.
- Social and economic justice.
- Favourable world order.
- Preservation and promotion of our values.

Our Strategic Vision

Nations adopt a national strategy in order to attain their national interests or goals. Clarity of strategic vision is very important if the national strategy is to take the nation on an optimal course to its desired national objectives. Let us, briefly, examine our strategic vision.

We are one of the oldest civilizations on Earth. Nearly, a sixth of the human race is Indian. Our country occupies a strategic location on the southern promontory of the Asian land mass and dominates large expanses of the Indian Ocean including the routes to the oil rich Gulf region, South East Asia and the Orient. These intrinsic attributes qualify, indeed demand, that India be a major player at the world stage.

By tradition, India has been a peace-loving and responsible nation. It has abjured aggression, espoused the doctrine of 'Ahimsa' or non-violence, led the non-aligned group of nations and played a constructive role as a member of the United Nations. This tradition clearly suggests that India should aspire to become a benign and moral superpower, rather than one, whose brute strength or wealth alone, confer on it, its place under the sun. Any examination of our strategic environment must be carried out against the backdrop of our strategic vision and the long term plans and strategies needed to realise that vision. By such an examination, we shall be able to predict the strategic environment of the decades ahead, and arrive at the appropriate force structure and equipment profile for our Army of the future.

Aim

The aim of this chapter is to visualise the likely national security environment in 2020 with special reference to the threats and challenges that may confront us at that time, and arrive at the most appropriate force structure and equipment profile for the Indian Army of 2020.

While the focus in this chapter is on the Army, it must not be construed that the Army can fulfil its missions without the active partnership of the Navy and the Air Force. Joint, or preferably, integrated tri-service functioning in war and peace will be an essential pre-requisite for success in all our operations. With this background, let us examine the geo-strategic environment we might face in 2020.

The Geo-Strategic Environment

Two major events, roughly a decade apart, have played a major role in shaping the current geo-strategic environment. The first being the demise of the Soviet Union. It brought the Cold War to an end, and conferred on the USA, an unchallenged pre-eminence in the world as the sole superpower. The second was the '9-11 Event'-the 11th September 2001 terrorist attacks on targets in Washington DC and New York. This impelled the USA to declare 'War on Terrorism', and attack Afghanistan and Iraq with a 'coalition of like-minded countries', with the purpose of ousting their regimes, which were sponsors of terrorist groups like Al Quaeda and were hostile to the USA. The USA believed that Iraq was in possession of weapons of mass destruction (WMD).

The impact of these two events are now being clearly felt in international affairs and by all indications, appear to be long lasting. We need to take note of the following major ramifications, which are specially relevant to India :-

- The USA has become hegemonic. Her style of diplomacy is increasingly becoming peremptory and coercive.
- The UN has been sidelined by the USA, which, acts at will, ignoring the need for UN's sanction.
- The USA has adopted the doctrine of 'Preemptive Military Intervention'. In consonance with this doctrine-threats, whether real and present or, perceived, are not allowed to mature, by use of military force.
- The USA has drawn a list of countries, which are 'of concern'

to it. Of these, it has dealt with Afghanistan and Iraq. North Korea and Iran await similar treatment by the superpower. Recently, India has voted in favour of a USA backed resolution against Iran possibly to secure military materials, nuclear technology and fuel for civilian purposes. If India resiles from her pro-USA stance in the late November 2005 voting, the USA may deny its expectations. This would amount to dictating India's foreign policy.

- China is neither amenable to coercion nor susceptible to being 'contained'. Besides, because North Korea is a protégé of China, the latter has a major role in USA's dealings with that country. The USA has also economically engaged China, as it provides a large market for US manufactured goods. The USA believes too, that as the USA-China trade gets increasingly intertwined, the likelihood of an armed conflict between the two will correspondingly reduce.
- The European Union, despite reservations on the part of some constituents, is for purposes of *realpolitik* pro-USA.
- Russia, because of her present economic debility, is supporting the USA or, at least, not opposing her. It may become more independent in its attitude as its economy recovers, a process that has already begun.
- Pakistan is a 'major non-NATO ally' of the USA and also its frontline state for the 'War on Terrorism'. The US has troops and aircraft on Pakistan's soil. It has been permitted to set up bases in return for huge subventions and to bail out Pakistan from the brink of a near-collapse economic situation. In effect, Pakistan has become a client state of the USA with a less than independent foreign policy.
- Terrorism, religious fundamentalism, nuclear and missile technology proliferation are pressing concerns for the US. It believes that these could ultimately pose danger to its 'homeland', something about which the USA is hypersensitive, or, even paranoid.

These are some of the ramifications of the two events i.e. the Soviet collapse and the 9/11 event, which shall continue to influence international relations in the next two decades or more. However, by 2020, some changes would have taken place with regard to the circumstances of the world's principal nations. These are enumerated below :-

- The USA will continue to be the preeminent power. Nevertheless, her 'edge' over China would have reduced to a small margin.
- China would be increasingly inclined to join issue with the USA, taking into account its envisaged near-superpower status. However, she would not risk her new found prosperity by being over-assertive with the USA and thus risk war.
- India would have caught up with China and achieved parity with China in many areas, but not military.
- Pakistan will continue to be the USA's client state, and in case the latter so presses, she may even enter into a comprehensive peace agreement with India. Otherwise, Pakistan would prefer to keep tensions alive with India in order to extract concessions and benefits from both China and the USA who will want an economically resurgent India to be reined in.
- The USA's 'War on Terrorism' may prove to be endless as, though the enemy has been rightly identified, the means being applied are all wrong, indeed, self-defeating.
- Radical religion will pose problems for the entire world as such. As radicalism flourishes in less developed countries, by 2020, there would also be a large number of very poor countries with radicalism well entrenched.

After this brief estimate of the geo-strategic environment in, 2020, let us turn to India's internal security environment.

ROLE OF THE INDIAN ARMY

Armies are maintained by countries in order to safeguard their core values and national interests from external aggression and internal subversion. The Primary and Secondary roles of our Army are as under :-

- Primary Role. Deter external aggression and, if deterrence fails, defeat it by force.

- Secondary Role. Assist the Government in overcoming internal threats, foreign sponsored or indigenous, and aid the civil authority when requisitioned for the purpose.

Capabilities Entailed by the Role

The capabilities that the Army must posses to fulfil its role must be identified in accordance with our 'Vision' for the Army. The capabilities, thus identified are as under :-

- Deterrent Capability. The Army should be so strong in both conventional and nuclear weapons, that potential aggressors are deterred.
- War Fighting Capability. If deterrence fails, the Army should be able to fight a successful war against the enemy, over any terrain, and in conventional as well as NBC warfare situations.
- Internal Security Management Capability. The Army should be able to deal with and manage internal security situations of various types like insurgency, grave law and order situations; and also render aid to civil power, when requisitioned under various situations including disasters, both natural and man-made.
- Force Projection Capability. The Army should be capable of operating 'out-of-area' as part of an integrated task force, when ordered by the Government.
- Peace Keeping Operations Capability. The Army should be able to undertake UN Peace Keeping Missions in any part of the world and inter-operate with Army components of other countries in such operations.

Though we presently posses all these capabilities in some measure, the desired level is yet to be realised in many areas. Resource inadequacy, lack of clear policy directions from the Government, frequent 're-thinks' on the part of the Army, failure of timely supplies of material and shoddy quality of what has been supplied, are some of the reasons attributable to the Army's inability to achieve and retain the desired level of capability at all times. Perhaps, even more important reason, is the knowledge driven Revolution in Military Affairs (RMA), which accelerates the process of obsolescence of equipment, doctrines and tactics. It is in this critical area of RMA that a lot of work needs to be done so that we can have adequate levels of the desired capabilities, at all times. Let us now examine whether the present structure of the Army needs to be altered to enable the Army to fulfil its assigned role better.

ARMY'S CAPABILITY ACCRETION

The challenges that the army is expected to face in the next decade are not likely to be any less formidable. An appraisal of the emerging threats in fact indicates an increasing complexity of the missions that the army may be expected to execute.

The basic character of the Army's responsibilities is unlikely to witness significant changes. Till the boundary disputes with China and Pakistan remain unresolved, Army's most important role of ensuring the nation's territorial integrity will retain primacy. Concurrently, as in the past, the Army will continue to remain embroiled in combating militancy, insurgency and terrorism. With the prevailing instability in the immediate and near neighbourhood, and the growing regional and global role of our country, the Army must also be prepared to undertake missions beyond our borders. It may be added that however much the Army may want to resist, it will continue to be drawn to tackle internal law and order situations and national manmade or natural calamities.

How has the Army fared in the last two decades in the discharge of its responsibilities? At considerable cost to itself it has barely managed to keep the lid on. Given the serious shortage of junior officers, and the indifferent and insufficient weaponry at its disposal, the Army it can be contended, has done exceedingly well. Regrettably the problems of the Army, and the stresses it is subjected to, are understood only by those who are in it. The MOD and the political leadership, or for that matter also the strategic community have a vague awareness, nowhere close to the ground realities. This explains the decades of inertia.

Exploiting the progressive decline of our conventional military capability all through the decade of the eighties, Pakistan launched a well orchestrated offensive through irregulars in Kashmir from about the beginning of 1990. When the momentum of this offensive seemed to be petering out Pakistan did not hesitate to gamble for higher stakes by resorting to Kargil. The Kargil fiasco and the growing domestic instability, however, did not dampen Pakistan's appetite for fomenting trouble for us. The terror attack on our Parliament in 2001 and 26 Nov. 2008-Mumbai is still fresh in our memory.

Over the last few years China too has begun to demonstrate bellicosity, tinged with arrogance, against us. Border intrusions with the purpose of intimidation coupled with force accretions in Tibet and along the LAC, portend problems for us. Its aggressive posturing on other fronts compounds the basket of our concerns.

Viewed from the national security perspective it emerges that our concept of military deterrence has failed or is failing. Clearly then, the Army's conventional war fighting capabilities must be brought to levels that promise if not absolute, sufficient deterrence.

So how do we go about building a credible dissuasive conventional military deterrence? For the past two to three decades the three services have been unsuccessfully trying to drive the process. It would be mindless to persist with the same approach. The responsibility must shift to the PM and his Cabinet Committee on Security. This is not going to happen without some precipitate action. How this is to be brought about is a matter that the services must address? The Army could do with a totally fresh appraisal to cover its overall strength, its structure and equipment profile, the quality of its man power, its leadership and its training. Such a review could perhaps be relevant and necessary for the Navy and the Air Force as well.

Technological advancements are taking place rapidly. Correspondingly the rate of obsolescence is also increasing. It is therefore imperative that we manage change with much greater sophistication so as to ensure available funds are utilized optimally. It follows that individuals charged with formulating qualitative requirements, induction plans and evaluation of systems must be competent and have the requisite grooming and experience. Even though this issue has been debated before no concrete remedial steps have yet been taken.

INFANTRY

The Infantry is the largest arm of our Army and the only arm which has perhaps never had a respite from combat from the time the Naga insurgency began in the fifties. Matters worsened when we sent the expeditionary force to Sri Lanka for Operation Pawan. Ever since, the Infantry has continued, without break, to climb the stress ladder.

Considering the Infantry's constant engagement, aware that all Army Chiefs from the early nineties have sought to give the Infantry the highest priority in terms of equipping and modernizing it. But if we were to carry out a critical appraisal of the Infantry in 2010 the report card of twenty years effort would be quite dismal. How ironical, especially when costs are lower and the systems involved are relatively not so complex? The story is eloquent testimony to the manner in which the country's higher defence management works.

Almost everything that a soldier needs, from the clothes and boots to the weapon he carries, is at present well below par.

Consider the 5.56 family of weapons that the Army is currently equipped. The Army was virtually bulldozed into accepting these weapons. It was told that indigenous R&D must be encouraged. Promises were made that in the production models the user will get a much improved and more reliable version and that a superior Mark 2 will follow. The DRDO also hinted that high volume orders from many foreign customers would be placed soon after the Indian Army accepted the induction and placed orders for delivery. The Army had no choice but to accept though none of the commitments materialized. It has lived with these weapons for more than a decade and paid an incalculable price. A good and reliable personal weapon we know does wonders to a soldier's confidence and morale. But we have failed in giving him such a weapon. Shouldn't there be review and people held accountable?

Conceptually the start point of capability-building and modernization has to be the individual soldier. So we must begin by giving him the best we can. Essentially what the soldier needs is a good and reliable personal weapon, comfortable clothing with stealth and concealment features designed to ergonomically accommodate everything he has to carry, the best protection (body armour) that portable weight permits, stabilized helmet mounted computer screens, sensors and night vision devices for observation and using his weapons, effective communications and position locating/ situational awareness systems. In addition he requires a host of sundry items like eye protection goggles, contemporary light bag pack equipment etc. The approach should be to look at the tactical vest and the helmet (protective gear) as a platform on which the future soldier systems are embedded so that weight reduction and mobility improvements issues are optimally addressed.

The resolve to modernize the infantry soldier has been there for long, but the process has been painfully slow. Ways have to be found to accelerate the process and do it comprehensively. We must therefore begin as of yesterday.

When considering assault rifles we have quite a few options available; each having its unique features. Let us briefly look at the 21st century trends in assault rifles. Essentially they are refinements to the systems developed in the previous decades. Some exciting options that could be considered are:-

- *Heckler & Koch HK 416 firing the 5.56x 45 or the HK 417 firing the 7.62×51 NATO rounds.* Both these weapons have updated features with Picatinny rails, a drop free magazine release, and some other smart features.
- *Israel's IMI Tavor TAR-21.* It has a compact bull pup design and uses the NATO 5.56x 45 cartridges. It can easily be set up for right or left handed shooters and has several modular variants that come with a standard reflex sight.
- *XM 8 from the US.* This has quite a few modular variants with inbuilt electronics such as a laser sight, round counter and integral infra red and visible sights.
- *South Korea's XK11.* This is an interesting new rifle that has a ballistic computer, a laser range finder and a digital scope that provides the soldier with combat data and enables night firing through thermal imaging sights. The product is still at a prototype stage but has considerable promise.

- *The AK Series*. The Kalashnikovs family of assault rifles is much too well known.

An important trend in small arms in the 21st century is that sophisticated electronics is now being built into the design of these weapons. There could be some justification for the approach we have now adopted. A few years ago we had considered integration of night sights in our tender for assault rifles. At that time there weren't many who were offering such embedded systems. To my mind the idea was right though the timing was wrong. But now, with most weapon manufacturers developing weapons with built in electronics.

Given the current employment of the Army and looking at the two vital needs of the infantry soldier i.e. his personal weapon and his body armour, it is difficult to decide which merits greater priority. What is but evident that on both counts the establishment has been found wanting.

Today we have all of the Rashtriya Rifles and a significant proportion of the Army deployed in combating militancy, terrorism and insurgencies. Of these how many of their personnel, are equipped with suitable body armour? And what are the constraints to procuring body armour? On both counts we will get answers that are far from convincing, particularly when today we have a host of companies in India manufacturing body armour and combat helmets. With a dynamic and inclusive approach we can harness the capabilities of these companies to give us quality protection suits and helmets at competitive prices. As a matter of fact with some support in terms of investment in R&D and inducements of assured orders, our companies can well become global leaders in protective solutions.

Assessments suggest that in the development of 'small arms protective inserts' (SAPI), technology today is at only the 40 percent level. Both in the case of X SAPI-silicon carbide and ceramic and E SAPI, and high molecular weight polyethylene (HMW-PE) and aramid fibers, there are possibilities that by improving the quality of resins and making the weave more unidirectional, weight to protection ratios can be substantially improved. The infantry also needs to acquire better surveillance and target acquisition capabilities as well as more potent fire power at the section level and above. A mission, terrain and adversary based analysis may suggest the induction of special weapons and surveillance systems on a regional basis. It can be assumed that such an exercise would have been undertaken.

ARTILLERY

In my reckoning Artillery modernization has not made any headway because of two reasons. The first is that-blinded by the labels of 'support' and 'supported', the Army has not yet grasped the full import of the modern artillery on tomorrow's battlefield. The second can best be described by just one word: jinxed.

However like the Infantry, modernization of the artillery has also been a matter of concern in the last decade or so. In these years much has apparently been done but unfortunately without any headway. Actually the process began in the early eighties. But other than 400 Bofors guns procured in the mid eighties we have nothing else to show.

The exercise to procure new towed and mounted self propelled tracked and wheeled 155 mm 52 calibre guns are on. We are also planning to induct a specified number of light weight 155 mm guns for certain areas and missions. It is important at this juncture to focus on ensuring that the process of evaluation and induction moves without any hiccups and delays.

As we induct these guns the space of the contact battle at the tactical level will increase to a 30 km envelop thus enhancing our ability to destroy, maneuver, and defeat. Similarly we need to pay more attention to the requirements of the Artillery at the operational and strategic level. In this context even though we have been inducting the Prithvi, the BrahMos and the Agni series, the process has been based on the developmental projects of the DRDO and not on the basis of a well thought through conceptual framework.

The subject of rocket and missile artillery thus merits deeper examination. We require more systems that can provide coverage between the 30 to 100 Km ranges. Besides, the liquid propellant based Prithvi imposes certain operational limitations. Admittedly the Smerch rocket system has filled this gap to some extent but much more needs to be done. Firing platforms like the guns and rocket and missile launchers are just one of the four pillars upon which comprehensive artillery capability is structured. The other pillars are communications to include artillery command and control systems, surveillance systems and the ammunition systems. In the Kargil war our communications and surveillance systems were not adequate. Thus the guns could be exploited to only 30 percent of their potential.

In principle surveillance and target acquisition capabilities must exceed our delivery systems ranges by at least 30 percent. The ideal would be 50 percent. We have been working on this for a while but more needs to be done.

We should be able to establish a comprehensive surveillance and target acquisition grid by using a mix of ground and air/ space based sensors to include satellites, aircraft, drones, helicopters and tethered balloons. On the ground besides, electro optical devices and thermal cameras we will also require a sufficient number of weapon locating radars some of which should be employable in the mountains. The surveillance grid must allow for transmission and exchange of data to all shooters and decision makers in real time. The problems of surveillance in the mountains merit special attention.

Advancements in ammunition technology have led to a dramatic enhancement in the lethality and destructiveness of the artillery. With improved conventional munitions (ICM) the kill capacity of the ordinary shell has gone up in multiples. Smart and intelligent munitions now permit pinpoint accuracy enabling the artillery to engage and destroy fortifications and tanks from long ranges. We must induct such sophisticated ammunition speedily. However while doing so the challenge lies in getting the mix right since sensor/seeker based munitions are relatively very expensive.

WEAPONS OF MASS DESTRUCTION INDIA

Ballistic Missiles

a. Prithvi I-Army Version (150 km range with a payload of 1,000kg)

- Prithvi II-Air Force Version (250 km range with a payload of 500kg)

  Prithvi III-Naval Version (350 km range with a payload of 500kg)

b. Dhanush is a System consisting of stabilization platform and missiles and can fire either the 250Km or the 350Km range missiles.

   Then the following year in December the missile's 350Km version was tested from the INS Rajput and hit the land based target

c. The Agni Missile system comprises of Agni I, Agni II and the Agni III 1500 Agni I uses the SLV-3 booster (from India's Space Program) for its first stage and a liquid-fueled Prithvi for its second stage.

d. On the other hand India's Agni II missiles have a range of the 1500 to 2500 kilometers. Unlike the Agni I, the Agni II has a solid-fueled second stage. India has also tested the Agni III IRBM with a range between 3000 and 5500km kilometres which has two stages. With a normal payload of 1000kg it can travel 5000km

e. The Surya-1 and-2 will be classified as strategic weapons, extending the Indian nuclear deterrent force to targets around the world. India currently is limited by the range of the Agni-3 missile.

   The Surya-1 will have an expected range of 6000-10,000 km. It reportedly has a length of 40 m and a launch weight of 80,000 kg (some reports indicate as much as 275,000 kg. As the missile has yet to be developed, the payload and warhead are as yet unknown. It is believed to be a three-stage design, with the first two stages using solid propellants and the third-stage using liquid. The first test flight is expected in 2009, but there may be delays. The Surya-is a longer-ranged variant of the Surya-1. It has a reported range of over 20,000 km.

f. The Shaurya missile is a short-range surface-to-surface ballistic missile developed by DRDO of India for use by the Indian Army. It has a range of 600 km and is capable of carrying a payload of one-tonne conventional or nuclear warhead. The Shaurya missile provides India with a significant second strike capability.

g. Sagarika is a nuclear capable submarine-launched ballistic missile with a range of 750 km. This missile has a length of 8.5 meters, weighs seven tonnes and can carry a pay load of up to 500 kg

CRUISE MISSILES INDIA

a. Nirbhay is a long range, subsonic cruise missile being developed in India. The missile will have a range of 1000 km and will arm three services, the Indian Army, Indian Navy and the Indian Air Force.

b. India has acquired around 200 3M-54 Klub for arming Talwar class frigate, Shivalik class frigate, Kolkata class destroyer and Sindhughosh class submarine The Russian 3M-54 Klub is a multi-role missile system developed by the Novator Design Bureau (OKB-8) with a range of 250Km-300Km and a average speed of .8 Mach with a maximum of 2.9 Mach

c. Popeye II, an air launched cruise missile capable of carrying nuclear warheads with a range of 80 Km can be launched from planes was given to India along with missile defence radars in a deal.

   The exact number transferred to India is unknown, but possibly 20 missile to perhaps 50 missiles could have been given with possibly more being built in India.

d. India has Soviet P-70 Ametist submarine-launched cruise missiles.

   The missiles can carry nuclear warheads and have a range of 50-65Km.

e. The P-270 Moskit is a Russian supersonic ramjet powered cruise missile capable of being launched from land and ships. India has most probably bought both land and ship variants which have a range of 120km.

f. Akash is India's medium range surface-to-air missile defence system The missile can target aircraft up to 30 km away, at altitudes up to 18,000 m. Akash is said to be capable of both conventional and nuclear warheads, with a reported payload of 60kg. Akash can be fired from both tracked and wheeled platforms.

NUCLEAR SUBMARINES

According to some accounts India plans to have as many as 20 nuclear submarines capable of carrying missiles with nuclear warheads. The Advanced Technology Vessel (ATV) is a Nuclear Powered Ballistic Missile Submarine being constructed for the Indian Navy at Visakhapatnam, India The ATV is an SSBN and will be armed with the ballistic missiles.

Once it is completed, it can be equipped with 6-8 nuclear capable Dhanush, Sagarika or Agni SLBM ballistic missiles and upto 12 BrahMos cruise missiles. It is also to be fitted with an advanced sonar system. The second and third submarines of the class may incorporate the Nirbhay as well. As of July 2007, the Sagarika missile as well as Dhanush had undergone three successful tests each. The ATV is to be unveiled on January 26, 2009 but trials will start later that year while induction is planned for 2010.

The INS Sindhuraj, INS Sindhuvir, INS Sindhuratna, INS Sindhushastra, INS Sindhukesari and INS Sindhuvijay are capable of launching 3M-54 Klub and BrahMos nuclear-capable cruise missiles.

India bought 10 Kilo class (in India known as Sindhughosh Class) submarine of which 6 have been refitted by the Russian Navy so that the they can launch cruise missiles such as nuclear capable BrahMos and 3M-54 Klub's 3M-14E variant.

The Submarine version of the BrahMos has been tested from static, underwater test stands in Russia and from the INS Sindhuvijay. As the Sinduvijay is similar to the other refitted submarines the test is considered a success.

MODERNISING THE INDIAN INFANTRY

Why has it taken the Army so long to conceive an upgrade package for the oldest, most potent and intensely employed fighting arm, the Infantry, even after the so-called revolution in military affairs? The foot soldier, the original and most versatile weapon system that is always taken for granted, has emerged from the dubious shock and awe strategy of recent campaigns as its ultimate arbiter. India has paid dearly for the neglect of its infantry in terms of cost, casualties and over-stretch of battle. But the Infantry has never let us down. Kargil was its finest hour. Gen VP Malik, the Army Chief of the time, wryly noted: "We will fight with what we have."

So when for the first time an international conference of Army and defence industry was launched last week to put the forgotten soldier centre-stage, some misgivings were natural. While Army Chief Gen JJ Singh outlined his vision for the soldier system of the future, the conspicuous and total absence of Government - MoD - robbed the conference of any sanctity. In sharp contrast, for a MoD-sponsored defence finance seminar earlier in the month, Government officials and ministers were stepping over each other at Vigyan Bhavan.

Free India's Army came into being in 1947 and within weeks, the Infantry soldiers landed in Srinagar to save J&K from being gobbled up by Pakistani tribal raiders. Since then, the Infantry has not ceased fighting proxy wars there and later, elsewhere too. A former Army Chief, Gen SR Choudhury, who was not from the Infantry, described the Infantry as the Army and vice versa. Field Marshal Montgomery said: An army is considered only as good as its Infantry.

The experience of four wars, several border skirmishes, two out-of-area missions, the ceaseless campaign to counter cross-border terrorism in Kashmir, numerous other insurgencies in the North-East, internal stability operations elsewhere in the country and UN peace keeping operations make the Indian Infantry the most battle-hardened and combat rich force in the world. The simple and uncomplaining infantryman has given so much to so many for so little. The modernisation of the infantry was first attempted - halfheartedly - in the mid-1980s by the Perspective Planning branch of the Army Headquarters. The bias for mechanised warfare, zealously pursued by Gen Sundarji, was so pronounced that the Infantry modernisation plan was skipped altogether. Guns, tanks, APCs were the weapons in demand. The Infantry was ignored. Had a modest upgrade package been undertaken at that time, infantry would have been more combat contemporary and effective.

Instead, till recently, some soldiers were still using World War II equipment and clothing. Shameful as it was, soldiers had to buy rucksacks and other accoutrements from the market. DRDO is still to come out with a light bulletproof vest. The Army failed to accurately visualize the nature of combat it would fight in the future. Pakistan-sponsored insurgency in Punjab did not alert the nation and the Army to the proxy war brewing in J&K. We defaulted on both counts - anticipating low intensity conflict and cross border terrorism and preparing the Infantry for it.

Despite the sustained counter-insurgency and counter-terrorism campaign in J&K and the North-East since the 1990s, the Army was sluggish in investing in the infantry. The first Gulf War reintroduced the fiction that wars could be won from the air. The air campaigns in Bosnia and Kosovo temporarily turned fiction into reality. But 9/11 broke the myth of supremacy of air power. Operation Enduring Freedom in Afghanistan lasted 76 days; 65 of these were air operations.

The 11-day land offensive secured a temporary and incomplete victory against the Taliban. Operation Iraqi Freedom on the other hand, fought for 20 days was bereft of any preparatory air campaign though a secret air war preceded it. Unhappily for the US/NATO-led coalition forces, despite their pyrrhic military victories, low intensity wars in Afghanistan and Iraq are continuing in full blaze.

The recent 34-day war in Lebanon and the ongoing campaign in Gaza demonstrate the limits of Israel's military power. Used to decisive victories in less than 10 days, Israeli Defence Forces (IDF) were badgered by Hassan Nasrallah's jihadi militia. Reliance on air power, tanks and guns in Lebanon as substitute for ground troops - infantry - was motivated by casualty aversion. We too have to be sensitive to casualties.

The wars in Lebanon, Iraq and Afghanistan spurred by the growing cult of Osama bin Laden and Hassan Nasrallah require a redefinition of the concept of power and military success. Success would necessarily be an inclusive military victory encompassing post-conflict stability and reconstruction. For this we need Infantry.

The Indian Army should not get overly seduced by high-sounding warfare like 'netcentric' that the West is being diverted into. This is not to suggest we ignore the strides in high-tech warfare. But as a former US NATO Commander noted recently: "This netcentric stuff is great but our men in Baghdad are being blown up with their Humvees by IEDs." He suggested that we address the battle we are fighting before switching to the one we will fight in the future.

India's supreme operational challenge is and will be the maintenance of internal security. Just last month, Prime Minister Manmohan Singh stated this ground reality. The Infantry is at the heart of counterinsurgency and counter-terrorism operations and may well get sucked into anti-Naxal operations as well. Keeping the Army operationally ready for both conventional and unconventional missions is imperative but the emphasis has to be on the business of the day: CI and CT.

The Indian Infantry is belatedly embarking on a modernisation programme to enhance its combat skills through increased lethality, communications, surveillance, mobility and suvivability. These force multipliers will enable the soldier to fight all-weather, 24x7 and on any terrain in the right battle-configuration albeit with the accent on LIC.

The GSQR for the Future-Infantry-Soldier-As a System (F-INSAS) must empower not encumber the soldier. DRDO must compete with domestic and international industry. DRDO has one more chance to make amends for its omissions and commissions. F-INSAS must strike the right balance between the surge of technology and sensibility of the soldier keeping the battle of the future in mind. Defence Minister AK Antony should accord F-INSAS the highest strategic priority.

INDIAN ARMY'S MODERN PLANS

Future conventional conflict on the Indian sub-continent will in all probability result from the ongoing low-intensity limited war on the Line of Control (LoC) with Pakistan or the unresolved territorial and boundary dispute with China and will be predominantly a land conflict. The Indian Army seriously lacks a potent firepower punch, especially in the mountain sector. Precision-guided munitions (PGMs) have still to enter service in numbers large enough to make a real difference. The reconnaissance, surveillance and target acquisition (RSTA) assets necessary for the optimum exploitation of even the existing firepower assets are grossly inadequate.

Automated command and control and decision support systems have been on the drawing boards for several decades but are yet to mature. In a future conventional war that will be fought under the nuclear shadow, manoeuvre will be extremely limited. This restriction will lead to much greater emphasis being placed on firepower to achieve the laid down military aim. Hence, it is imperative that artillery modernisation is undertaken with alacrity so as to generate firepower asymmetries on the future battlefield. After a long spell of keeping the powder dry, action on modernisation of the Indian artillery is livening up once again. Since January 2008, the Ministry of Defence (MoD) has issued three global tenders for 155mm guns and howitzers for the mountains, the plains and self-propelled guns for the deserts.

Summer and winter trials are expected to be held over the next one year and, red tape permitting, contracts may be awarded as early as in the first half of 2010. Artillery firepower had paved the way for victory during the Kargil conflict. Despite the lessons learnt in Kargil, modernisation of the artillery had continued to lag behind. The last major acquisition of towed gun-howitzers was that of about 400 pieces of 39-calibre 155mm FH-77B howitzers form Bofors of Sweden in the mid-1980s. This gun had proved its mettle in the Kargil conflict. Just when a contract for 120 tracked and 180 wheeled self-propelled (SP) 155mm guns was about to be concluded after years of protracted trials, South African arms manufacturer Denel, a leading contender for the contract, was alleged to have been involved in a corruption scam in an earlier deal for anti-material rifles (AMRs). The other two howitzers in contention, from Soltam of Israel and BAE (Bofors) of Sweden did not meet the laid down criteria according to the COAS and Army

HQ recommended fresh trials, setting the programme back at least three to four years.

Another key issue was that the howitzers that had been offered were technology demonstration models and not guns that were in actual service with the home country armies. The probability of the next conventional war breaking out in the mountains is far higher than that of a war in the plains. With this in view, the artillery recently conceptualised a requirement for a light-weight towed howitzer of 155mm calibre for employment in the mountains. Neither the present Bofors howitzer nor its replacement will be capable of operations in the mountains. A light-weight 45-calibre 155mm howitzer weighing less than 5,000 kg, with a light but adequately powered prime mover, is ideal for the mountains. The gun-train should be capable of negotiating sharp road bends without the need to unhook the gun from the prime mover.

The two British 45-calibre 155mm howitzers that competed for the US contract for a similar howitzer some years ago – the UFH (Ultra-lightweight Field Howitzer) and the LTH (Light-weight Towed Howitzer) – could be considered for licensed production with transfer of technology. In January 2008, the MoD floated a Request for Proposal (RfP) for 140 pieces of ultra-light 39 calibre 155mm towed howitzers for use by the Indian Army's mountain formations and, presumably, by its rapid reaction divisions – as and when these are raised as it will be easy to transport by air. 140 howitzers will be adequate to equip seven medium artillery regiments and will cost approximately Rs 3,000 crore. The RfP has been reportedly issued to UK's BAE Systems (which now owns Bofors), for the M777 howitzer claimed to be the lightest in the world at under 4,220 kg, and to Singapore Technologies for the Pegasus SLWH.

India has floated a global tender for the purchase of 400 155mm towed artillery guns for the Army, to be followed by indigenous manufacture of another 1,100 howitzers, in a project worth a whopping Rs 8,000 crore. The RFP was issued to eight prospective bidders including BAE, General Dynamics, Nexter (France), Rhinemetall (Germany) and Samsung (South Korea). An RfP has also been issued for 180 wheeled self-propelled guns for around Rs 4,700 crore for employment by mechanised forces in the plains and semi-desert sectors.

Since the Bofors 155mm Howitzer was introduced into service, the indigenously designed and manufactured 105 mm Indian Field Gun (IFG) and its (not so) light version, the Light Field Gun (LFG), have joined the 75/24 Indian Mountain Gun, the 100mm Russian field gun and the 122mm Russian howitzer on the obsolescence list. Approximately 180 pieces of 130mm M46 Russian medium guns have been successfully "up-gunned" to 155mm calibre with ordnance supplied by Soltam of Israel. The new barrel length of 45 calibres has enhanced the range of the gun to about 40 km with extended range ammunition.

A contract for the acquisition of two regiments of the 12-tube, 300mm Smerch multi-barrel rocket launcher (MBRL) system with 90 km range was reported to have been signed with Russia's Rosoboronexport in early-2006. This will be a major boost for the long-range firepower capabilities of the army. If this weapon system had been available during the Kargil conflict, Pakistan's brigade HQ and forward airfield at Skardu and other targets deep inside POK could have been hit with impunity. Extended range (ER) rockets are being introduced for the 122 mm Grad MBRL that has been in service for over three decades. The ER rockets will enhance the weapon system's range from 22 to about 40 km. A Rs 5,000 crore contract has also been signed for the serial production of the Pinaka MBRL weapon system, another DRDO project plagued by time delays and completed with help from Larsen and Toubro and the Tatas.

Modernisation Plan

The modernisation plan of tube artillery alone is likely to cost Rs 13,000 crore. The major acquisitions will be of initial lots of 400 towed howitzers of 155mm calibre, with a barrel length of 52 calibres, costing about Rs 4,000 crore, 140 ultra-light weight 155mm towed howitzers, with a barrel length of 45 calibres, costing Rs 3,000 crore and 180 SP 155mm howitzers costing Rs 5,000 crore. The "Shakti" project for a command and control systems for the artillery, called Artillery Combat Command and Control System (ACCCS), has reached the stage of maturity and is now being fielded up to the regimental level. The BrahMos supersonic cruise missile (Mach 2.8 to 3.0), with a precision strike capability, very high kill energy and range of 290 km, was inducted into the army in July 2007.

It is a versatile missile that can be launched from TATRA mobile launchers and silos on land, aircraft and ships and, perhaps in future, also from submarines. Fifty BrahMos missiles are expected to be produced every year. Efforts are underway to further increase its strike range. BrahMos Aerospace has orders worth Rs 3,500 crore from the army and the navy, which has opted for the anti-ship as well as the land attack cruise missile (LACM) versions. These terrain hugging missiles are virtually immune to counter measures due to their high speed and very low radar cross section and are far superior to sub-sonic cruise missiles like Pakistan's Babur. Chile, Kuwait, Malaysia and South Africa have shown interest in acquiring this missile.

The Indian army is extensively engaged in ongoing internal security (IS) and counter-insurgency operations (CI) and simultaneously needs to prepare itself for a future border conflict that may spill over to a larger conventional war in the plains. In keeping with these twin requirements, Army HQ have apparently decided to upgrade the IS and CI capabilities of infantry battalions as well as enhance their Infantry firepower-mobility-EW (electronic warfare) punch for a possible war in the plains against Pakistan or in the mountains against China. The Army Chief's modernisation vision is to "adapt to high-end technology, improve night-fighting capability… (and) information technology, information warfare and network centric warfare."

Despite its large-scale employment on border management and extensive commitments in Internal Security and Counter Insurgency operations, infantry modernisation had been languishing for several decades when the Ministry of Defence (MoD) finally cleared a visionary plan to modernise the army's infantry battalions by according "in principle" approval in the form of Modification 4B to the war establishment (WE) of a standard infantry battalion in 1998. However, no funds were specially sanctioned for this purpose till the BJP-led NDA government approved the expenditure of Rs 3,500 crore in September 2003. Thereafter, approval had to be sought on file for each new weapon system or piece of equipment on a "case-by-case" basis as has become the norm. It is by now well-known how each such case chronicles the saga of an uphill struggle to get approval first from the MoD, then MoD (Finance) and, finally, the Ministry of Finance (MoF). All this is only possible after the DRDO has first certified that the weapon system or equipment in question cannot be developed and manufactured indigenously and such a certificate is hard to come by.

While 250 Kornet-E anti-tank guided missiles (ATGMs) with thermal imaging sights have substantially increased the anti-tank capability of infantry battalions, most efforts to modernise the equipment held by infantry and Rashtriya Rifles (RR) units are aimed at enhancing their capability for surveillance and target acquisition at night and boosting their firepower for precise retaliation against infiltrating columns and terrorists holed up in built-up areas. About 200 hand-held BFSRs with practical ranges up to seven to eight km where clear line of sight is available, 2,000 hand-held thermal imaging devices (HHTIs) with ranges up to 2,000 metres for observation at night and stand-alone infra-red, seismic and acoustic sensors with varying capabilities have enabled infantrymen to dominate the Line of Control so completely that infiltration has come down to almost a trickle.

The newly acquired weapons, which complement these surveillance and observation devices, include: 1,500x84 mm rocket launchers, including some disposable ones; 1,000 AMRs (anti-material rifles); 8,000 UBGLs (under-barrel grenade launchers); 4,000 new generation carbines; 300 bullet proof vehicles; and, several hundred accurate sniper rifles. However, the numbers acquired and the ammunition stocks are still inadequate and need to be made up more rapidly. While the INSAS 5.56 mm assault rifles have now been in service for almost 10 years and proved to be effective, the light machine gun (LNG) version is still facing teething problems and the carbine version for close quarter battle has not found favour with the army. New 5.56 mm assault rifles of bull-pup design with an integrated laser range finder and grenade launcher are under development. Efforts are also being made to provide infantry platoons and sections with integrated GPS-based navigation system, secure light-weight walkie-talkie radio sets and better protective gear with a helmet that incorporates a built-in head-up display.

The mechanised infantry is now equipped with the BMP-2 ICV Sarath of which over 1,000 have been built since 1987. A new variant is the 81 mm Carrier Mortar Tracked Vehicle (CMTV) that is based on the chassis of the Sarath ICV and has been indigenously developed to enhance the integral firepower available to mechanised infantry battalions. Other variants include a command post, an ambulance, armoured dozer and engineer and reconnaissance vehicles. Mechanised reconnaissance and support battalions need better surveillance radars, fire-and-forget ATGMs and effective night fighting capability. However, their capabilities can be upgraded on a lower priority compared with infantry battalions that are engaged in border management and IS/CI operations.

The army's infantry battalions also need their own mini or micro UAVs like Elbit's Skylark or Rafael's Skylite, among others, to partly reduce the extent of patrolling necessary in internal security environment and to improve their surveillance capability in conventional conflict. These UAVs should have a range of about 10 to 15 km, should be light-weight (less than 10 kg), hand-launched, carry a single payload, e.g. a daylight video camera or infra-red camera for night operations, and should be inexpensive enough to be dispensable. A mini ground control station should be authorized at battalion HQ for planning and control. Ideally, these should be indigenously designed and developed and locally manufactured.

New DRDO Project

A new DRDO project, that is reported to be ongoing, aims to equip future soldiers with lightweight force multipliers. Soldiers of the future will have miniaturised communication and GPS systems, small power packs, weapon platforms and smart vests with fibre-optic sensors. The soldiers will also have better and lighter combat fatigues, boots, belts, ammunition pouches, rucksacks and rations in the form of meals-ready-to-eat. Though somewhat akin to the US Army's Land Warrior programme, the Indian Army programme for modernisation of infantry battalions will result in only incremental changes. However, these would be significant enough to make a difference on the battlefields of the Indian sub-continent. The infantryman's average combat load is approximately 27 kg, including the 3.06 kg 5.56 mm INSAS assault rifle and its "on weapon" ammunition. If this can be reduced by even a few kg, it will enable the soldier to improve his agility in battle and counter-insurgency operations. Ultimately an infantryman has to be prepared to engage in hand-to-hand combat and agility can make a difference between life and death.

For over 350 infantry battalions, plus about 150 Rashtriya Rifles, Assam Rifles and Territorial Army battalions, these major changes will be extremely costly to implement and will spill over at least 10 to 12 years – that is, if the funds can be found. What is certain is that there is no alternative to making the financial commitment that is necessary to enhance the operational capabilities of the army's infantry battalions. Without modernising this cutting edge of its sword, the army will soon begin to resemble the armies of India's lesser neighbours.

The indigenously designed Arjun main battle tank (MBT) has been in the pipeline for over two decades. Though the tank has many good features, it has consistently failed to meet the army's GSQR for an MBT and orders have been placed for only 124 tanks to be manufactured. The lack of progress on the Arjun MBT had slowed down the pace of armour modernisation. India then signed a deal with Russia to acquire 310 T-90S tanks in the year 2000. Subsequently, India began to assemble these tanks at Avadi. It has recently been reported that in addition to these, India has decided to acquire another 347 T-90S tanks and assemble them within the country.

The first Indian assembled T-90S (Bhishma) rolled off the production line on January 8, 2004. While T-90S Russian tanks have provided new teeth to India's strike formations in the plains and corrected the imbalance that had resulted from Pakistan's acquisition of T-80 UD from Ukraine and the Al Khalid tanks jointly designed with China, a large number of T-72 (Ajeya) tanks are still awaiting modernisation. The lack of a suitable fire control system and night fighting capability are major handicaps. As soon as the obsolescent Vijayanta tanks are phased out of service, it will be time to also discard the old T-55s as well as they can no longer be either upgraded or modernised. Armour modernisation is now proceeding apace and can be classified as a success story.

The air defence (AD) of mechanised forces is another area that is crying for attention. The Kvadrat missile system that has been the backbone of AD for strike formations since the early 1970s are now ageing and need urgent replacement. With the DRDO's indigenous Akash medium-range and Trishul short-range missile projects not making major headway, it is time to start looking at import substitutes. In fact, the assets of Army Air Defence corps of the army are grossly inadequate to provide effective protection against enemy aircraft during war. This young corps requires substantial capital infusion to really come into its own.

Another DRDO project that is way behind schedule is the Nag anti-tank missile system. The antiquated Jonga-mounted SS-11 B1 anti-tank guided missile (ATGM) system has been replaced in missile battalions by MILAN shoulder-fired ATGMs. However, a vehicle-mounted missile system like the Nag is definitely necessary for reconnaissance and attrition tasks. The experimental Plan AREN tactical communications system for strike formations needs early replacement. The ability to carry broadband data needs to be enhanced in particular. Even the more recent static communications network called ASCON lacks ISDN capability for the real-time transmission of maps and streaming video.

While some Stentor long-range BFSRs have been in service for over a decade, medium-range radars are still to be acquired. At least about 30 to 40 weapon locating radars (WLRs) are required for effective counter-bombardment, especially in the plains, and only a few have been procured so far. Israeli Searcher-I unmanned aerial vehicles (UAVs) have been introduced into service but these are few in number and it will be a long time before these will really make a difference by providing a real-time surveillance capability so that ground forces can initiate action even as a fresh input is received. Only a small number of Searcher – II UAVs, with an upper ceiling that makes them suitable for the mountains, have been acquired.

An automated command and control and decision support system for use by the General Staff is still a far cry and so are supporting systems like the battlefield surveillance system and air space management system. The urgent requirement of real-time satellite reconnaissance systems has still not been accepted despite the nuclear overhang under which the armed forces now operate. Even though the cameras on India's remote sensing and cartographic satellites now have sharply enhanced resolutions, less than one metre, military-grade photographs of still better resolution are needed to be purchased from the open market. These sources may dry up quickly during war.

A "system of systems" approach must be followed so that scarce RSTA and communications resources can be synergistically configured and optimally exploited. The war in Iraq fought in March-April 2003 was based on the concept of "network-centric warfare" in which surveillance sensors, targeting systems and "shooters" are fused together in a seamless "system of systems" that reduced response time between the acquisition of a target and its destruction to 15 to 20 minutes. While such a system may take over a decade to establish, a beginning must be made right away.

PGMs are increasingly gaining currency as weapons of choice in conflict on land, both to accurately destroy critical hard targets quickly as well as to avoid or at least minimise collateral damage. During the Gulf War I in 1991, despite all the CNN-generated hype of smart bombs flying unerringly through ventilators, PGMs formed less than 10 percent of the total high explosive dropped over Iraq and were rather inaccurate. The "collateral" destruction of an air raid shelter harbouring women and children has been too well documented to bear recounting. The coalition forces did not destroy a single Iraqi Scud missile launcher. In Kosovo, PGMs accounted for about 30 per cent of the ordnance dropped and accuracies had improved considerably by 1999. In the post-September 11, 2001 retribution inflicted on the Taliban militia and its al Qaeda supporters in Afghanistan, the share of PGMs had risen to nearly 60 percent. In Gulf War II in Iraq, the ratio of PGMs went up to nearly 70 per cent. The Indian artillery does not have any PGMs worth the name. Only limited quantities of the Russian

Krasnopol PGM have been imported for the Bofors 155 mm howitzer. Among others, the Bofors Bonus PGM is a suitable candidate, subject to successful trials in the deserts and the mountains.

Finally, the approach to army modernisation must be more focused; the priorities must be clearly established and then adhered to. The government must give a firm commitment in terms of funds and the Ministry of Defence must streamline its procedures and processes for speedy procurement of high priority weapons and equipment. It is time to institute a rolling, non-lapsable defence modernisation fund of Rs. 25,000 crores as a viable method of ensuring that defence procurement is not subjected to the vagaries of annual budgets. The present situation is disturbing and, if allowed to go on indefinitely, will seriously compromise the army's preparedness to fight the next border war that inimical neighbours like Pakistan can be expected to thrust on India.

MODERNISING THE INDIAN INFANTRY

Why has it taken the Army so long to conceive an upgrade package for the oldest, most potent and intensely employed fighting arm, the Infantry, even after the so-called revolution in military affairs? The foot soldier, the original and most versatile weapon system that is always taken for granted, has emerged from the dubious shock and awe strategy of recent campaigns as its ultimate arbiter. India has paid dearly for the neglect of its infantry in terms of cost, casualties and over-stretch of battle. But the Infantry has never let us down. Kargil was its finest hour. Gen VP Malik, the Army Chief of the time, wryly noted: "We will fight with what we have." So when for the first time an international conference of Army and defence industry was launched last week to put the forgotten soldier centre-stage, some misgivings were natural.

While Army Chief Gen JJ Singh outlined his vision for the soldier system of the future, the conspicuous and total absence of Government-MoD-robbed the conference of any sanctity. In sharp contrast, for a MoD-sponsored defence finance seminar earlier in the month, Government officials and ministers were stepping over each other at Vigyan Bhavan. Free India's Army came into being in 1947 and within weeks, the Infantry soldiers landed in Srinagar to save J&K from being gobbled up by Pakistani tribal raiders.

Since then, the Infantry has not ceased fighting proxy wars there and later, elsewhere too. A former Army Chief, Gen SR Choudhury, who was not from the Infantry, described the Infantry as the Army and vice versa. Field Marshal Montgomery said: An army is considered only as good as its Infantry. The experience of four wars, several border skirmishes, two out-of-area missions, the ceaseless campaign to counter cross-border terrorism in Kashmir, numerous other insurgencies in the North-East, internal stability operations elsewhere in the country and UN peace keeping operations make the Indian Infantry the most battle-hardened and combat rich force in the world.

The simple and uncomplaining infantryman has given so much to so many for so little. The modernisation of the infantry was first attempted-halfheartedly-in the mid-1980s by the Perspective Planning branch of the Army Headquarters. The bias for mechanised warfare, zealously pursued by Gen Sundarji, was so pronounced that the Infantry modernisation plan was skipped altogether. Guns, tanks, APCs were the weapons in demand. The Infantry was ignored. Had a modest upgrade package been undertaken at that time, infantry would have been more combat contemporary and effective. Instead, till recently, some soldiers were still using World War II equipment and clothing.

Shameful as it was, soldiers had to buy rucksacks and other accoutrements from the market. DRDO is still to come out with a light bulletproof vest. The Army failed to accurately visualize the nature of combat it would fight in the future. Pakistan-sponsored insurgency in Punjab did not alert the nation and the Army to the proxy war brewing in J&K. We defaulted on both counts-anticipating low intensity conflict and cross border terrorism and preparing the Infantry for it. Despite the sustained counter-insurgency and counter-terrorism campaign in J&K and the North-East since the 1990s, the Army was sluggish in investing in the infantry.

The first Gulf War reintroduced the fiction that wars could be won from the air. The air campaigns in Bosnia and Kosovo temporarily turned fiction into reality. But 9/11 broke the myth of supremacy of air power. Operation Enduring Freedom in Afghanistan lasted 76 days; 65 of these were air operations. The 11-day land offensive secured a temporary and incomplete victory against the Taliban. Operation Iraqi Freedom on the other hand, fought for 20 days was bereft of any preparatory air campaign though a secret air war preceded it. Unhappily for the US/NATO-led coalition forces, despite their pyrrhic military victories, low intensity wars in Afghanistan and Iraq are continuing in full blaze.

The recent 34-day war in Lebanon and the ongoing campaign in Gaza demonstrate the limits of Israel's military power. Used to decisive victories in less than 10 days, Israeli Defence Forces (IDF) were badgered by Hassan Nasrallah's jihadi militia. Reliance on air power, tanks and guns in Lebanon as substitute for ground troops-infantry-was motivated by casualty aversion. We too have to be sensitive to casualties.

The wars in Lebanon, Iraq and Afghanistan spurred by the growing cult of Osama bin Laden and Hassan Nasrallah require a redefinition of the concept of power and military success. Success would necessarily be an inclusive military victory encompassing post-conflict stability and reconstruction. For this we need Infantry.

The Indian Army should not get overly seduced by high-sounding warfare like 'netcentric' that the West is being diverted into. This is not to suggest we ignore the strides in high-tech warfare. But as a former US NATO Commander noted recently: "This netcentric stuff is great but our men in Baghdad are being blown up with their Humvees by IEDs." He suggested that we address the battle we are fighting before switching to the one we will fight in the future.

India's supreme operational challenge is and will be the maintenance of internal security. Just last month, Prime Minister Manmohan Singh stated this ground reality. The Infantry is at the heart of counterinsurgency and counter-terrorism operations and may well get sucked into anti-Naxal operations as well. Keeping the Army operationally ready for both conventional and unconventional missions is imperative but the emphasis has to be on the business of the day: CI and CT.

The Indian Infantry is belatedly embarking on a modernisation programme to enhance its combat skills through increased lethality, communications, surveillance, mobility and suvivability. These force multipliers will enable the soldier to fight all-weather, 24x7 and on any terrain in the right battle-configuration albeit with the accent on LIC.

The GSQR for the Future-Infantry-Soldier-As a System (F-INSAS) must empower not encumber the soldier. DRDO must compete with domestic and international industry. DRDO has one more chance to make amends for its omissions and commissions. F-INSAS must strike the right balance between the surge of technology and sensibility of the soldier keeping the battle of the future in mind. Defence Minister AK Antony should accord F-INSAS the highest strategic priority.

INDIAN ARMY 2020

A nation's military is a major but unstated factor in international Realpolitik, howsoever moderated and underplayed, in acknowledgement of international sensitivities. Nevertheless, its existence and capabilities percolate into the public domain, domestic as well as international, and its presence, even unstated, becomes a background presence, which provides a sense of hard-edge backup to the national establishment for undertaking effective front line diplomacy. It is, therefore, essential in the national interest that the armed forces are upgraded and updated on an ongoing basis, something which governments have been traditionally loath to acknowledge and undertake, the Indian government perhaps more so than others in this respect. Historically, it is to the credit of the Indian Army that it has fulfilled its role as an organ of the state, and undertaken all assigned tasks successfully, except in the Sino-Indian border war of 1962 and reclamation of Indian territory in the Aksai Chin plateau, on the Sino-Indian border in Tibet, for which reasons have to be sought elsewhere. It has functioned effectively in every type of role, in spite of the general lack of a supportive government environment by way of adequate finances, resources, equipment, personnel policies, or higher political direction. The modernization and upgradation of the Indian Army to function in a 21st century environment is, therefore, a priority task for the present as well as successive governments to undertake.

The new millennium opened literally with a thunderclap, as the world witnessed America's new Day of Infamy on live media, with the demolition of the World Trade Centre in New York on September 11, 2001, in an air-assault by Al Qaida fidayeen. In his speech to the Congress on September 20, 2001, President George W Bush proclaimed America's 'War on Terror'. In its aftermath, the tensions of the recently terminated Cold War appeared to revive in a different manifestation, which mutated almost seamlessly into the new conflict that spread rapidly outwards, and impacted Afghanistan and Iraq. In fact, the War on Terror seems to have replaced the earlier geo-political confrontation of the Cold War with another worldwide confrontation, this one an ethno-religious clash of cultures (if not of entire civilizations) between neo-con America and Jihadi Islam.

The doctrines of pre-emptive intervention and regime change by the military superpower and high intensity holy war by non-state terrorists are set to overwhelmingly shape the security environment of the new millennium, and will dominate India's perceptions and security stances in at least the middle term future. Numerous local and regional extensions and variations of the conflict have sprung up all over the world, extending from immigrant communities in Europe, all the way to Indonesia, Thailand, Malaysia and the Philippines in South East Asia, traversing enroute hotspots in Russia and Eastern Europe, Chechnya, Central Asia, Afghanistan, Pakistan, Kashmir, as well as other parts of India, and Bangladesh, with branch lines to Chinese Turkestan along the Silk Route. Some of these new wars have subsumed ongoing confrontations, others are taking the form of proxy wars, sub-ethnic insurgencies, terrorism, narcotics, organized crime, illegal migration, environmental poaching, as also high intensity flare-ups over disputed borders, and perhaps with others yet to come (who knows?) involving exclusive economic zones, oil, seabed and water resources. India's relationships with the Peoples' Republic of China, as well as its strategic surrogate Pakistan, have generally been adversarial, but now repairs to these traditional contentions are being attempted. But any attempts at reconstruction will have to take into account the wider context of the new realities of the War on Terror.

To India, these realities will include, amongst others, the massive and seemingly unstoppable 'peaceful rise' of the Middle Kingdom immediately next door, with its unspoken but implicit connotations of military super-capabilities in the not too distant future, the come-back of Islamic jihad in South and South East Asia, the emergence of 'Maobadi' militias in Nepal on India's doorstep, closely interlinked with their fraternal confederates of the newly consolidated Communist Party of India (Maoist) and other Naxalite affiliates in a nascent Compact Revolutionary Zone, which reaches deep into the Indian heartland. India, shining or not, is nevertheless on its way to be an emerging power whose pluralistic society is under direct attack by the new conflict, which demands the closest attention and can be ignored only at peril; whose ultimate dimensions are as yet unclear. Till that time, there are only wide open questions, difficult, if not impossible to forecast from the present perspective.

Thus, at one extreme, putting a way-out positive spin on the current trends in Indo-Pak and Sino-Indian relations, the possibilities of turning swords into ploughshares appear endless. For instance, with the current upsurge in people-to-people relationships between India and Pakistan and general improvement in the civil environment, could for example a South Asian Federation become a practical reality in 2020, just as the European Union is today, (including, necessarily, resolution of the Kashmir and Siachen problems to the satisfaction of all parties concerned)? Would such a solution emerge as a match winner, or would there still remain some warm embers of national interest, pride and resentments, which would continue to smolder, perhaps requiring to be extinguished later? Would an international border held only by paramilitary forces replace the Line of Control and Actual Ground Position Line?

Ultimately, what impact would all these developments have on the force structure of Army 2020 in terms of mechanized and holding forces for plains and desert warfare; holding forces for the Line of Control and Actual Ground Position Line, and also the ditch-cum-bund and other defense assets and infrastructure painstakingly and painfully developed along the entire front with Pakistan? Also, if and when outstanding issues with the Peoples' Republic of China are resolved on a permanent basis, what would be the end results for forces holding the Line of Actual Control in Northern, Central and Eastern Commands, right from the Kara Koram Pass in extreme northern Ladakh down to Kibithoo in extreme eastern Arunachal Pradesh? On a similar spin, if the internal security situation also improves to the same extent, will civil administrations manage without continuous recourse to the Army as at present, reducing these unpleasant, thankless, and irksome commitments in aid to civil power, perhaps with substantial savings in manpower in terms of the Rashtriya Rifles? Therefore, at the politically upbeat end of the scale, with conflicts, both domestic and international, being resolved, Army 2020 might well evolve into a minimalist organization, lean perhaps to the point of cadaverousness, based primarily on high technology and special forces, supported by airpower, which many today see as a classical model for the new world.

However, there are also more down market perceptions too, whose darker prognoses cannot be totally set aside. Amongst these are the massive and seemingly unstoppable 'peaceful rise' of the Middle Kingdom immediately next door, with its unarticulated but implicit connotations of military super-capabilities; the come-back of Islamic jihad on India's doorstep in the Islamic Republic of Pakistan, Afghanistan, Bangladesh and Southeast Asia; the emergence of 'Maobadi' militias in Nepal on India's immediate doorstep, with a corresponding Compact Revolutionary Zone of their fraternal confederates, the People's War Group established deep within the Indian heartland; could all suggest a 'Future History' in much deeper tones of sepia.

Taking an in-between perception of the two extremes, it would be realistic to assume that the world would perhaps continue to remain an uncertain and uneasy place, where the only certainty would be uncertainty. Threats would be undefined, unexpected and also omnipresent, in shapes and forms, which cannot be visualised clearly at present. Army 2020 will, therefore, have to be designed to function in an amorphous security environment with capabilities to operate across the entire spectrum of conflict from low intensity warfare to the ultimate unthinkable Kurukshetra of nuclear conflict.

Except in the unlikely event of a major reversal turnabout in India's traditional political worldview within the next decade or so, the role of the defense forces in 2020 will remain unchanged from the traditional one of homeland defense – protection of the territorial integrity of Indian territory by land, sea, or air. This will be consistent with the perceptions that all governments in office, regardless of their political philosophies or domestic policy, have taken all along since Independence, in which international military alignments through power blocs, mutual defense treaties, or major expeditionary commitments overseas (except of course on United Nations missions) have been eschewed.

However, the perception of homeland defense has never passively ruled out pro-active or pre-emptive interventions within or outside the country, wherever considered necessary in the national interest, as have been undertaken on numerous occasions earlier by the Indian Army. This cannot, and indeed must not be wished away or forgotten. Military intervention in the national interest, to consolidate and nurture the fledgling nation, commenced almost immediately after Independence and through the early years of the Republic, with operations in the (then) princely states of Kashmir, Hyderabad, and Junagadh. The historical process continued with the assimilation of Portuguese colonies in 1961, absorption of the Sikkim Monarchy, assistance and support to the brutalized people of East Pakistan – now Bangladesh – in 1971, attempted peacemaking in Sri Lanka in 1987-1990, the Maldives in 1988, or more recently, the carefully harmonised anti-insurgency operations with Myanmar and Bhutan against separatist elements along contiguous border areas. Similar contingencies may arise in the future as well, and there is no need to be in any manner apologetic about them, though some ventures can certainly be criticized for incoherent political direction and poor military planning. In addition, the Indian Army has also very successfully displayed its capabilities for operations other than war (OOW) in these regions by way of training missions and assistance in natural calamities, whenever requested by the host countries. Such contingencies could very well arise in future too.

Viewed from the final months of 2004, Indian Army 2020 is only fifteen years ahead on the timeline, within the current 15-Year Defense Perspective, and not really all that distant at all in terms of successive Five Year Defense Plans. The building of the New Army is, therefore, already in progress with the ongoing Tenth, and the future Eleventh, Twelfth and Thirteenth Five Year Defense Plan series. If these proceed even approximately on schedule (which incidentally, has almost never been the case!), Army 2020 should be in place within the Thirteenth Five Year Defense Plan (2017-2022). But defense planning has traditionally been low on the scale of national priorities, with myriad hurdles in the process of planning, decision-making and production. Political decision-making and effective follow through action by the government have been glacial in terms of results actually achieved. Desperate attempts to expedite the process, even during national emergencies like Kargil 1999, ultimately backfired into low grade, ill informed and crudely partisan political confrontations around the Tehalka sting operation, the CAG Report, and the so-called Coffin-gate scandals, which rocked the political firmament of the time. Their spill-over effect severely inhibited the official decision-making process, and perhaps damaged it beyond repair. The evolution of Army 2020 will have to live with this and evolve as best as it can. The crux of the issue, as always, will be sustained availability of adequate finances. Finance ministers controlling the nation's purse strings (including in the current dispensation) generally do not look benignly on resources diverted from the national kitty towards defense, and dole them out grudgingly at the best of times. Plans for Indian Army 2020, integrated into the overall perspective of the Defense Services, are therefore, critically interlinked with the national effort in terms of resources likely to be allotted, as also to timely political and financial decision making. This is likely to be a fluctuating process, very much influenced by the course of geo-political and economic developments, as well as political philosophies and attitudes of future governments regarding adequate and sustained financial support for defense planning. All these imponderables would impact heavily on the Defense Plan series, and therefore, on the profile of Army 2020, but in what manner and to what effect, remain questions only the future can answer. Meanwhile, an almost continuous flow of revolutions in military affairs has been underway for over two decades now, which should certainly be incorporated into the profile of Army 2020.

The Indian Army has traditionally been manpower intensive, which many modern intellects disparage as a hangover from the Second or even the First World War era. But it must be understood that these apparent anachronisms linger on even at present, due to certain economic as well as operational compulsions. At one level, the inability of the Indian Army to shed manpower is due to lack of resources to replace it with high-end technologies, primarily because of the generally low priority accorded to defense planning, and inadequate resource allotment. In the absence of equipment, manpower intensive alternatives, somehow have to persist almost by default. The unsatisfactory hybridization, which created the current Reorganized Army Plains Infantry Division – RAPID – is a good example of this. In this case, the divisional structure was reduced by a brigade, on the assumption that manpower thus reduced would be replaced by force multipliers and surveillance. Needless to say, the Army waited for these in vain, because the financial resources for the technological makeover were simply never allotted. It is to be seen whether these difficulties will persist in future as well. By present indications, it seems that they would still be around for quite some time. At another level, mountain and jungle terrain in the northern and eastern regions combined with extensive deployments on counter insurgency, established operational imperatives for organizations with adequate manpower. Here, sheer technology, though helpful, was not the dominating factor, and there was no substitute for numbers of well-trained 'boots on the ground', as American forces in Iraq are painfully learning the hard way. So, in New Age organizations, manpower versus technology will have to be implemented carefully and judiciously. At present, there is an intense debate within the military and the rest of the strategic community on the shape of warfare in the future, and the type of army required to meet future threats. Will a traditional conventional army, even if technologically upgraded, be adequate to handle these when they occur? Now that the process of re-construction is already under way, what kind of an Army 2020 should emerge at the end of it? How and to what extent will it or can it reflect the operational compulsions of that future time? The answer to these and other similar questions must be clearly understood, which is that Indian Army 2020 must retain the basic configuration of a conventional army, and not be mutated by radical doctrinal surgery into some kind of heavy constabulary. The New Army must possess integral multi-role operational capabilities across the entire spectrum of conflict, whether nuclear, conventional, or low intensity. Any undue emphasis or insistence on a tailor-made orientation focusing primarily on any particular level of warfare would be dangerously misplaced. To effectively undertake its task of land warfare for homeland defense, India requires a large army, with an armory ranging from land-launched strategic weapons at the high intensity end of the spectrum, to special operations forces at the low intensity end. The middle levels will continue to be bulked out by conventional forces, with adequate manpower – armor, artillery, infantry, as well as integral army aviation, backed up by the requisite support and logistics elements. The basic organizations of the Army require extensive technological upgradation, but are otherwise stable and time-tested under a wide variety of environments. They are flexible enough for structured regrouping for various contingencies. Changes to the existing pattern should be introduced only after careful deliberation.

Amongst other emerging factors are strategic weapons systems, which are still a comparatively recent acquisition and whose command and control methodologies are yet to be fully stabilized. The Strategic Forces Command has been recently established as the designated inter-services agency for overall management of these high-end assets. The new organization is logical and was originally scheduled to function directly under the much awaited Chief of Defense Staff, but since this appointment is yet to be implemented, it has now been placed de facto under the Chiefs of Staff Committee, through the Integrated Defense Staff. It still remains to be seen how the final shape of the new Command emerges, i.e. whether in the classical sense of a separate command with direct control of operational, logistics, and personnel, or as a functional command for operational employment of dedicated strategic components held with each individual Service.

In the Indian context, perhaps the latter would be more practicable. However, whatever the command structure model ultimately adopted, it must also be optimally calibrated to fulfill the important aspect of 'command satisfaction' within its hierarchy, an aspect not often considered, or, if so, ignored or disregarded. Each Service operates in its own physical environment, and land-based strategic systems are within the Army's domain. Army 2020 must incorporate an integral component of strategic forces, which can be operationally emplaced under the Strategic Forces Command.

A word about Army Aviation, which must be another vital area of focus for Army 2020. Airpower dominates the battlefield, and must be employed to achieve maximum synergy.

However, in the inter-services context, this eminently profound article of faith has been allowed to acquire an extended meaning of single service ownership of all air assets. To the Army, airpower is essentially firepower, surveillance and target acquisition from the sky in close or distant support of ground operations extending up to the operational depth of the tactical battle area. Given the advances in technology, these tasks can now be undertaken by manned as well as unmanned flight platforms, covering a range of unmanned air vehicles / remotely piloted vehicles (UAV / RPV), ground launched precision-guided missiles, and rotary wing ground combat aviation (attack and assault helicopters). These aerial platforms operate primarily in the environment of the land battle, either independently or in a supplementary role to the air battle, often without diverting high-end airpower from its primary tasks. Army 2020 will have to build up integral air resources for itself, particularly in rotary winged combat aircraft (attack and assault helicopters, airborne early warning, communications and medevac) integral to Army Aviation, which must become the primary agency of rotary wing airpower.

But for all this to be effective within the given timeframe raises the vital issue of the attitudinal and cultural reorientation of the defense forces into a synergized joint-service environment. While acknowledging the supreme importance of individual Service identities and aspirations, by 2020, the Indian Army individually, as well as the Defense Forces collectively, must no longer be allowed to function as independent disconnected entities, without the required inter-service synergy for fullest exploitation of their respective capabilities.

Army 2020 will, therefore, have to be organized, equipped, trained and culturally energized to take its place within an operational triad in conjunction with maritime and aerospace power, functionally interlinked through an integrated politico-military Higher Defense Organization, and a common framework of joint-service doctrines and joint command structures. It takes three to tango, but nevertheless unless the joint services environment is simultaneously developed and implemented, Army 2020 (as indeed Navy 2020 or Air Force 2020) cannot be employed to its fullest capability and effect. In some senses, provision of an enabling environment of jointmanship (a clumsy term!) and stamping them on the individual ethos and culture of each Service may well be the most challenging task, which should be accorded an overall priority higher than many other issues. In this context, the major area of reconstruction of Indian Army 2020 (and the other Services) might well be in reform of traditional mindsets and approach to battle.

2020 : INDIAN ARMY

National security, is that ambience, in which a nation is able to protect and promote its national values, pursue its national interests and aspirations, in spite of, or, in the absence of, external or internal threats, real or perceived. Threats to national security may impact on any aspect of a nation's life, ranging from its territorial integrity and internal cohesion to its economy, political structures and institutions, diplomacy, national leadership, national character, morale and so on. The armed forces of a nation have a vital role to play in meeting these threats.

INDIA'S NATIONAL INTERESTS

India's national interests, simply stated, are as follows :-

- National sovereignty.
- Unity and integrity of the country.
- Democratic and secular polity.
- Economic development.
- Social and economic justice.
- Favourable world order.
- Preservation and promotion of our values.

Our Strategic Vision

Nations adopt a national strategy in order to attain their national interests or goals. Clarity of strategic vision is very important if the national strategy is to take the nation on an optimal course to its desired national objectives. Let us, briefly, examine our strategic vision.

We are one of the oldest civilizations on Earth. Nearly, a sixth of the human race is Indian. Our country occupies a strategic location on the southern promontory of the Asian land mass and dominates large expanses of the Indian Ocean including the routes to the oil rich Gulf region, South East Asia and the Orient. These intrinsic attributes qualify, indeed demand, that India be a major player at the world stage.

By tradition, India has been a peace-loving and responsible nation. It has abjured aggression, espoused the doctrine of 'Ahimsa' or non-violence, led the non-aligned group of nations and played a constructive role as a member of the United Nations. This tradition clearly suggests that India should aspire to become a benign and moral superpower, rather than one, whose brute strength or wealth alone, confer on it, its place under the sun. Any examination of our strategic environment must be carried out against the backdrop of our strategic vision and the long term plans and strategies needed to realise that vision. By such an examination, we shall be able to predict the strategic environment of the decades ahead, and arrive at the appropriate force structure and equipment profile for our Army of the future.

Aim

The aim of this chapter is to visualise the likely national security environment in 2020 with special reference to the threats and challenges that may confront us at that time, and arrive at the most appropriate force structure and equipment profile for the Indian Army of 2020.

While the focus in this chapter is on the Army, it must not be construed that the Army can fulfill its missions without the active partnership of the Navy and the Air Force. Joint, or preferably, integrated tri-service functioning in war and peace will be an essential pre-requisite for success in all our operations. With this background, let us examine the geo-strategic environment we might face in 2020.

THE GEO-STRATEGIC ENVIRONMENT

Two major events, roughly a decade apart, have played a major role in shaping the current geo-strategic environment. The first being the demise of the Soviet Union. It brought the Cold War to an end, and conferred on the USA, an unchallenged pre-eminence in the world as the sole superpower. The second was the '9-11 Event'-the 11th September 2001 terrorist attacks on targets in Washington DC and New York. This impelled the USA to declare 'War on Terrorism', and attack Afghanistan and Iraq with a 'coalition of like-minded countries', with the purpose of ousting their regimes, which were sponsors of terrorist groups like Al Quaeda and were hostile to the USA. The USA believed that Iraq was in possession of weapons of mass destruction (WMD).

The impact of these two events are now being clearly felt in international affairs and by all indications, appear to be long lasting. We need to take note of the following major ramifications, which are specially relevant to India :-

- The USA has become hegemonic. Her style of diplomacy is increasingly becoming peremptory and coercive.
- The UN has been sidelined by the USA, which, acts at will, ignoring the need for UN's sanction.
- The USA has adopted the doctrine of 'Preemptive Military Intervention'. In consonance with this doctrine-threats,

whether real and present or, perceived, are not allowed to mature, by use of military force.

- The USA has drawn a list of countries, which are 'of concern' to it. Of these, it has dealt with Afghanistan and Iraq. North Korea and Iran await similar treatment by the superpower. Recently, India has voted in favour of a USA backed resolution against Iran possibly to secure military materials, nuclear technology and fuel for civilian purposes. If India resiles from her pro-USA stance in the late November 2005 voting, the USA may deny its expectations. This would amount to dictating India's foreign policy.
- China is neither amenable to coercion nor susceptible to being 'contained'. Besides, because North Korea is a protégé of China, the latter has a major role in USA's dealings with that country. The USA has also economically engaged China, as it provides a large market for US manufactured goods. The USA believes too, that as the USA-China trade gets increasingly intertwined, the likelihood of an armed conflict between the two will correspondingly reduce.
- The European Union, despite reservations on the part of some constituents, is for purposes of *realpolitik* pro-USA.
- Russia, because of her present economic debility, is supporting the USA or, at least, not opposing her. It may become more independent in its attitude as its economy recovers, a process that has already begun.
- Pakistan is a 'major non-NATO ally' of the USA and also its frontline state for the 'War on Terrorism'. The US has troops and aircraft on Pakistan's soil. It has been permitted to set up bases in return for huge subventions and to bail out Pakistan from the brink of a near-collapse economic situation. In effect, Pakistan has become a client state of the USA with a less than independent foreign policy.
- Terrorism, religious fundamentalism, nuclear and missile technology proliferation are pressing concerns for the US. It believes that these could ultimately pose danger to its 'homeland', something about which the USA is hypersensitive, or, even paranoid.

These are some of the ramifications of the two events i.e. the Soviet collapse and the 9/11 event, which shall continue to influence international relations in the next two decades or more. However, by 2020, some changes would have taken place with regard to the circumstances of the world's principal nations. These are enumerated below :-

- The USA will continue to be the preeminent power. Nevertheless, her 'edge' over China would have reduced to a small margin.
- China would be increasingly inclined to join issue with the USA, taking into account its envisaged near-superpower status. However, she would not risk her new found prosperity by being over-assertive with the USA and thus risk war.
- India would have caught up with China and achieved parity with China in many areas, but not military.
- Pakistan will continue to be the USA's client state, and in case the latter so presses, she may even enter into a comprehensive peace agreement with India. Otherwise, Pakistan would prefer to keep tensions alive with India in order to extract concessions and benefits from both China and the USA who will want an economically resurgent India to be reined in.
- The USA's 'War on Terrorism' may prove to be endless as, though the enemy has been rightly identified, the means being applied are all wrong, indeed, self-defeating.
- Radical religion will pose problems for the entire world as such. As radicalism flourishes in less developed countries, by 2020, there would also be a large number of very poor countries with radicalism well entrenched.

After this brief estimate of the geo-strategic environment in, 2020, let us turn to India's internal security environment.

INDIA'S INTERNAL SECURITY ENVIRONMENT, 2020

India is a rapidly developing country with a GDP growth of seven percent. It has a huge reserve of technical manpower and strong liberal political culture, a youthful population more than half of which will be below 30 years of age in 2020. It also has strong and apolitical armed forces. Our present concerns, which may persist in future are as under:-

- The present rate of population growth is 1.6 percent. It is imperative to bring it down to one percent by 2020-2025.
- The political culture in the country has deteriorated over the years. Communalism, sectarianism, regional parochialism, and sub-nationalism are on the rise. There is growing criminalisation of politics and a culture of 'vote banks' has taken root. Politicisation of the bureaucracy and the police, is well-established. The Armed Forces have, so far, been able to remain insulated from politics. Unless these evils are overcome, in 2020, we may have a nation whose internal security environment will be extremely unhealthy.
- Distributive justice with regard to sharing of revenues and the fruits of development is an imperative, if radical left movements, currently active in the country, are to be eliminated by 2015 or so.
- The separatist movements in the North-East and J & K must be amicably resolved.
- Black money and drug trafficking must be put to an end as they not only ruin the economy but also corrupt the youth.

Attention to the above areas of concern will enable India to achieve desired internal security by 2020. Let us now identify the threats and challenges India is likely to face in 2020.

THREATS AND CHALLENGES TO INDIA : 2020

Military Threats

- India is not likely to face a military threat from the USA or China because of its strength, both military and economic.
- A medium level military threat may arise from Pakistan if it fails to make adequate economic and political progress,

or, its leadership passes to radical elements, or, the country as such, fails and lapses into a state of anarchy.

- Bangladesh may pose a very low level threat if it decides to encourage demographic 'aggression' by using its over-sized armed forces in support.
- Threats of non-state groups armed with WMD could become a reality. They could be acting on their own initiative or, at the behest of a sponsor nation. This dimension of WMD would warrant war-like response from us.

Challenges. Apart from military threats, a number of non-military challenges may have to be faced by our Army in the 2020 time frame. These are as follows:-

- Human resources of appropriate quality may get drawn to the more lucrative civilian sector. The terms and conditions of service and satisfaction levels of personnel, must be made more attractive. We should also enroll more short service personnel than regular cadres to reduce pension liabilities and for better career management of officers.
- Funds allotted to the Armed Forces should be sustained at a level of three per cent of GDP for at least 12 to 15 years so as to ensure requisite modernisation and making good existing shortfalls.
- Defence Research and Development Organisation (DRDO) must be upgraded qualitatively and top quality scientists should be inducted into it. Rightfully, their expectations of pay and research facilities will be high. These must be met.
- Private sector participation in defence R & D and development of complete systems by them, must be facilitated. Government should fund their defence research projects and give them guarantees of sizeable orders to encourage their partnership with the DRDO.
- Scientific and technical manpower will be eagerly sought by other countries. To overcome this 'brain-drain', we should improve the working conditions and research facilities in our country.

- The IT driven revolution in military affairs requires that the Army 'manages' these changes in a systematic and smooth manner. We need to create an integrated force working in an 'unified battle space'; seamless communications; extensive exploitation of IT with excellent 'cyber security'; top quality space based and terrestrial surveillance systems and fully operationalised C4I2 systems. This convergence of various technologies and capabilities will bestow the forces with much enhanced force-multiplier benefits through Network Centric Warfare (NCW). We have a long way to go in this regard.
- Internal contingencies of various types could retard or block the Army's effort to achieve optimal development in the next 15 years. We need to be prepared with suitable contingency plans to overcome these 'drag' factors.

Extreme Contingencies. In the unlikely event of our prognosis being grossly in error, the following extreme contingencies could occur :-

- The USA, in a bid to prevent China from superseding her as the superpower, provokes China to a war with possible use of nuclear weapons.
- China, in frustration with the US-India Axis and to teach India a lesson, may declare war on us.
- Pakistan may join China in the war against India, or, allow to be used as a proxy to support China in a 'holding' mode.

Nature of Warfare in 2020

We have already seen that war with the USA and China (and, indeed, other advanced countries) is most unlikely. War with Pakistan may however occur, as also minor skirmishes with Bangladesh. Such engagements may have the following characteristics :-

- They will be of short duration, say, a week or less.
- Penetration in depth is unlikely to be attempted by either side.
- 'Cold Start' will be attempted whenever possible to achieve surprise and maximise gains.

- The entire border is likely to be activated with shallow thrusts, very heavy firepower and short span manoeuvres.
- Nuclear weapons may not be used; their use may, however, be threatened.
- Special Forces and coup-de-main forces will play a major role.
- Integrated action by all three services will be crucial for the enhancement of our combat power vis-à-vis the adversary's.
- Levels of technology employed in the wars will be higher than at present.
- Wars will end in stalemate, with little or no gain, and heavy losses to military as well as civilian targets.
- In the case of Bangladesh, the threat is of such a low level as to be non-serious. However in the skirmishing, the danger of casualties to unarmed civilians will be great and will need to be handled with firmness and imagination.

VISION : INDIAN ARMY: 2020

The foregoing threat assessment and the likely nature of any future war we may be required to fight, including the extreme contingencies we have listed, should give us the 'Vision' of the Indian Army, 2020. We may state this vision as follows:-"The Indian Army, 2020 will be an optimally equipped and weaponised force, with the capability to operate effectively in an integrated joint services environment, over the entire spectrum of conflict, in a regional context." The vision statement spelt out above, is appropriate to the restrained aspirations of this huge and benign country, whose ethical values and traditions inhibit it from anything less modest than what has been stated. It also ensures that this country shall never again have to undergo the humiliation of foreign conquest, as in the past; hence the emphasis on optimal strength, under all conditions of warfare.

ROLE OF THE INDIAN ARMY

Armies are maintained by countries in order to safeguard

their core values and national interests from external aggression and internal subversion. The Primary and Secondary roles of our Army are as under :-

- Primary Role. Deter external aggression and, if deterrence fails, defeat it by force.
- Secondary Role. Assist the Government in overcoming internal threats, foreign sponsored or indigenous, and aid the civil authority when requisitioned for the purpose.

Capabilities Entailed by the Role

The capabilities that the Army must posses to fulfill its role must be identified in accordance with our 'Vision' for the Army. The capabilities, thus identified are as under :-

- Deterrent Capability. The Army should be so strong in both conventional and nuclear weapons, that potential aggressors are deterred.
- War Fighting Capability. If deterrence fails, the Army should be able to fight a successful war against the enemy, over any terrain, and in conventional as well as NBC warfare situations.
- Internal Security Management Capability. The Army should be able to deal with and manage internal security situations of various types like insurgency, grave law and order situations; and also render aid to civil power, when requisitioned under various situations including disasters, both natural and man-made.
- Force Projection Capability. The Army should be capable of operating 'out-of-area' as part of an integrated task force, when ordered by the Government.
- Peace Keeping Operations Capability. The Army should be able to undertake UN Peace Keeping Missions in any part of the world and inter-operate with Army components of other countries in such operations.

Though we presently posses all these capabilities in some measure, the desired level is yet to be realised in many areas. Resource inadequacy, lack of clear policy directions from the Government, frequent 're-thinks' on the part of the Army, failure of timely supplies of material and shoddy quality of what has been supplied, are some of the reasons attributable to the Army's inability to achieve and retain the desired level of capability at all times. Perhaps, even more important reason, is the knowledge driven Revolution in Military Affairs (RMA), which accelerates the process of obsolescence of equipment, doctrines and tactics. It is in this critical area of RMA that a lot of work needs to be done so that we can have adequate levels of the desired capabilities, at all times. Let us now examine whether the present structure of the Army needs to be altered to enable the Army to fulfill its assigned role better.

STRUCTURE OF THE ARMY : 2020

General. It is idle to claim that our organisations have 'stood the test of time and war' and, therefore, need not be tampered with. The nature of wars we are likely to face has changed. The battle zone is virtually transparent to surveillance devices. The range and lethality of weapons has increased many times over. Precision guided munitions have replaced the old area-neutralisation munitions. Means of mobility have increased. And the convergence of Information Technology, computers, all-weather sensors, communications and firepower resources has vested commanders at various levels, with unprecedented real-time knowledge of the situation as also the ability to alter it at will. These developments necessitates a review of our existing force structure.

Macro-level Restructuring. The Army has always been regretting the blunting of the 'Combat Edge' it had over its traditional adversary. The calculation of force ratios between the adversaries was hitherto done on a service to service basis-our Army versus the opponent's, our Navy and Air Force versus the opponent's. This gave us a skewed idea of the capability of our armed forces as a whole vis-à-vis our adversary. Wars are not fought service wise. All the services have to join during combat. In such a milieu, the three services should be integrated into one strong unified force with-unity of command and control, total synergy in operations, and much superior and economical employment of the resources available to the armed forces. There is bound to be great opposition to this idea, just as in the case of formation of the Andaman and Nicobar Command (ANC) in 2001-2002. There is no escaping the military logic of creating suitably constituted integrated theatre commands and functional (non-territorial) commands for the Armed Forces as a whole. The benefits that will accrue are : cohesion among the services, synergy leading to maximisation of combat power, better exploitation of the RMA brought about by C4I2 enabling Network Centric Warfare (NCW), strategic and intra-theatre flexibility in handling of resources and, above all, classic unity of effort. No specific solutions are offered for the creation of such integrated theatre commands. If the idea suggested above raises discussion on this important issue, our aim would have been achieved. Hopefully, this idea too, is NOT put into cold storage like the creation of the post of Chief of the Defence Staff!

Reorganising the Present Army for 2020. The resistance to change for macro level restructuring of India's Armed Forces, is likely to be stiff. It may, therefore, not be achievable in the 5-10 years timeframe. However, within the existing organisation of the Army some meaningful reorganisation can be brought about. The following suggestions could be considered :-

- Intelligence and surveillance organisations must be strengthened and modernised.
- Additional Special Forces (SF), patterned broadly on the present organisation, need to be raised. These units should be capable of functioning in very small groups, for prolonged periods, within or beyond the combat zone. Their tasks could include covert special reconnaissance; target specific raids; unconventional operations to organise resistance groups and conduct guerilla warfare in enemy territory; penetration of terrorist organisations for intelligence purposes; and counter-terrorism in all its manifestations including WMD. The personnel must be endowed with very high level of practical intelligence, initiative, mission orientation and excellent linguistic competence appropriate to the area where they are to operate.

- Special Rapid Action forces for offensive or reactive employment at the Corps level and an Army reserve with adequate airlift resources including for light tanks/ICVs, needs to be created.
- Information Warfare Units need to be created at each Corps to carry out psychological operations.
- An amphibious formation suitably grouped with other elements for out of area operations should be raised.
- As the proxy war and insurgencies abate, the existing RR force may be scaled down suitably and kept as a reserve force for the same tasks as before.
- Conventional forces, which are today considered to be 'holding' forces, should be enabled to take up 'cold start' offensives by grouping with them mechanised forces, airborne/ heliborne forces as the case may be. This will give the 'strike' forces a forward launch pad for their tasks.
- Strategic forces need to be built up to 'deterrent' levels against a major power like China. The more forbidding the weapon the more likely it is to deter the enemy. The nuclear arsenal must, therefore, be enlarged and diversified to include thermo-nuclear weapons. To ensure guaranteed second strike capability, submarines capable of launching thermo-nuclear weapons must be available.
- Air defence of the field force must be upgraded considerably.
- Army logistics must be improved by equipping transport units with high mobility vehicles. Heavy lift helicopter units of the Air Force should be made available to them on a guaranteed basis for training and operations.
- The survivability aspect of personnel needs to be addressed. The soldier must have lightweight personal protective clothing, excellent night vision device, light and accurate automatic weapon, 'walkie-talkie' type of radio communications and each section must have a portable anti-aircraft missile firing capability.

We have suggested what could be done to better utilise the presently available forces to give us the desired capabilities. The question, whether the existing organisation of the field army into corps, division and brigades should be retained, or a more flexible organisation of 'task forces' directly controlled by a divisional or corps headquarters should be introduced, needs to be considered by the Army. The organisation so created should not only be tactically sound, it should also result in substantial savings in manpower for the Army. Overall, with a switch to the Task Force mode, significant savings of manpower can accrue even at present.

Equipment Profile

Mechanised Forces. T-90 tanks are likely to be the mainstay for the next two decades and after mid-life upgradation. The next generation of Infantry Combat Vehicles (ICV) should be in service by 2010 or so. Part of the ICVs should be wheeled. All mechanised forces should be NBC proof, better protected, and have greater speed and night fighting capability. Artillery. Multiple Launch Rocket Systems (MLRS) with range in excess of 120 kilometers, SSMs of the Prithvi family with solid propellant, self-propelled guns (both tracked and wheeled) of the same calibre, some long range rifled mortars and a higher availability of precision guided munitions form the bulk of the Artillery 'wish list' for 2020. Better radio sets, better equipment (both radar and opto-electronic) for target acquisition and survey, upgraded computers for both gun and observer ends and advanced systems of fire direction and damage assessment are also needed. The use of remotely piloted aerial vehicles working in conjunction with long range MLRS will help shape the future battlefield in depths, hitherto not attained. It will also alter the battlefield into a non-linear one.

Infantry. The Infantry needs to be upgraded to produce very high volumes of fire using a range of weapons. Surveillance by radars and other sensors will give the Infantry added ability to 'kill' enemy tanks and other hard targets. The next generation of ATGW should be in service by 2015, giving the Infantry greater lethality. With improved personal protective clothing, better night vision capability and the ability to shoot down attacking aircraft with section level anti aircraft guided missiles, the infantryman of Army 2020 will be a very formidable soldier indeed.

Bibliography

Ajey Lele: *Strategic Technologies for the Military : Breaking New Frontiers*, Sage, Delhi, 2009.

Amitabh Sikdar: *India and China : Strategic Energy Management and Security*, Manas, Delhi, 2009.

Anil, K.C.: *Military and Democracy in South Asia : Challenges, Politics and Power*, Sumit Enterprises, Delhi, 2009.

Asha Gupta: *Military Rule and Democratization : Changing Perspectives*, Deep & Deep, Delhi, 2003.

Atar Singh Jadoan: *Defence Military Geography of South East Asia*, Anmol, Delhi, 2001.

Bandita Sijapati: *A Kingdom Under Siege : Nepal's Maoist Insurgency, 1996 to 2003*, The Printhouse, Delhi, 2003.

Bosson, James E. : *Tibetan Treasury of Aphoristic Jewels*, Bloomington, IN: Indiana University Press, 1968.

Cole, Alan : *Mothers and Sons in Chinese Buddhism*, Stanford, CA: Stanford University Press, 1998.

Deepak, B R : *India and China : 1904-2004 : A Century of Peace and Conflict*, Manak, Delhi, 2005.

Digumarti Bhaskara Rao: *Military Conversion : Impact on Science and Technology*, Discovery, Delhi, 2003.

Digumarti Bhaskara Rao: *Military Conversion : Impact on Science and Technology*, Discovery, Delhi, 2003.

Evelyn Goh, *Meeting the China Challenge: The U.S. in Southeast Asian Regional Security Strategies*, DC: East-West Center, 2005.

Gao, Mobo: *The Battle for China's Past: Mao and the Cultural Revolution*, London, Pluto Press, 2008.

Geremie R. *Shades of Mao: The Posthumous Cult of the Great Leader.* Armonk, N.Y.: M. E. Sharpe, 1996.

Huntington, S.P.: *The China Defence Modernisation Military and the State*, N.Y., Vintage Books, 1964.

Jagannath P. Panda: *China's Path to Power : Party, Military and the Politics of State Transition*, Pentagon, Delhi, 2010.

Jones, W.H.: *The Government and Politics of Indian Military*, London, Hutchinson, 1971.

Kansakar, V. B. S.: *"International Migration and Citizenship in Nepal"*. Kathmandu: Central Bureau of Statistics/UNFPA, 2003.

Kapur, C.K. : *Chinese Military Modernisation*, Manas, Delhi, 2003.

Kumar, Raj : *Weapons and Military Technology*, Sumit Enterprises, Delhi, 2009.

Lamrimpa, Gen : *Realizing Emptiness: Madhyamaka Insight Meditation*, Ithaca, NY: Snow Lion, 2002.

Major Donovan: *Air Defence Power*. Sampson Low. London, 1940.

Parmanand. *The Nepali Congress since Its Inception: A Critical Assessment*. Delhi: B.R. Publishing, 1982.

Posen, B.R.: *The Sources of Military Doctrine*, Ithaca, 1984, Cornell Univ. Press.

Prabir De: *India and China in an Era of Globalisation : Essays on Economic Cooperation*, Bookwell, Delhi, 2005.

Randall Forsberg: *The Arms Production Dilemma: Contraction and Restraint in the World Combat Aircraft Industry*, Cambridge, Massachusetts: MIT Press, 1994.

Rosen, P.: *Societies and Military Power: India and its Armies*, Ithaca, Cornell University Press, 1996.

Shaun Narine, *Explaining ASEAN: Regionalism in Southeast Asia*, Boulder, CO: Lynne Rienner Publishers, 2002.

Sutton, J., *Technology and Defence Market Structure*, MIT Press, Delhi, 1998.

Index

L

M

N

O

P

S

T

W

❑❑❑